LAW, NARRATIVE AND REALITY

Law and Philosophy Library

VOLUME 30

The titles published in this series are listed at the end of this volume.

BERT VAN ROERMUND
Tilburg University,
Tilburg, The Netherlands

LAW, NARRATIVE AND REALITY

An Essay in Intercepting Politics

KLUWER ACADEMIC PUBLISHERS
DORDRECHT / BOSTON / LONDON

A C.I.P. Catalogue record for this book is available from the Library of Congress.

ISBN 0-7923-4621-1

Published by Kluwer Academic Publishers,
P.O. Box 17, 3300 AA Dordrecht, The Netherlands.

Sold and distributed in the U.S.A. and Canada
by Kluwer Academic Publishers,
101 Philip Drive, Norwell, MA 02061, U.S.A.

In all other countries, sold and distributed
by Kluwer Academic Publishers Group,
P.O. Box 322, 3300 AH Dordrecht, The Netherlands.

Printed on acid-free paper

Printed in the Netherlands

TABLE OF CONTENTS

PREFACE

To a certain extent, this book is a translation of *Recht, verhaal en werkelijkheid*, published by Coutinho (Bussum, 1993). Chapters 1, 5 and 9, however, differ considerably from the original. At the basis of the Dutch book were arguments already submitted in 'Narrative coherence in legal contexts', in C. Faralli and E. Pattaro (eds.), *Reason in Law,* vol. III., Milano, A. Giuffrè Editore, 1988, pp. 159-170; 'Justice, Rights, and Human Dignity', in *The Windsor Yearbook of Access to Justice*, 7, 1987, pp. 46-65; 'Narrative coherence and the guises of legalism', in P. Nerhot (ed.), *Law, Interpretation and Reality*, Dordrecht - Boston, Kluwer Academic Publishers, 1990, pp. 310-345; 'The Instituting of Brute Facts', in *The International Journal for the Semiotics of Law / Revue internationale de sémiotique juridique*, 4, 1991, pp. 279-308. For chapters 1 and 9 I used the following materials: 'Law is narrative, not literature', in W.J. Witteveen (ed.), *Law, Rhetoric and Literature* (Special Issue of the Dutch Journal for Legal Philosophy and Legal Theory), 23, No. 3, 1994, Zwolle, Tjeenk Willink, 1994, pp. 221-227 (with a response by R. Weisberg, pp. 228-229); and 'Seeing Places: On Prepositions in Law', *The International Journal for the Semiotics of Law / Revue internationale de sémiotique juridique*, 6, 1993, pp. 249-270. Chapter 5 was rewritten on the basis of 'The Instituting of Brute Facts'.

All papers published earlier were re-edited to fit within the framework of this book. I want to thank the editors and publishers involved, but especially Coutinho Publishers for graciously having given permission and support in reworking the original book. I am indebted to Deborah Charles Publications (http://www.legaltheory.demon.co.uk) for granting permission to re-use the papers which originally appeared in *The International Journal for the Semiotics of Law / Revue internationale de sémiotique juridique*. I also want to thank dr. Hans K. Lindahl, who previously translated the original into Spanish (Madrid, Tecnos, 1996) and challenged me to improve upon many points in my text. Special thanks go to Hildegard Penn, who carefully edited the English manuscript, and to Marjo van Dinteren, who transformed it into a camera-ready print. Without their sustained efforts and their sense of perfection I would have been lost.

Bert van Roermund

INTRODUCTION

Perhaps I am too sensitive, or too rude; it is my experience, in any case, that discussing problems of law or legal theory in terms of 'narrative coherence' gets on lawyers' nerves. They become impatient when someone tries to convince them of the quite received view that law should be and is presumed to be coherent. They become suspicious when they are asked to learn still another fashionable word for what - if anyone knows - *they* know about coherence in law, fed up as they feel after having swallowed hermeneutic, rhetoric, cybernetic, semiotic, etc. jargon. They even become slightly aggressive, at least in my country, when they hear coherence in law epitomised as 'narrative': for 'nar' in Dutch means 'fool' or 'jester'; and should not law be taken seriously?

In spite of all the annoyment this book is about law and 'narrativity', that is to say: the characteristic structure of tales, or stories, in contradistinction to other genres of texts, for instance, poems, academic treatises, prayers, or, indeed, scores of music. Its title is purposively ambiguous. By putting a simple comma after 'law' I leave it to the reader to decide what the best title is: either an enumeration of three terms, promising an argument about the relationships among them, or a characterisation of law in both terms: narrative and reality, strongly suggesting an opposition. But what kind of opposition? Can we trust our intuitive expectation that it will be about the opposition between the verbal and fictive nature of narratives on the one hand and the hard and true reality on the other? It will turn out that we cannot.

When notions from a specific branch of contemporary theory of literature, such as narratology, are introduced into the theory of law, they require careful philosophical investigation before any profit can be claimed. This entails, as far as I can see, at least two interdependent tasks:[1] to relate the concept of narrativity to a comprehensive philosophy of law, and to use it in the analysis of rich and complex data for such a philosophy.[2] This is precisely what this book seeks to accomplish. But before

1. Cf. Castañeda (1980: 13 ff).

2. These tasks are by no means identical, nor are they each other's infinite delay. They require flexible co-operation between lawyers and theorists of law (including philosophers) creating and accepting mutual challenges, in spite of their mutually repulsive charges. For philosophy's institutional illness is, as Wittgenstein diagnoses (*Philos. Invest.*, § 593), the

this two-pronged enterprise can be embarked upon, a good deal of work will have to be dedicated to carving out the exact shape of this idea of 'narrativity' in relation to law. And prior even to all this I believe it necessary to explain, in order to avoid misunderstandings, how my argument relates to some projects in contemporary legal philosophy, and why it deviates considerably from other projects which, judged by the similarity of words, look akin to it, but are in fact rather different.

Broekman and 't Hart, in the late seventies, were among the first legal philosophers who advocated exploring the relationship between law and narrativity[3], the latter on the basis of his Vico research, the former on that of his acquaintance with both structuralism and the work of Walter Benjamin.[4] Their thesis was that law, like fairy-tales, legends and other *genres* of texts, in fact always says the same thing, at least in the sense that it always uses the same structures, the same categories and the same procedures to talk about social reality, even to the point where social reality itself becomes the very product of such legal discourse. In a slightly more technical vocabulary, they held that there is a limited number of reductive operations applied to social life by legal doctrine and its strict, though flexible, conceptual apparatus. Thus legal doctrine construes and transforms the goings-on of social life into, for instance, sets of legal facts, or cases. The 'it' of a case has to be construed as a function of the answers to questions like: who did *it?* what caused *it?* what balance is disrupted by *it?*[5] Such a format ignores the possible relevance of other questions, like: Is agency the proper category is this case? Is it possible to have a discussion of infinite causal chains? What order is presupposed in speaking of a disrupted balance? Broekman and 't Hart also stressed that these strategies of legal language are hiding from us and that we are hardly able to criticise them, because we are encapsulated by a powerful gen-

one-sided diet of thinking with only one kind of example, while variety of cases is of the essence of law and legal doctrine. On the other hand, the law's institutional pressure is towards instrumentalism and (short-term) applicability of whatever concepts can represent the law within a specific political context; thus, it tends to be impatient of philosophical pluralism, pervasiness, circularity, scepticism, etc.

3. Cf. Broekman - 't Hart (1980); Broekman (1979), (1982); see also more recently his (1993); the last essays of the collection by 't Hart (1983), more recently his (1991).

4. See Broekman (1971), (1973); 't Hart (1979), which was his doctoral thesis at Leuven (1978).

5. See Broekman (1982)[1979].

eral conception of language. This conception wants us to believe that language is a tool or an instrument in the hands of a user, by which this user can transmit his intentions to other users. The instrument has the form of a code, that allows us to link (inner) meanings to (outer) signs. Because of the dualism between the inner and the outer world, as well as between the subject and the object of language use, they referred to this conception of language as 'cartesian'. To confront cartesianism in law, they looked for a theoretical opening in law to acknowledge its commitment to certain structures of discourse that relate to the truth and values our culture wants to hold on to. Their hope was that if we can show that what law believes to be 'the world out there' is in fact not just contingent on the laws of nature but even more on the laws of man, i.e. on a proclaimed rather than an observed truth, this would mean a liberation from the self-indulgence our culture shows in its allegedly universal orientation towards humanness and its conception of law as a moral service to mankind. The conception of language preparing for this liberating potential they called 'narrative'.

Note that this was not a plea for an extrinsic 'application' of (post-) structuralist literary theory on law. The aim was to contribute to a theory of law, based on the presupposition that law and language emanate from a common cultural background, and to criticise some common basic presuppositions. Among these are that language and law are both:

- objects in the hands of a subject: language is an instrument in the hands of the 'competent speaker', while law is an instrument in the hands of the 'competent authorities';
- objects of order and ordering yielded by voluntary agreement and submission all subjects involved, i.e. the idea of the social contract as the basis of language and society;
- objects laid down in a code (a grammatical or a legal one), maintained and enforced by a power that spreads over the whole of society.

It should be stressed that this was a view on the level of legal theory, which is not to say that it was unimportant or irrelevant to legal practice. But its critical ring was heard by lawyers as an allegation that they were the willing executives of a bourgeois culture, unaware of the overwhelming powers that had washed their brains. And they were not quite without arms against this philosophical *savoir critique*. For one thing, if philosophers could tell lawyers how to escape from cartesianism in actual legal practice, they would in fact advocate that law is just a manner of applying philosophical insight - which would not only be a claim that lawyers would find hard to believe, but also one that could only emanate from the kind of cartesianism under criticism. For another thing, if philosophers could not tell how to escape from cartesianism after having explained why lawyers would never find their way out, what difference would this critique make? At the most, it would boil down to a truism that no-one professionally involved in law will deny, to wit, that there is an irreducibly 'casuistic' aspect to law and that cases in law are always constructs of law.

I think that these initial views suffered from a lack of empirical analysis, and that this is one of the main reasons why their critical intentions were misunderstood. The theory of narrative was invoked to provide a 'new' and 'post-cartesian' framework in the philosophy of law, an incantation that was supposed to be sufficient in itself to condemn all legal doctrine as 'uncritical' while all the real work was still to be done.[6)] Part of the work was done in the course of the eighties, when the topic of 'law and narrative' became popular in a variety of approaches. One may think of the debate between Dworkin and Fish on the analogy between legal decision-making and writing a (chain-)novel (1982-1983)[7)]; of the powerful, but somewhat ignored argument made by Cover (1983) on narrative and nomos; of MacCormick's paper on narrative versus normative coherence (1984); or of Dworkin's reception of hermeneutics in his work (1986). Other authors approached the topic from quite different angles, for instance, Jackson (1988), who developed a narrative model of fact construction in the trial, based on a semiotic appraisal of social psychology; or J.B. White (1985; 1989), who renewed his efforts to picture legal language as a powerful device to gain access to justice. Publications by Lenoble, Ost, Van de Kerchove and Gérard centred largely around the same issues in the French discussion, while Ballweg, Ladeur, Seibert and Sauer, among others, contributed to the German debate. We may witness the growing interest in the issues of the *International Journal for the Se-*

6. Even as late as the beginning of the nineties Witteveen (1990: 180), in an anthology on narrativity and the humanities, states with regard to law that '(...) only few narratological analyses are available'.

7. The first round of their debate in the 1982 issues of *Critical Inquiry* re-appeared Mitchell (1983) and afterwards in, respectively, Dworkin (1985) and Fish (1989). Dworkin (1986) and Fish (1987; also reprinted in his (1989)) continued the discussion. The final round is to be found in Brint & Weaver (1991).

miotics of Law / Revue Internationale de Sémiotique Juridique (since 1988), in the papers delivered to the Congress of the International Association for Philosophy and Literature (Atlanta, 1989), or in an international pattern-card on legal interpretation edited by Nerhot (1989). Apparently, 'narrativity' has become a key-word that has managed to attract authors from very different backgrounds. Increasingly one has presented analyses of legal files, trying to build a bridge between the specific problems of legal practice and the reflective interests of philosophers: Balkin, Den Boer, Jackson, Landowski, Ost, Sobota, Van de Kerchove, Seibert, Schlag, Witteveen - to mention just a few.

The variety of approaches is so great that we are know confronted with the antipode of the problem just mentioned: without a clear-cut hypothesis regarding the specific character of narratives, these analyses will remain isolated, individual enterprises. At this stage, Broekman's insight, which is very similar to Cover's, regains relevance: one should not look for extrinsic application of literary theory in the field of legal theory, but for an intrinsic relationship between law and narrative, or to the narrative dynamics of law itself. This is the programme this book intends to join. Though I start by asking what kind of knowledge hides in (legal) narratives, I aim at answering the question, what of our (legal) knowledge can be said to be narrative. The book therefore combines narrative analysis, conceptual justification and legal theory.

Thus locating my project on the map of contemporary jurisprudence makes it clear that I keep a distance from what is presently known among legal theorists as the Law and Literature Movement, although I am also indebted to it. I intend to pay my debt by briefly discussing two of its main topics in the remainder of this Introduction. But these discussions merely prepare the ground for what I consider to be a different approach to the narrative aspects of law. Let me state the differences before discussing the two topics. First of all, my argument is not about literature, but about a structure of language use called 'narrative'. Secondly, this structure is not regarded as on a par with other patterns we may discover in studying the use of (legal) language. It is, in particular, not one of the many rhetorical devices which the actors involved in legal procedures may use (consciously or not) to pursue their goals. Rather, narrative structure, although emerging to the surface of language use, is an epiphenomenon of the way we refer to the object of thinking, in our case legal thinking. This object we may call 'the world', or 'reality'. As the word 'narrative' characterises this harpooning of 'the world' by thinking, I am using it as a predicate in the theory of knowledge, that is, as an epistemological term. A third reason why the Law and Literature debate is not at the heart of my enterprise, is that, in my view, a theory of knowledge in law is not equivalent to a theory of legal interpretation. In fact I will criticise one of the main presuppositions favoured by almost any theory of interpretation, namely, that interpretation is representation. Moreover, I want to believe that a theory of legal knowledge should try and prove its pertinence in giving an account of the core concepts of the main areas of law, such as democracy, punishment, or contract, rather than of the nature of interpretation.

This is all not to say, of course, that my argument has not profited from the topics discussed in the contemporary debates on law and literature, nor that I did not find inspiration in the works of authors who contributed to these debates. But it does explain why this book largely ignores the canonical topics and authors in the province of jurisprudence that commonly shows the sign 'narrative', and why it discusses the issues brought up by authors like Kelsen and Schmitt, Atiyah and Fried, Kant and Rousseau, Wittgenstein and Castañeda - thinkers who never would have considered to use a word like 'narrative'. And yet, the fact that they did not use the word does not entail that they were not aware of the matter. Thus, my argument does not claim to be 'original' in the sense of 'self-made', though it wants to pay tribute to the origins of philosophy. For similar reasons lawyers should not get nervous about the word 'narrative': it does not try and persuade them to embark on something different from doing law. It refers to their core-business, in particular the foundations of their discipline. It's their thinking I characterise as 'narrative', only to challenge them to really *think* as lawyers.

Setting aside, now, the issues of 'legal restrictions on literature' (cf. obscenity) or 'literary style in legal argumentation' (cf. the inspiration a novelist may derive from reading the *Code civil*), I think that the debate centres around two focusses. One is about the educational function of literary fiction for all students of law. The other is about the nature of interpretation in law, which supposedly could be clarified by a similar process in the interpretation of literary texts. Sections 1 and 2 discuss these issues. Section 3 announces the line of argument I would like to follow and gives a bird's eye view of the chapters of the book.

1 Learning through literature

What is sold today as 'a narrative approach to law' is clearly a manifold of things. I am convinced that they are all not only perfectly legal, but also quite interesting in their own right. We should, however, become less liberal when some of the salesmen claim that their stuff has philosophical meaning, or - which amounts to the same thing - constitutes the basis of a new jurisprudential 'theory'.

One may respond that philosophy itself is a good many things; so what is the point of rebutting a manifold of claims in the name of philosophy? But the fact that (the history of) philosophy is an amalgam of heterogeneous, even contradictory or incompatible approaches, does not justify the claim that philosophical argument can conceive *of itself* as an amalgam of heterogenous and even contradictory or incompatible cognitive attitudes. In trying to make a philosophical argument, one will have to take a position on what philosophy is and what it is not. In the case of law and literature, philosophers will be interested in the internal rather than the external link between the two. That is to say: they will primarily ask whether or not the two terms of the relationship have meanings that are necessarily intertwined. They have an interest in the general structure of the ways *we think we have to* understand reality, in this case: the built-in reciprocal reference between law and literature. At the end of the day, this is a matter for conceptual debate rather than for empirical research. But undoubtedly this debate should start from experience.

When we turn to the manifold of relationships between law and narrative, it is obvious that not all of these relationships are philosophically feasible in the sense described above. A recently popular branch of research in 'law and narrative' has been to scan works of literary art on what is said about 'the law'. From Shakespeare to Kafka, from Kundera to Sophocles, the great literature offers us many a scenery in which the law is portrayed, at times in glorious, at times in embarassing positions. The thesis added is that lawyers can learn a great deal about law by looking into that mirror, to the benefit of both themselves and their clients, not to mention the legal system and society at large.[8] This is a good example of a thesis which I find perfectly legitimate in its own right (or, let us say, in the perspective of legal education), but rather flawed from a philosophical point of view. I am quite willing to believe that lawyers can learn a great deal about law by reading literary art about law; and not only lawyers, but also (perhaps even more so) philosophers of law. We should, therefore encourage both lawyers and legal philosophers to devour as much literature with legal scenery as they can. But saying or believing this much is not very pertinent to the general structure of understanding in which law and literature are intertwined. I can easily imagine other ways in which lawyers and philosophers can acquire innovative ideas about law, and I have no difficulty in advocating these ways on an equal footing with reading literature. For one thing, there are other forms of art apart from literature which may be as inspiring to the proper legal attitude as literature, for instance film, theatre, painting and sculpture; yes, why not music?[9] Then there are other things than art which are very useful in learning some basics about law in society. One may, for instance, learn a lot from survival training or transcendental meditation, by engaging in social service for a year or so, by living on the dole for six months or by spending a week in jail. Note that some of these techniques are in fact used to bring people to new or better ideas about law and society - especially people who despise all works of literary art and classify them as 'bullshit'. If I, a middle-class academic philosopher, happen to think that people can learn much about law from literature, I am in fact cherishing a psychologi-

8. See, for instance, J.B. White (1973, 1985 and 1990), though with gradually developing shifts in focus; furthermore, Posner (1988) and, in a philosophically far more interesting way, Nussbaum (1995). In a critical vein, R. Weisberg (1992), although he admits, for instance, p. 5: 'Literature provides a lively and accessible medium for learning about law in an ethical way.' Cf. also p. 34 ff. I should add, however, that I have much greater sympathy for Weisberg's first thesis, 'the poetic method for law', which amounts to the idea that we should come to appreciate 'how law means', in a way similar to 'how literature means' (cf. p. 4). But then again, (a) is not that what the 'new rhetorics' (Perelman c.s.) has pointed out ever since 1958, if not 'the old rhetorics' (Aristotle, Quintillian, Cicero); (b) are we not going around in circles? In 1960 Gadamer taught us that exegesis of (biblical) texts and interpretation of (statutory) law are extremely relevant to acquire adequate ideas about hermeneutics. Today, legal theorists, including Dworkin, lean heavily on Gadamer claiming to clarify from his hermeneutical insight what interpretation in law is like.

9. Cf. Jerome Frank's analogy of legal interpretation or decision making, and 'making' music.

cal belief about what kind of people will learn from what kind of sources. I do not take a philosophical stand.

If I did, some rather curious consequences would follow. Firstly, I would have to accept that reading the appropriate kind of literature would be the thing that law enforcement officials could command citizens to do in order to make them know and, indeed, abide by the law, so as to prevent them from committing crimes. For what goal would 'learning about law' serve if it were not, in the final analysis, for enforcing the law? And by what right would only law students be so privileged that they may enjoy the profits of this allegedly excellent educational device? Secondly, I would come close to accepting censorship. For if there is literature which gives us insight in the basics of law, how it works and what it requires, there will probably also be literature which does the opposite, or which gives us the 'wrong' idea about law. Would it not be the responsibility of the authorities to expel texts by, for instance, Jean Genet from the classrooms? And why are we so sure that *Crime and Punishment* would pass the test? Does it give us the *right* idea about law? Thirdly, our theory of the sources of law would have to revised. If there would be an intrinsic relationship between law and literature, legislators, litigators and judges would be allowed to refer to what literary pieces say about the law on a par with what the constitution, a statutory rule or a precedent tells them. For all these reasons it seems wise to distinguish our views about good legal education from philosophical or jurisprudential views.

It will be objected that I have put forward a rather naïve view on literature as art, together with a naïve view about the way in which we may be said to 'learn' something from it and to derive 'ideas' from it.[10)] Of course, one might say, art does not 'teach' us lessons in the same way as manuals or textbooks do, that is, by appealing to our cognitive capacities. A good piece of art holds us captive, it fascinates us, and indeed *moves* us from here to there in the most literary sense we can imagine: it moves us from a safe and established point of view of our reality and it brings us to points of view from which we can see reality in a light hardly dreamt of. It appeals to our capacity of imagination. It brings possible worlds to our senses, and, thus, before our mind's eye. Now, once a possible world is before our mind's eye, once it has been presented to us by the imagina-

10. Weisberg, however, does speak (ibid.: 4) about the *what* of literature as '(...) the rationalized rearticulation of its "lessons" for law.'

tion, it has gained what we may call the quality of virtual reality. This does not mean, necessarily, that we can make it come true. But by the sole fact that it has become accessible by imagination, it becomes an important point of reference from which we can try to redefine the order of the world we actually live in.[11)] We may come to see this actual world from a new practical and/or intellectual point of view. This may supply us with new names and predicates which may evoke new practices, or it may offer us comfort or reconciliation so that we can endure the world we live in. By challenging our established understanding of the world, art sustains our existence in it.[12)]

I acknowledge that this is only the beginning of a philosophical account of art, which hardly escapes the level of triviality. It suffices, however, to see that the way in which we can said to 'learn' from art is indeed not only a complicated one, but also one which is not so easily put on an equal footing with social or military service, survival training, or a good stay in prison. An artificial programme *to learn something about 'real life'*, although it can have its healthy effects, is quite different from an artistic event in which we gain *the very experience that 'real life' is not a pre-established given*. I submit, therefore, that art is as vital for a society as is its legal system. But what I also want to maintain is that this insight does not bring us to the original claim we were investigating: that there is some intimate relationship between law and narrative which we can get hold of by paying attention to law and literature.

The first thing we should note is that in this type of argument there is an unjustified assumption that speaking of narrative is the same as speaking of literature, or, in any case, as speaking of art. This assumption is not only unjustified, it is also highly counterintuitive. 'Narrative' is just a rather solemn word for what everyday language prefers to call 'a story'.

11. Cf. Ricoeur (1983-1985, I: 120) 'Le choc du possible, qui n'est pas moindre que le choc du réel, est amplifié par le jeu interne, dans les oeuvres elles mêmes, entre les paradigme reçus et la production d'écarts par la déviance des oeuvres singulières. Ainsi la litterature narrative, parmi toutes les oeuvres poétiques. modélise l'effectivité praxique aussi bien par ses écarts que par ses paradigmes.'

12. The terms 'counterfactual' and 'alternity' for this kind of *mimetic* relationship between the imagined 'other world' and the lived world were used by George Steiner in *After Babel* (1975: 222). This sense of 'counterfactual' should be distinguished from the *discursive* sense in which Habermas has used it in his theory of communicative action ever since 1971.

Many stories are perfectly good stories, but they are not, by the same token, literary art; at least, they do not belong to what seems to be a special realm called 'literature'. My uncle used to tell a limited set of rather amusing stories at family parties, but it was clear that they would not make it all the way up to literature. Many a bewildering story is told on the psychiatrist's sofa or at the local police station, but no publisher of literary art would be interested in seeing it printed. In playgrounds and classrooms, children tell one another stories as if their lives depend on it (in fact, their lives do depend on it), but neither their teachers nor they themselves conceive of these stories being interchangeable with the literary texts in their classrooms. Of course, it is safe to say that literary narratives are paradigms of good storytelling, but we should be careful not to reverse that claim and assert that storytelling is the same as producing literature. So, when it is stated that there is some liberating force in narratives which law should be sensitive about, it is important to know whether or not this alleged liberating force is located in what is special about narratives, or in what is special about art.[13)]

Let us assume that the liberating potential of literature, or of art in general, is philosophically feasible. So, what we seem to gain from locating the interesting thing about law and literature here, is that we can drop the perhaps oversophisticated category of 'narrativity': supposedly, reference to the artistic quality of literature suffices to give an account of its allegedly liberating potential. But the price one has to pay for taking this horn of the dilemma is the burden of proof for the assertion that law is sufficiently like literary art in relevant respects in order to assemble a similar liberating force and build it into its categories. One will in fact have to argue a rather close analogy between law and literature *on the aesthetic level*. Such an analogy is very counter-intuitive. One will have to cope with salient differences, such as the use of violent force, the prominent role of doctrine, the weight of predictability, the need for 'officials' - all present in law, but absent in art. The only direction this argument can take, as I see it, is the metaphor of the counterparts attracting and supplementing each other in mutual captivity. But this metaphor only works if one gives an account of the embracing whole which the mutually supplementing counterparts are parts of. This would make the aesthetic bond

13. In this respect, I disagree with Ricoeur (1983-1985, I: 118 ff), and his categorisation of narratives as a subset of works of literature.

even more enigmatic, if not suspect.

At this point, the similarity of law and literature as two forms of institutionalised judgment becomes apparent, and it will be tempting to embark on an argument to the effect that there *is*, indeed, this close analogy on the very points just mentioned. The argument would go as follows. Access to literature is guarded in a way analogous to access to justice - if it is allowed to refer briefly to a major thesis of a Kafka text read by Derrida.[14] There are 'officials' in literature, there is the weight of a certain 'predictability', there is a prominent role for 'doctrine' or literary criticism, and there is even an aspect of 'violence' contained in the way in which the world of literature can disturb or defend the world of right and wrong. The canonical character of literature and the positive character of law are of much the same ilk, so one could say. What happens in law and what constitutes it (to wit: authoritative judgment and the appeal to authoritative judgment), is also at the basis of literature in the double sense of canonical art production and art consumption. Their middle term is authoritative judgment, or rather, the way in which judgment is always tied up with pre-established institution and authority. Therefore, the appeal to the authority of law and the appeal to the canon of literature mirror each other.

Note, however, that this resemblance carries us in a direction opposite to the one we wanted to go. For the appeal to literature in legal theory is now justified by the fact that the counterparts of law and literature are, in the final analysis, not opposite at all. They are said to be supplementary in the sense that they reciprocate each other's order and legitimation, as two hands washing each other. What seems to be the liberating force of art is mixed up with and exchanged for the authoritative judgment of literature as an institution. This is a category-mistake: we switch from the aesthetic to the institutional angle on literature. The force of literary art, however, is already domesticated if it is supposed to be found in the canon of 'literature'. Not to obey the established laws of its genre is the first and foremost quality of a work of literary art. This is not to say that there is no liberating force in literary art. On the contrary, I have pointed out that its primary stake is to challenge the authority our judgment is tied up with. I have asserted only that the quality of 'belonging to literature' is different from the quality of 'having artistic impact'. I conclude, therefore, that the

14. Derrida et al. (1985: 87-139).

topos of 'law and literature' is not within the scope of a narrative approach to law which is philosophically feasible. For one thing, referring to 'literature' is not tantamount to referring to narrative, but also referring to 'literature' is not tantamount to referring to art.

2 Interpretation in law and literature.

The other horn of the dilemma was to locate the interesting thing about narratives in what is special about narrative itself as a specific structure of language in use, not as something intrinsically artistic. I think this is the only philosophically viable way to go. It leads to an account, not of the role narratives should play in order to get a more vivid or anecdotic style of law or legal parlance, but of the epistemological bond which narratives forge with what is narrated.

But here, too, there are different approaches; and not all of them seem equally attractive from the outset. In particular, I find it difficult to support the view that 'interpretation' is the hallmark of law, that legal interpretation is analogical to interpretation in general, and that the interpretation of narratives is the paradigm of interpretation in general. The protagonists of this threefold mistake[15)] fight their battle on the nature of interpretation in general, assuming that interpretation is about narratives and that law is about interpretation. They seem to forget the challenges to which these claims are open:

(i) It is far from obvious that the interpretation of narratives is paradigmatic of interpretation in general. The suggestion is that all texts under interpretation become objects to be operated on by cognitive skills exercised by the interpreter. To the extent that 'interpretation' even becomes a model of human knowledge at large, this view - pushed to its limits - wants us to believe that our lives are treated as such objects at moments when we ask ourselves 'how to carry on'. But it is far from evident that these 'objects' are as passive as they are believed to be. The least we can say is that they urge the interpreter to look or listen from a specific *position.* Whatever we may want to say about a painting, our account cannot ignore the position of the spectator dictated by its perspective. Neither can

15. See the theory of legal interpretation submitted in Dworkin (1986) and the discussion with, e.g., Fish and Fiss. Cfr. footnote 7.

we understand Greek tragedy unless we accept the position assigned to us by the chorus[16]. If it is really true that these 'objects' of interpretation situate us, they do more than take us to the point where it is up to us to decide about how to proceed. Then they have their impact on our cognitive attitude, without any warrant in advance that these forces will always bring about the same attitude. Narratives might require an attitude different from that required in understanding philosophy, poetry, mathematics or, indeed, law.

(ii) It is equally challengeable that legal interpretation can be regarded as a species of the genus 'interpretation' without more ado. Although Gadamer (1975) takes legal interpretation as one of the paradigm cases from which we can learn what interpretation is about and as the starting point of his impressive account of interpretation in general, there are two difficulties. One is that Gadamer used legal interpretation as a case in point to focus on what he calls 'Applikation' and did not imply that interpretation is like legal interpretation in every respect. The other is that all legal scholars in Germany who referred to Gadamer for their theory of legal interpretation (e.g. Larenz, Hruschka and Esser) altered his theory on a few decisive points so as to adapt it for legal purposes.[16] What these legal authors try to restore is the role of the doctrinal system in legal interpretation. Although common law countries are not familiar with the true meaning of the word *Dogmatik*,[17] they will be as familiar as civil law countries with the constraints on interpretation generated by law being a system, and a system in a specific way at that; namely, a quasi-provisional system of framing practical knowledge to solve social conflicts. Neither acquiring nor manipulating this knowledge comes down to interpretation; institution building, procedural policy and (sometimes) coercion are equally essential.

(iii) The last problem with the interpretational view is that it takes the notion of interpretation for granted, discussing at the most whether its most characteristic gesture is towards a (counterfactually) imagined or a (factually) committed 'community of interpretation'. The relevance of that discussion, staged by Dworkin and Fish in various rounds of debates[18],

16. See Tindemans (1996).

16. See chapter 6 for Gadamer, Larenz and Esser.

17. For an extensive historical and epistemological account of the notion, see Herberger (1981).

18. See footnoot 7 and 15.

is perhaps rather limited: it is the old philosophical issue of ruling out scepticism. There are two ways around that issue, but no direct attack. One is to say that it is always possible that we are deluded by an evil demon: even our firm belief that we are not deluded is a delusion. Then our efforts to find 'the truth' are in vain, but we will never know it. If we would find out, on the other hand, a second way around scepticism would open itself to us. Then we would have to acknowledge that at least scepticism is true and, thus, there would be at least one thing we could not be sceptical about. The Dworkin-Fish discussion has this familiar, in fact Cartesian ring: it may well be that a counterfactually imagined 'community of interpretation' is a rhetorical ploy of a factually committed community with real interests, motives, institutions and power plays. But either we will be quite happy to accept that one of the rhetorical strategies this community has is to critically examine its rhetorical strategies by imagining a counterfactual community of interpretation, or we will ask whether the critic would be inclined to admit that his own sceptical position is just another rhetorical device. In short: we take, of course, an *interest* in truth, but then we take an interest in *truth*. Now in sorting out different ideas of truth, we may want to examine the notion of interpretation and its presuppositions. I therefore propose to reach beyond the Dworkin-Fish debate and challenge one of its basic presuppositions. For what is not questioned in this debate is the simple logic presupposed by even the most radical hermeneutics, namely that interpretation is always already an operation on something not-interpreted. It is this last resort of hermeneutical theory that a narrative account of law, in my view, will address. It will do so on the basis of an hypothesis that expresses what is characteristic of *narrative*; not art, and not text.

3 Overview of the argument

I referred already to the epistemological bond which narratives forge with what is narrated. I call this bond the 'interception of reference'. I will present it in more detail in chapter 1, to tie it down to the theory of knowledge in chapter 5. A very superficial characterisation, a clip rather than an abstract, would be the following preview. What narratives do is to do to make and to intercept reference to a world 'out there', by both making and intercepting reference to a world 'in here'. Thus, they maintain their ontological claims by retarding instead of either fortifying or dissolving them. Conceptual discourse is non-narrative in the sense that it puts retardation of ontological claims to an end by judgement. Judgement either affirms or negates such claims, thus either fortifying or dissolving them. Therefore, narrative discourse questions conceptual discourse in a specific respect. Now the discourse used in shaping our social relationships, in politics, in families, in trading, is essentially conceptual. Therefore, it involves ontological claims, pertaining to what is the case or what should be the case.[19] Now my thesis is that law is an institution that maintains these claims by retarding them. No doubt, legal discourse is conceptual discourse. But it is, at least in principle, a kind of self-questioning conceptual discourse. Retarding, in the case of law, does not mean fleeing from conceptual discourse and retreating to story-telling. It means engaging in such discourse by tactically diverting it from the many immunizations of truth-claims and ideals posited in socio-political relationships. By implication, it can never be an overt tactic, for the same reason as a narrative cannot overtly question. It can only obliquely challenge the ontological commitment with which it is told: otherwise it would be disguised as deceit.

The core of this book, then, is that law has to do with narrative, in the sense that this strategy of intercepting reference to either a hypostatised world or a wishful imagination is at work in law and produces its healthy effects in society. We should neither underestimate the extent to which this is the case, nor the force with which it is concealed by the official ideology of law that it is the case. More specifically, I claim that where stories depend on an alternating logic between Event and Interpretation, law depends on a similar alternating logic between Fact and Norm (Chapter 1). A narrative reading of law is one which systematically digs out this relation of interception on different levels of facticity and normativity, if it is allowed to use these rather pompous substantives. There is such a relationship between facts and norms on the level of the case as it is presented to the officials in a court of law (Chapter 2). It also emerges on the level of the legal system itself which prefers to present itself to us as one normative block (Chapter 3). In a third form it plays a role on the level of legal decision making - which is, after all, mapping the 'facts' of the case

19. I regard claims pertaining to 'what should be the case' as ontological, as they refer to states of affairs, whereas deontic claims, expressing 'what is to be done', do not.

on to the 'norms' of the system (Chapter 4).

In order to build this hypothesis on solid philosophical ground I will continue by arguing that interception of reference is primarily an epistemological paradigm, not an artistic one (though the arts are very good in using it), and that it goes against the grain of a different epistemological paradigm dominant in legal thought (and probably even thinking in general): representationalism. Representationalism is the view that knowing is *nothing but* representing: either representing the world outside in our belief (reflection) or representing our belief in the world outside (projection). Note that representationalism is defined as a philosophical exaggeration: knowing is *nothing but* representing. Narrativity goes against the grain of this philosophical absolutism. It is not a critique of the representational character of thinking as such; on the contrary, it respects representation in thinking. What it does not respect is that re-presenting is all there is to thinking. It reminds us that there is a primordiality of presenting in thinking, which the little preposition 're-' tries to get rid of. Once, however, that much is appreciated, an even more dazzling question discloses itself to us. If it is true that the preposition 're-' hides from the presenting character of thinking, what about the next preposition 'pre-' in 'presenting'? What does 'pre-' conceal or try to get rid of? It seems to suggest a primordiality of 'being' hiding in 'presenting'. Indeed, we are on the verge of metaphysical critique (Chapter 5).

The next step in the argument, however, will take us back to law, although we will stay on the level of the theory of knowledge. I will defend the view that representationalism assumes a specific theoretical format in legal contexts, which is called legalism. Taking a cue from Wittgenstein's critique of representationalism, I will explain how legalism can take on different guises. These guises often pose as so many efforts to refute legalism, while, on my account of the matter, they reinstall it under a different name. With due respect to the authors I selected for discussion, I will explain why, in my view, Larenz's theory of 'types', Esser's theory of 'agreement' and Aarnio's theory of 'forms of life' are examples of the guises of legalism (Chapter 6).

Once we have analysed law from this point of view of alternating interception of reference, it becomes fascinating to learn how law is able both to maintain and to intercept its logic in self-presentation. From this angle, it is possible to detect in what sense reference to 'the people' in a democracy is both advocated and mitigated by law (Chapter 7). It is possible to detect to what extent the notion of 'crime' is both promoted and restricted by law (Chapter 8). It is possible to detect how radically opposite views on the sources of (contractual) obligations can be given their respective due (Chapter 9). All of these lessons point to one central idea: law is not just integrity in principled politics, as Dworkin would have it,[20] but self-intercepting, and, thus, self-questioning integrity. Law is aware that 'principles' constitute only one of the two forms general meanings can take. The other form is narrative. From this, it does not follow that the law *can express* itself as if it (or, for that matter, its subjects) had an option here. It has not, therefore it cannot.

20. Cf. his *Law's Empire* (1986).

CHAPTER 1

A HYPOTHESIS ABOUT NARRATIVES

1 All about 'about'

Not too long ago, we could do without narratology and be quite happy in analysing stories. Notions like 'point of view', 'perspective' or 'voice' were rather old-fashioned but reliable tools in understanding how a text relates its tale to us, its readers. We were perfectly able to ask and answer questions like the following: From which point of view, framed (by the text) as being inside or outside the text, is a story told? Within which perspective are references established? By which voice meanings ordered and distributed? Does the story touch upon other points of view, inside or outside the text? Does it touch upon not only other characters', but also the author's and the reader's points of view?[1)] Take, for instance, the first sentence of *Through the Looking Glass*:

> One thing was certain, that the *white* kitten had had nothing to do with it - it was the black kitten's fault entirely.

It makes quite a difference in understanding this text, whether we put these words in the perspective of an outsider, a storyteller, or in the perspective of the main character, Alice. Indeed, who's voice is this? Who is so certain? Has the reader the same reasons to be as certain as Alice? Has this first sentence already to do with the chess problem the former is invited to solve through the series of adventures the latter is related to have experienced? This is the kind of questions we can analytically ask concerning such a first sentence. A second example could be derived from Rousseau's *Confessions*: two, three or even four layers of referents can be

1. Cf. Chamberlain (1990: 3): 'Narrative perspective has been described as the essence of the narrative art (...). It plays an essential role in the writing and reading of texts and has become a major issue in the theory that narrative gives rise to. Different theoretical approaches have sought to define it with terms such as 'person', 'point of view', 'reflector', 'voice', 'central consciousness' and 'focalization'.' Chamberlain questions the notion of perspective. I will return to this in chapters 5 and 6.

detected in certain tokens of the pronoun 'I' in this 'autobiographical' text: the author, the narrator, the main character, the main character in retrospect, etc. Sometimes they are congruent, sometimes not - and this is what makes the text intriguing. Careful and close reading rather than theory seemed to be involved in giving an account of such intricacies.

'Narratology' came into being by the time Walter Benjamin noted, in his famous essay *'Der Erzähler'*, that the storyteller and the story had been fading away for some ages. It arose, not to play the part of the zoo rescuing the last copies of a species, but because it saw stories everywhere: in myths, fairy tales, music, stained-glass windows, film, dance, etc., but certainly also in the works of both literary fiction and science. It seemed that there had to be something common in all those stories, something which could be framed as an object of study. They seemed to obey a certain code of stories whatever the way in which they materialised, whatever they meant to say and whatever interpretative approaches they mobilised. This common code was called 'structure' and the aim of the study was to explicate the 'logic' or the 'grammar' of this structure. One tried to establish elementary components of stories (or a particular kind of stories, such as fairy tales), to style them into variables and parameters, and to make hypotheses about the algorithms that might govern the possible relations among these variables. It appeared that it was possible to formulate powerful generalisations on this grammatical structure of stories. These generalisations were data for philosophical questions (Barthes) and paradigms for theoretical analyses on whatever could be regarded as an analogous realm of culture, including law (Greimas). In the meantime, it became clear to most of these theorists that it was *very* difficult to maintain a workable distinction between form and content. This was not *just* because demarcation in science is always a tricky enterprise, but *mainly* because the generalisations themselves tended to absorb and explain content aspects. For instance, from specific relations between the variables 'destinateur' and 'destinataire' in law, hypotheses were inferred about 'the point' of the institution 'law', conceived as being a narrative itself.

At this very point of 'point', the 'logical' tradition of narratology met with a different approach to texts in general and stories in particular. Just a different approach? No, rather the archenemy of logic: rhetoric. Rhetorical analysis of stories (in terms of 'point of view', for instance) has been practised in literary contemplations from of old, but this approach gained attractiveness when it appeared that the sophisticated apparatus of 'structural' semantics/semiotics/semiology came down - when all was said and done - to an enriched restatement of the old problem: What is it, for a story, to have a point?[2] Although this question would never be the same again after structuralism, it was still the question to which E.M. Forster's well-known example[3] referre phrase [1]

[1] The king died, and then the queen died

is not a full-fledged narrative, but more like an enumeration. However, [2] is a complete, though admittedly very short narrative:

[2] The kind died, and then the queen died of grief.

A little pause to look at this example may suffice to see what is at stake here. Forster's tiny narrative [2] connects two ways of telling 'what happened': it announces a sequence of events in temporal priority and *then* adds a qualification 'of grief', which makes this priority significant. It puts the events in perspective and gives the enumeration a point, indeed a plot, which supposedly is missing in [1]. The reader or hearer of the story is supposed to grasp the more-than-temporal character of the sequence and, by the same token, the plot of the story, from a body of general background knowledge or beliefs about the reasons why something happens, for instance how people, in particular queens, come to die. These qualifications of the order put forward are not always explicit. Sometimes they are hidden, or marked by a semantic blank, leaving the interpretation to the reader. For instance, in the well-known example [3]

2. Greimas's 'actantial' model. For an exposition with regard to law, Jackson (1985) can be seen as the mould of what 'having a point' amounts to for classes of narratives.

3. See Forster (1974: 60). Forster makes a distinction between 'story' en 'plot', limiting 'story' to 'a narrative of events arranged in their time-sequence', while 'plot' stands for 'also a narrative of events, the emphasis falling on causality'. In my view, this is a questionable way of making the distinction, for instance because the temporal order is bound to lead to distinguishing between more and less significant moments in time, presupposing a minimal plot; unless, of course, there is truly an enumeration with neutral conjunction, but then there is no story in the first place. That is why I slightly alter Forster's thesis by means of the word 'full-fledged', doing justice to another place in the book: 'A story, by the way, is not the same as a plot. It may form the basis of one, but the plot is an organism of a higher type (...).' (ibid.: 20)

[3] They married and had children

the enumeration is structured by the connective 'and', which is by no means neutral as to the order of the first and the second terms, like conjunctive operators in logic or mathematics. Again the order is tacitly interpreted as a temporal one, over and above the conjunction of propositions: they married first and then had children. That there is even more to this 'and' than temporal order, is brought to light when the story is told in reverse order [4]:

[4] They had children and married.

Now we feel that the morals of a particular society, thus normative meanings, come to play a role in the conjunction, which qualifies the enumeration. And if they do in [4], they already did in [3]. It is widely accepted that such wants and beliefs are determinative for the coherence we detect or construe in a story. And it is also a rather accepted view that, in virtue of this determining function, they are at the roots of additions, omissions and transformations involved in putting a coherent story together from a huge number of possible, heterogeneous narrative elements.

When I say that these wants and beliefs are general, I only imply that they are more than arbitrary or subjective; I do not specify in any way the sense in which they can be said to be general. There is, surely, a variety of modes at work here. Wants and beliefs can be general in a number of respects. Sometimes they will be global, sometimes quite local; at times highly institutionalised, at times very implicit; sometimes very much felt inside, sometimes enforced by coercion; sometimes detailed, sometimes vague. But this is not the most important thing. The only thing I submit for endorsement is that they form the grid that shapes our conception of reality. Indeed it generates, to a large extent, though not completely, what we call 'reality'. Not wholly, but often more than we admit, we see what we want to see. Every policeman can corroborate this from his experience with depositions of 'what happened'. The problem, however, becomes much more complicated if we do not only have to admit that we see what we want to see, but also that we think what we want to think. For then it is much more difficult to show by means of tests and experiments that we are wrong, let alone that it is possible to show how to develop strategies to become more right.

To return to Forster's paradigm, we may venture the thesis that - perhaps for pedagogical reasons - he made too easy a distinction between [1] and [2]. The difference is perhaps more relative than he suggested. Taking a cue from Hayden White, we may say that [1] is the paradigm of a chronicle, while [2] is that of historiography. But if such is the case, then it would be feasible to assume that entry [1] in the chronicle would have a date, and that this date is an element in a series of dates. Even then a selection is made by virtue of certain wants and beliefs. For unless this series is nothing more than a calendar in which all days are mentioned, whether something happened or not, the series will contain *the most important* dates. They will be important in presenting a story and contributing to the story having a plot, for instance the rise and fall of a kingdom. Then the (implicit) reading of [3] would perhaps be something like [1a]

[1a] The king died and then (oh, disaster) the queen died.

In this implicit reading [1] becomes rather similar to [2]. The important thing is that stories are not stories by virtue of being merely 'about' something, but just as much in virtue of being 'all about' something.

2 The double hierarchy of Event and Interpretation

It is, to carry the argument one step further, by no means accidental that in our paradigm case the events come first and the qualification second. Although in full-fledged stories the order may be less perspicuous, the simple paradigm case cannot help but reveal that it is based on an insurmountable presupposition of narratives; that the narrative is itself the presentation, articulation, modification, interpretation, evaluation, or whatever, of something (the events) which is conceived of, by the story itself, as independent of and prior to the articulation, modification, etc.[4] This rock-bottom distinction is mostly called the distinction, indeed the hierar-

4. From here I follow a line of argument in Culler (1981: 169 ff), the chapter on 'Story and discourse in the analysis of narrative'.

chy between *Discourse* and *Story*, or *Meaning* and *Event*.[5)] The word 'hierarchy' characterises the priority of the one term over the other, in this case Event (E) over Meaning or, as I will call it for reaons of transparancy in the remainder of the argument, Interpretation (I). Even when we characterise a discourse as fiction, we only understand it by using this very hierarchical framework: the narrative can only be narrated (and received) in virtue of the presupposition that there is something 'outside' the story to tell something *about*; though in that case we do it 'with a wink' to what we trust to be a *real* distinction between Event and Interpretation. To put it in the words of the previous section: If there is one thing that stories are 'all about', it is that they are 'about' something out there. This is why fairy-tales begin with the famous '*Once* upon a time *there* was ...'. The seemingly innocent reference to time and space outside the narrative is the immediate legitimation that a story has begun.

Jonathan Culler has argued[6)], however, that it is of the essence of narratives to prompt the hearers to a second presupposition, which is as necessary as the first one. This second presupposition entails a hierarchy, too, between Event and Interpretation. But it is the exact inversion of the one in the previous section. According to this presupposition, the narrative can only be understood if one acknowledges that the 'events' referred to are *not* independent of and prior to the Interpretation, but are rather the products of discursive forces, restrictions and requirements. To support his thesis, Culler cites Greek drama, modern novels, Freud's report on the famous Wolfman case, Nietzsche's analysis of causation, and William Labov's research on 'natural narratives' in everyday life. His *locus classicus* is the play *Oedipus Rex*. The action of this drama is, without doubt, based on the gradual revelation (Interpretation) of the meaning of a past occurrence (Event). The event of 'Oedipus killing an old man at the cross roads' gets the meaning of 'Oedipus being guilty of killing his own father'. In this respect, the normative judgment of guilt is the consequence

5. Bal (1980: 14) makes the same distinction by means of the terms 'geschiedenis' (history) en 'verhaal' (story). It is '(...) based on the difference between the sequence of events and *the way in which* these events are represented' (my translation). See also Ricoeur (1983-1985), III: 275): 'Raconter quoi que ce soit (...), c'est le raconter *comme* s'il s'était passé.'

6. Culler (1981: 1972 ff). But note also (in Dutch) Verhoeven (1966).

of the antecedent judgment of fact. This is the first presupposition. We may frame it as a hierarchy of reading [H.1]:

[H.1] $E \rightarrow I$ (Event prior to Interpretation).

But the opposite presupposition is also present. Careful reading of the text makes it clear that Oedipus' guilt is never established by the crucial evidence which the old shepherd is expected to give as a former eyewitness at the crossroads. Although this witness is found at last, and although it has been said before in the play by Oedipus himself that his testimony will be all-important, the shepherd is never asked to tell what happened at the crossroads. In fact, what makes the play a tragedy is that this final proof is omitted. The hero knows his destiny already and himself erases the possibility of innocence. He knows the prophecies, he knows the curse on Thebes, he understands from the shepherd that he is Laius' son and he has not forgotten that he once killed an old man at the crossroads and reported that event in public. From all these narrative lines of signification one crucial *event* arises, which needs no further testimony as it is the keystone of the topology of the text: Oedipus acknowledges that he then and there killed his father.

> Oedipus becomes the murderer of his father not by a violent act that is brought to light, but by bowing to the demands of *narrative coherence* and deeming the act to have taken place.[7)]

It is precisely this bowing as a personal act which distinguishes the hero in classical drama from the main character in an arbitrary blood-and-thunder - play. This recognition of his own identity requires the revelation of an origin as a first cause, an origin which is, paradoxically, the effect of its effect, the present cause of past effects. This reading can be framed in a second hierarchy [H.2]:

[H.2] $I \rightarrow E$ (Interpretation prior to Event).

It should be stressed, as Culler does in fact, that this second reading of the text is not *better* than the first one. It does not *replace* a naïve, deluded, or

7. Culler (1981: 174); my emphasis.

somehow incorrect reading. Both hierarchies between Story and Discourse, Event and Interpretation are essential to understanding the text in its interesting aspects. And what is more, we cannot invoke a higher-order hierarchy to harmonize the two opposite ones, for the categories of Event and Interpretation are absolutely basic to the readability of the text. So each of the hierarchies

> (...) works by the exclusion of the other; each depends on a hierarchical relation between story and discourse which the other inverts.[8)]

To put it in other words: The Event will take the place of the ultimate *interpretans*, i.e. the interpreting term, as this is the way in which it can hold on to its place as the ultimate *interpretandum*, i.e. the term to be interpreted. The narrative presupposes *and* intercepts the references to an independent world, precisely by making such a world the keystone of the interpretation and renouncing its own interceptive strategy. The hierarchy of interpretation and event, of thinking and reality, is rendered undecidable and floating. This double bind of poles I will call the interception hypothesis.

It is rewarding to have a short look at other examples given by Culler. That Freud's investigations in psychoanalysis are a main source, will come as no surprise. The Wolf-man is a celebrated case.[9)] At first, Freud defends that something must really have happened with his patient at the age of one and a half (in the family bedroom where he slept, he had watched his parents copulating). In a later writing he returns to the case, though rather casually. Now he points out that it is *undecidable* whether there has been this primordial scene or not. And he adds that it is really not very important either. The scene can also be the focus (and in that sense the product) of significations based on perceptions at a later age (for instance watching copulating dogs at the age of four). Only one who is keen on the instrumental value of the story, for instance for pedagogical reasons (parents, don't let your children sleep in your bedroom!), will be interested in whether the primordial event really happened. It does not make any difference to one who is interested in communication with and care of a patient.

But examples are not restricted to the realm of psychoanalysis. For one

8. Culler (1981: 175).
9. For the first reading, see Freud (1918: 156 ff); for the second, Freud (1918: 166 ff).

thing, Culler himself refers to research on everyday storytelling by William Labov, which clearly indicates the same double hierarchy as set out above. The story in the pub or at the party should be 'worth the telling' and avoid the risk of 'so what?' innuendos. The story demands so much to be 'about' something that *that* is what it is 'all about' in the first place. But in order to meet that demand effectively, the storyteller as well as the hearer has to carefully hide the traces that would disclose the presence of his thought in what should constitute the not-just-thought, to wit, the event. For another thing, it is quite possible, once we get the drift of Culler's thesis, to come up with other examples. One set of examples that particularly leaps to mind are the founding stories of communities in politics or religions. Here it is all too common that what is presented as 'the original event' that founded the whole movement is, at the same time, the keystone or focus of what one wants to come true. For instance, in christendom, the gospels tell us the story of the life of Jesus Christ while, at the same time, this life is narrated as what ultimately tells us the message. Or, to take the birth of a nation like France in the era of modernity: the Revolution is both the event that caused a rupture with the Ancien Régime and the final self-interpretation of the new legal order, which rewrites the event as unequivocal and homogeneous in order to generate its basis of legitimation. Probably the story of 'how philosophy came into being' does not escape the same grammar. Western philosophy sets itself on stage by telling the story ('from muthos to logos') of, for instance, Socrates strolling around in ancient Athens, challenging citizens about their idea of man and what he ought to do. Plato's dialogues are, on the one hand, a report of this 'event', while on the other hand Socrates' role is what makes these dialogues into a coherent whole, even where mythic stories take the place of arguments.[10)]

If Culler is right, as I believe he is as far as narratology is concerned,[11)] we may even try to go one step further. From Culler's account it follows, that 'narrative coherence' generates events in some sense of the word, and that it is the discursive upshot of those events in another sense. What has to be conceived of as an event prior to all interpretation turns out to be also the interpreting notion *par excellence*. This, now, is an

10. As in *The Republic* and *Phaedo*.

11. In chapter 5 I shall present some epistemological amendments, as I cherish the old-fashioned belief that a theory of literature is not per se a theory of knowledge.

important *performative* aspect of narrative texts. By mobilizing the two presuppositions mentioned above, the text succeeds in creating its own 'situation', at least in the sense of an epistemic attitude with which it should be told, heard or read. It is like the urge of a statute or a painting that can make you stand in a certain place rather than another in order to make you look at it properly, while, at the same time, you cannot but deny that it is the causal source of your taking up that position. We may perhaps say that each story has its point, but that all stories have, as narratively coherent stories, a point in common: they can only 'make' their points if and when they are told, heard or read from this double-bind attitude. The attitude which narratives encourage us to adopt, is something like: 'Do not act as if you must decide: either event or interpretation.' But we are bound to make this decision constantly, otherwise we would not be able to act (in the world) or to think (about the world). So the only possible way to obey the command is a sort of eternal 'reversing the charges': if you feel forced to attach interpretation to events; try to find out which of these interpretations generate events: and if you find yourself confronted with generating events from interpretations, try to appeal to what is prior to all signification.

Why do narratives have these curious habits? To narrate is, essentially, to make up for what is left out in conceptual (scientific or philosophical) thinking, to wit, the *singularity* of whatever singular thing, or the *eventuality* of whatever singular occurrence one is trying to give an account of. Conceptual discourse can propose *that, how* and *why* something exists or happens, but only at the cost of leaving something out: the irreducible singularity of this specific something. Narratives are justified by being about something non-discursive, since *that* is a powerful way of presenting this something in its singularity or eventuality. But this is still too simple a way of putting it. If it is true that narratives are not just constituted, but *justified* by being about something non-discursive, when they take an interest in being about some non-discursive event as much as they can, they have to avoid one particular danger of their own rhetoric strategy: they should avoid the pretension of being a totally adequate *representation* of the event in question as a singular event. For if they would *claim* to have the power which conceptual discourse does not have (to have found a key to the inaccessible eventuality of things), they would, at the same time, destroy the basis of their justification. For in that case they would not only claim that 'eventuality' is accessible after all, but also that they can (if only they would) give a (necessarily non-narrative!) account of what counts as adequate accessibility. They would turn into (no doubt *bad*) conceptual discourse. Narratives have an elegant way of coping with this danger: they trace a sort of self-denunciatory circle around an event. They intercept their own referring devices to the outward world by referring to this world as the focus of their own coherence.

It will perhaps be said that this a primitive dualism. A dualism it is in a certain sense, but I am not sure whether it is primitive. What I have tried to say is this: The phenomenon of *narrative* coherence prompts us to assume an attitude of recognizing *ontological* incoherence, or the radical dualism between Event and Meaning. The presumption of ontological incoherence prohibits human thinking to claim truth on the basis of ontological *Letztbegründung*, because this would, necessarily, be a piece of hypostatising either *that* we think or *what* we think. On the other hand, the presumption of ontological incoherence neither entails a dualistic 'reality' (metaphysical dualism) nor a dualistic conception of knowledge (epistemological dualism). On the contrary, precisely because we give up hypostatised rockbottoms, thinking and knowledge become a matter of *making* coherence, without there being an a priori guarantee or *rule* (which is always a rule in someone's, some class's, some time's *hand*) to decide what counts as coherence. So, in the end, *narrative* coherence evokes *epistemological* coherence by paying tribute to ontological incoherence.

3 A strong hypothesis

The dual interception of reference in narratives is the core of the hypothesis I want to investigate in its relation to law. It seems to me that it is the strongest hypothesis available with regard to narrativity. Perhaps Culler is not the only one to defend it, but I think he has formulated it in the most pertinent way and has drawn the most far-reaching consequences. A brief discussion of a view that is paradigmatic of many contemporary theories will show this.

One of the authors who bring this view to the fore is Hayden White. In his essay 'The value of narrativity in the representation of reality' (1981), he explains that a historical story, a narrative about things that 'really' happened in the past, is brought about by operating on a huge amount of disorderly elements. Some of these are selected, others dropped, still others reconstructed or even constructed from almost nothing, in order to make a meaningful pattern arise. The same goes for other than strictly historical narratives, in as far as all stories require story-independent goings-on.

The main criterion for significance in historical narratives, White submits, is of a political nature. Decisive is what contributes to a pattern that is meaningful for the culture or the community to bring its own history to the fore; that is to say, the sociopolitical order or identity of this culture or group. But in order to frame such a story as a story about 'what really happened', the epiphenomena of this decisive criterion have to be removed from the surface of the story. The events have to be shown as 'brute facts' rather than literary constructs, let alone the disseminations or reflections of a unbridled want or belief. Thus, the decisive criterion of sociopolitical meaningfulness will only be implicit in the story as it is told.

Subsequently, White arrives at a distinction of hierarchies similar to Culler's: the truth value of the narrated events is always also a function of the coherence of the story itself.

> Common opinion has it, that the plot of a narrative imposes meaning on the events that comprise its story level by revealing at the end a structure that was immanent in the events *all along*. What I am trying to establish is the nature of the immanence in any narrative account of *real* events, the kind of events that are offered as the proper content of historical discourse. The reality of these events does not consist in the fact that they occurred but that, first of all, they were remembered and, second, that they are capable of finding a place in a chronologically ordered sequence. (1981: 19)[12)]

Through this process of composing a plot, the 'real events' are moulded into a unison of meaning, which, as contingent reality, they cannot possibly harbour and which cannot be immediately 'sensed' from them by experience. The convergence can only arise from the imagination and ideals which we allow ourselves to cherish in the first place. And precisely in order to conceal this compositional process and make it the most effective it can be, its product has to be stiffened as reality *par excellence*.

It cannot be doubted that White's thesis is close to Culler's. But there is, nevertheless, a considerable difference to be appreciated. Culler seems

12. Cf. a later publication: White (1986: 21).

to see narrativity as an escape from, or at least a rebuttal of, representational thinking. His most interesting and daring proposition is not that what initially looks like a report on hard and fast reality is, on closer examination, a construed projection. The most challenging part of his view is that, on still closer examiniation, the demarcation of reality and interpretation becomes involved in an infinite process of interception and suspension, in which we can neither transcend nor abandon the poles of the relationship. In this context, Culler uses the term 'undecidability': there is no theoretical synthesis to be worked out between [H.1] and [H.2] that could warrant a higher order of understanding. White, on the contrary, refrains from taking this radical stand. He seems to hold on to the belief that, at the end of the day, we are able to sort out appearances and reality in an objective and final way. His view is that a large number of narrative elements in stories that pose as 'story-independent reality' are to be unmasked as reflections of a pre-established sociopolitical self-conception, directives of action or morals to be included. But this does not amount to departing from representationalism; it just means that a story represents something different from what it seems or pretends to represent on its face, and tries to cover up the traces of this strategy of hiding.

It seems to me that what White tries to do, put to its limit, resembles a Foucaultian programme. In his first volume on the history of sexuality, *La volonté de savoir,* Foucault (1976) argued that 'sexuality' is to be seen as the product of a *discours*, that is to say,[13)] an ensemble of strategies of thinking, speaking and acting. To those who object that at the basis of all these strategies there are, undeniably, the brute facts of a natural passion or urge from which they originate, he responds that this very idea of a natural urge is the paragon of discursive productivity. This is the keystone that has to be generated in order that the whole edifice shows meaningful coherence. Unlike Culler, Foucault only emphasises one side of the interception. He wants us to replace our usual hierarchy [H.1] with a better one [H.2], claiming that everything we call 'reality' is in point of fact a dis-

13. I derive this definition of *discours* from Jan M. Broekman (1973). I have pondered on translating the term itself by 'linguistic tissue' because, like in a tissue, the representing front is very opaquely, but still systematically matched onto (and, reversely, produced by) the knots and threads at the back.

cursive construct.[14)]

This claim, in my view, comes down to turning the tables within the framework of a common and decisive presupposition. This presupposition is that there is a relation of representating or picturing between knowledge and reality. What Foucault does is to reverse the order of this relation: our epistemic claims are not picturing reality, it is rather the other way round: reality is a picture of our epistemic claims (to be disguised as power claims rather than truth claims). Thus, the pole of Event can be reduced to the pole of Interpretation. The interception hypothesis goes one step further: it attains the self-evidence of the relation of representation, without denying the necessity or the possibility of constantly making a provisory, rather than a final distinction between appearance and reality. It is a strategy to deal with both of the poles at the expense of neither one and, thus, to escape from reductionism. That is why I think that Culler's hypothesis is the stronger one compared to Foucault's and probably also to White's.

One may be inclined to ask if it is not too strong to be fruitful. Characterizing the opposition between [H.1] and [H.2] as 'undecidable' seems to lead a priori into a dead alley. Although I painfully tried to avoid the word 'deconstruction', it will be clear to philosophical insiders that this is the label under which Culler's views have to be stored.[15)] And if this is the case, one usually gets suspicious: what else can be expected from deconstruction than destruction? To put it in another way: Does not the Culler approach consist of forcing a text into the shackels of contradictory readings, only to step backwards and claim from a safe position outside the text that there is no sense at all to discover, that every meaning is neutralized by another, that we are left with sheer aporia and 'undecidability'?[16)] Lawyers especially will be tempted to wonder what good

14. Under the revealing title *Oublier Foucault* (1977), Baudrillard explained this pitfall in Foucault's approach. According to Baudrillard, Foucault forgets that he is still committed to the claim of privileged access to a higher - order reality linked up with his theory. After having written the first part of the history of sexuality, Foucault changed to a different paradigm of analysis, which escapes the criticism.

15. Cf. Also the explicit title of his later work, *On Deconstruction.*

16. Readings (1991: 136) believes that there is reason to criticise Culler's approach from views taken from Lyotard. Although Readings mainly focuses on Paul De Man's work, Culler is involved to the extent that the latter has supported De Man's project in public. If Reading's objections are aimed at De Man, they also aim at Culler. Their core lies with this approach denying the historicity of the text, as it always and only goes for carving out

could come from a theory that celebrates 'undecidability', as it so clearly seems at odds with everything society expects from law. Is it not this stepping back that generates the alleged aporia, as if it were the spatial object of a 'gaze'? Indeed, is not the aporia brought to light only in order that deconstructive analysis closes itself, instead of the aporia being something really 'there' in the text? Is there anything more to it than creating an opposition between the representation of an act (representing an event) and the act of representation (the event of representing)? Maybe the ironic gaze is able to detect that the representation of [H.1] is premature, but does not realise (i) that it represents the event of representation according to the selfsame logic, thus obeying [H.2], and (ii) that it therefore falls short of the alleged 'original event' which [H.1] posits. In still other words: Should not the interception hypothesis be applied to itself?

I believe that this criticism is a misfire, though it may be useful in preventing too naïve an interpretation of the interception hypothesis. It is right that 'deconstruction' is all too often looked upon as a philosophical permit to rip any text apart into ever so many aporias, ignite the gaze of complete confusion and knock off to the next job. The problem lies with the word 'any'. I have no difficulty with feeling bewilderment in the confrontation with, for instance, a work of art that, under certain forms of analysis, shows insoluble aporias of experience. I even think that some philosophical texts can be contemplated from this, what I would like to call an aesthetic, point of view. But what I doubt is whether that would take into account what the text presenting a philosophical theory wants to be as much as the analysis arguing that it does not succeed in achieving what it wants to be, namely a truth claim. Such criticism 'from outside' is self-destroying: it must either stage itself as the only escape from falsity, or concede that it is itself just another way of generating non-sense.

The stakes with Culler's model of narrative are different.[17)] The aporias it tries to reveal are not construed from a standpoint outside the text, but are valid inside the text, i.e. for the protagonists of the story itself. This is what the Oedipus example clearly shows. Oedipus is the first to bow to the demands of narrative coherence. And it is because Oedipus bows first that the audience is able to see the tragedy of the story they have involved themselves in. Oedipus allows them to 'find him guilty',

some essential meaning leaving the rest behind as rubbish.

17. Also those in De Man's project, in my view.

but not as if they were his jury. The spectators look into a mirror: if they confirm Oedipus' guilt, they cannot but acknowledge that they themselves are guilty in the first place. In particular, they will become aware of the fact that they already bowed to the demands of narrative coherence and found Oedipus guilty long before he himself did. They saw fate coming and rendered their judgment prematurely. Why do they not take the sight from their own eyes? Of course, it is not true that there is no difference between the standpoint of the spectators and that of the protagonists. The important thing is that there is no ontological warrant for the difference: it can be challenged in an ongoing process of interpretation. Not only is there no last interpretation, but there is also no first event to be interpreted, not even at the meta-level of understanding itself. This is what allows us to conceive of history as suspension rather than hypostatisation of our favourite epistemology, which is representationalist through and through.

A last objection against the interception hypothesis could perhaps be based on the observation by (again) Hayden White, referring to Hegel's philosophy of history. White believes, as we learned, that coherence in a historical narrative is politically determined. I think that there is reason to generalize this observation to all narratives and not to restrict it to historical narratives. However small the circle is that poses as the recipient of a story, the point of the story will always be dependent on the self-conception of this circle as a limited and structured whole, surrounded by the larger circle of what they call their society. We could say that each narrative presupposes a society to have identified itself already and - to phrase it in Lefort's terms - to have already bestowed legitimacy upon the place where power resides by virtue of that identity. In other words: White believes that the instance of the Law (as legitimate power) would have to precede every story, as narrative coherence is always dependent on the viewpoint of legitimate power.

This may be true in itself, but it does not solve the problem that the Law (or simply, authority) also is not just something self-identical 'out there', but an instance that has its own history, even if, by necessity, it is unable to analyse itself as the product of history in the very speech act in which it claims authority, i.e. in enacting laws. It would lose its impact as norm-enacting authority if it were to pose as the product of contingent historical causes.[18] Here also, there is interception in both directions. History is not a representation of authority, even if it always refers to it; but neither is authority a reflex of history, even if it is generated by it. To reinforce their own position, both terms of the relationship have to acknowledge what they are *not*.

The interception hypothesis seems to me the strongest hypothesis, and one that rises to some important preceding objections of implausibility. That is why it will be taken under scrutiny in the following chapters. This investigation will develop in three stages. Firstly, the explanatory force of the hypothesis is tested against legal texts from three different contexts: relating the facts, closing the system of norms and applying the norms to the facts in legal decision making. Then, secondly, the results will be accounted for in a larger epistemological framework: the critique of representationalism and its legal guise, legalism. The last chapters, thirdly, will elaborate on the jurisprudentional consequences of what I prefer to call a narrative approach to law, only - as J.L. Austin admitted when he coined 'linguistic phenomenology' - 'that's rather a mouthful'.

18. Derrida (1985).

CHAPTER 2

NARRATIVE COHERENCE AND THE FACTS OF THE CASE

The hypothesis of interception between the variables E and I can only be tested if these variables take on different values. Although the hypothesis is derived from storytelling in the plain sense, its epistemological scope is much more embracing than that. So, what we will do is explore this scope by gradually altering the context. The first context, however, will be quite close to the one from which the hypothesis was derived. Because a typical and, indeed, a large part of what lawyers do in actual practice (in drafting, litigating, decision making, etc.) is to lay out the facts of a case in a legally 'relevant' way. Thus the case is a value of I, while the raw materials they build it from can be regarded as a value of E. Our question then becomes whether reciprocal interception occurs at this level of building a case.

1 Relating facts

What lawyers call a case is by no means a neutral description of the problems that occurred in real life. Every lawyer knows that. A case is a construct, often laboriously tinkered from reports and records, testimonies and confessions, observations and interpretations. All these materials are qualified from a certain angle, to wit, the question whether or not they bear (prima-facie) relevance to a decision in the case at hand. Thus, in a sense this case has to exist before it is constructed in full. Some of these materials - for instance police records - are sometimes framed in categories so clearly derived from the nomenclature of the law that important questions of relevance are already answered before the case has been constructed. When a police officer sits before the blank screen of what is to become 'a case' he or she knows very well which elements of the complex situation to eliminate, which to accentuate in order to make the public prosecutor do his job. Whether he goes so far as to frame the suspect is another thing, but he certainly frames the case. However that may be, a case is only a case if it is possible to describe it *coherently* in legal categories.

In his Lund-lecture,[1)] Professor MacCormick introduced the notion of narrative coherence along with normative coherence. Both concepts, in juxtaposition, function in his account of justified legal reasoning. The latter refers to matters of law: coherence of legal norms is to be considered

> (...) a function of its justifiability under higher-order principles or values, principles and values being extensionally equivalent; provided that the higher or highest-order principles and values seem acceptable as delineating a satisfactory form of life, when taken together.[2)]

The former refers to a test of truth or probability in questions of fact and evidence upon which direct proof by immediate observation is not available (MacCormick 1984: 245; 248f). Criteria of narrative coherence allow us to draw inferences from statements of evidentiary facts to propositions about unperceived events. Such a test justifies decisions about what content of belief will constitute the case to be judged. MacCormick also highlighted the epistemic background of the explanatory force which narrative coherence appears to have. Human beings make their world an intelligible world for themselves, which requires the presuppositions, (a) that whatever we perceive is real (the phenomenal world matches the noumenal world) and (b) that whatever is real is rationally related under some explanatory principle to whatever else is real. Both (a) and (b) have to be regarded as tentative and provisional for at least three reasons: (i) the revisability of our explanatory schemes, (ii) the incompleteness of information and (iii) the delusoriness of our perception.

I think that MacCormick's analytical distinction between normative and narrative coherence is blurred in the actual construction of a case. A specific part of the background which allows us to process a coherent account of facts in law is certainly a sort of 'knowledge' that pertains to not just common or scientific sense, but to what Hayden White calls the sociopolitical identity of the group in which the decision procedure evolves and which is accounted for in terms of normative convictions: basic values, ideals, wants and needs. An even more specific part is constituted by the format in which this broader type of 'knowledge' is allowed to enter legal

1. MacCormick (1984: 235-251, esp. 245 ff).
2. MacCormick (1984: 28).

language, that is to say, through the sieve of doctrinal concepts. This double constraint, reference to political identity and reference to doctrine, is decisive in the way in which the facts of a case are processed. Let us see how it works when we make a laboratory-like setting of texts with legal relevance, comparing them by means of close-reading techniques. In its plainest form the question is: How is it that stories in law are told in order to get the facts clear? We will see the question answered by applying the interception hypothesis.

Below I present in two columns two versions of the facts of the same case: a case of euthanasia tried in The Netherlands.[3)] It concerns an old lady who wants to be freed from her sufferings and asks a medical doctor to give her a lethal injection - which the doctor does after many hesitations and deliberations. When we recorded the texts, the case was before an appellate court, and it was expected to come before The Netherlands Supreme Court as well. But I will refrain from telling either the sequence of decisions or the legal consequences, as in this stage I am interested in the way in which the facts of the case are related. In other words, I am curious about the way in which background convictions in law are rhetorically mobilized and processed in order to construct a case. I am aware that many details of the case give rise to moral questions, which may receive varying answers. But again, I leave that point aside, to deal with nothing but 'the facts' - which will be quite a lot.

2 A case in synopsis

These two narratives stem from different sources. The left-hand column renders Discourse I (DI), which is the story told by the litigator of the defendant, i.e. the physician. It is a part of his plea (under the heading 'the facts') before a court of appeal.[4)] Discourse II (DII) is a recital of

3. Cf. Rb. Alkmaar, 10th May 1983 (NJ 1983: 407). For the reader's information: This District Court declared the doctor not guilty; the Court of Appeal found him quilty (Hof Amsterdam, 17th November 1983, NJ 1984: 43) but refrained from punishment; the Netherlands Supreme Court overruled that decision (27th November 1984, NJ 1985, 106) and referred the case to the Appellate Court at 's-Gravenhage (10th Juin 1985 and 11th September 1986, NJ 1987: 608). The latter ruled as the District Court at Alkmaar.

4. Cf. Sutorius (1984: 51).

the facts by a lower court in its formal statement of the grounds for its verdict. The different elements of the two stories are put in synopsis, so that similar episodes are juxtaposed. For the convenience of the reader I give fictional names to the main characters of the stories: Mrs. Burlow and her practitioner, Dr. Shope. On reading and comparing the texts we will soon enough find that there are different demands of coherence in the two columns.

DI

On the 8th of March 1976, 89-year-old Maria B. moves to a service flat in P., because of her advanced age. She becomes a patient of Dr. S. Maria B. is a lively, mentally alert woman, who values her independence very highly. In the course of the years, her body functions less and less well and symptoms of old age, like moving with difficulty, deterioration of sight and hearing, attacks of dizziness, increase considerably.

On the 14th of April 1980, she signs a so-called declaration of euthanasia, which she hands over to her medical doctor. Earlier, Maria B. had asked her doctor several times if it would be possible for him to end her life through medical intervention - a request to which Dr. S. had not responded.

On the 16th of September 1981, she falls, breaks her left hip and announces that she only wants to be operated upon if she is not going to survive the operation. The surgeon refrains from operating. She is transferred to the infirmary at the serviceflat and is confined to her bed, awaiting her death. Walking is impossible; after a few months she is also unable

DII

(The court)

Considering that the suspect (P.L.S., eds.) has declared in court - reported in essence i.a., that he has been a general practitioner at P. since 1st January 1974; that Mrs. M. Burlow, born at H. on the 27th of November 1886, has been his patient since 8 March 1976; that she lived in an apartment on R. 513 at P., in serviceflat W.;

That during the past years Mrs. B. had asked him several times whether he would end her life through medical intervention;
That the matter had rested there;
That she had handed him at a given moment a declaration of euthanasia, which he accepted;

to sit. Her sight and hearing deteriorate rapidly and from time to time it is hardly possible for her to speak. She is now 94 years old. The necessity of a catheter and her absolute dependence on nurses for washing, tools and care in general emphasize for Maria B. - who remains mentally perfectly clear-headed and aware - her gradually increasing debasement. This experience is further reinforced by the fact that communication with her environment is hardly possible, due to diminishing sensory functions. Her requests to her doctor to shorten her life become increasingly urgent. During the last week of her life her condition gets considerably worse. She is not able to drink any more and loses consciousness for a period of time. After a few days, however, a small change for the better occurs, though drinking remains difficult and eating impossible. As soon as communication to a limited extent becomes possible again, it turns out that she had expected to die and cannot accept that this did not happen. She asks her son to come and see her, and begs him to arrange euthanasia, a request that she repeats to her doctor and to Dr. B., his assistant. Thereupon a number of talks take place between the patient, her son and the two doctors, which result in Dr. S. decision finally to comply with Maria B.'s urgent wish on Friday morning of the same week. On this Friday morning there is, first, a long talk between mother, son and daughter-in-law: farewell is said and she declares how grateful she feels to her doctor ('Honour this doctor') and also to her son and daughter-in-law for accepting her decision. Furthermore, she ar-

That the request to end her life became more urgent during the last week and that her general condition made this request explicable;
That her mental faculties remained intact all the time;
That her physical faculties were visibly deteriorating;
That, when the son's request to comply with his mother's wish was added, he decided to yield to her intense and serious desire;

That he has had, at her request, a final talk with her, her son, Mr. van S., her daughter-in-law, and his assistant, A.B., on 16th of July 1982 at about 11.00 a.m.;

ranges some details concerning her cremation and the expression of thanks to a number of good friends. At about 11.30 a.m. the doctor and his assistant arrive. They ask Maria B. whether she insists on her explicit wish, which she affirms without any restriction ('If it is possible, please, doctor, immediately; let's get on with it, not another night.'). Then, the doctors leave the room for a moment, offering the family the opportunity for a last farewell. After that, at 11.44 a.m. the doctor gives Maria B. an injection, which makes her fall asleep.	That it became evident again at that moment, that she had only one wish: to die as soon as possible; That he has complied with her request immediately after that talk; That on 16th of July 1982, at 11.44 a.m. he gave her an intravenous injection of 6 cc Sterolid (10 mg/cc), as a result of which she partly lost consciousness;
At 11.55 a.m. a second injection is given causing her to go into a coma. And at 12.03 a.m. she is given a last injection, which causes Maria B.'s respiration to halt, as a result of which she dies.	That at 11.55 a.m. he injected her with 2 cc Pethidine (50 mg/cc), after which she went into a coma; That at 12.03 a.m. he injected her with 3 cc Cunarine (1.5 mg/cc), after which she died at 12.08.

3 Analysis

By comparing the two narratives, we may establish that they are not simply about the same 'event' and, thus, not merely variations of representation, but that they also generate *different* 'events'. Let us note some slight, but yet striking differences in the internal coherence of DI and DII.

1) DI is a discourse primarily focused on Mrs. Maria B., while DII is clearly focused on Dr. S. This is already evident in the very first sentence: DI mentions B. first, DII mentions S. first. Also, the stories start at different stages: in DI Mrs. B. looks for a practitioner after having moved to a new place and finds Dr. S., whereas in DII Dr. D. finds Mrs. B. as one of his patients. Time indications (dates) function in DI to pinpoint moments in the contact between B. and S. from B.'s point of view, in DII from S.'s point of view.
2) Moreover, it is clear that DI is closer to B.'s actual biography than

DII: the former starts with some details about B.'s age, her decision to move because of her age, etc., as an immediately relevant context for what follows. From the beginning of DII, more or less the same data can be derived, but here they function as adequate means to identify B. and S. as the legal subjects (rather than persons in everyday social life) involved. This becomes clear from the fact that B.'s place of birth is mentioned, which is hardly relevant to the situation in which she found herself during the last period of her life.

3) In DI the 'action' of the narrative is the increasing tension between B.'s physically degenerating condition and her acute awareness of it, or indeed disgust at it. This increase is presented as producing the increasing urgency of the requests for euthanasia. DII focuses directly on this increasing urgency of requests as the 'action' of the narrative whereas, Mrs. B.'s condition comes in as a (possible) explanation (from the court's perspective?) of only the final stage of the series of requests.

4) The link between Mrs. B.'s final request and Dr. S.'s final decision in DI is narrated by referring to a number of talks between patient, doctor, assistant-doctor and the son, indicating a common quest for an acceptable solution. In DII, however, the link is rather designed as a process of bargaining by two quasi-contractual parties, demanding and offering until they agree about the exchange of goods.

5) In DI emotive expressions, though used quite sparingly, are essential to focus on the 'decisive moment' of the injection; they are altogether lacking in DII, except where reference is made to the urgency and intensiveness of Mrs. B.'s wish to die by way of euthanasia.

6) It is remarkable that DI is narrated in the present tense, aiming at coherence in prospect. It recounts the sequence of events as a coherent development from one stage into a succeeding stage. Each stage is a new one for the agents involved. Here the reasonableness of sequences is narrated as an agent would see it, without having knowledge of what will appear to be the case in hindsight. DII, on the other hand, is in the past tense, aiming at coherence in retrospect, i.e., a coherent account in which each stage can be explained from a previous one.

7) It is obvious that DI is twice as long as DII. However, if we count tokens of words in the semantic field of 'request', 'desire', 'ask', their frequency in DI is 10, while in DII 12. So their relative density in DII is much greater. Moreover, no less than 5 tokens occur in DII before Mrs. B.'s deteriorating physical condition is mentioned explicitly for the first

time. In DI this number is 0. So it seems to me that in DII the narrative line of B.'s request is much more prominent than in DI.

8) The synopsis maps the stories' elements onto each other, so that they take the same space on paper. Thus it comes to light which element in one story corresponds to a blank in the other. Corresponding to the five empty spaces in DII are the following narrative elements on the left-hand side:

(a) history of increasing illness
(b) history of increasing illness
(c) history of increasing illness
(d) conversation; deliberation
(e) conversation: thanks, goodbye, last wishes

Of course there are also (small) blanks in the left-hand column, corresponding to three narrative elements (a') - (c') in DII:

(a') composition and dilution of the first injection
(b') composition and dilution of the second injection
(c') composition and dilution of the third injection

9) Although it will certainly have been irrelevant during the trial, in DI we do not find an indication of the date on which S. gave the injection. It appears from DII that this must have been on the 16th of July 1982. But we do know from DI that it was a Friday: the Friday of the week in which there had been intensive deliberations between B., her family and the two practitioners involved, and the decision was taken to end her life. This week is depicted only as 'the last week of her life'. We may conclude from this that in DI time is seen as determined from the perspective of the act, not (as in DII) the act from the perspective of time. Time in DI is a narrated time frame, without reference to the calendar outside the story.

4 Interpretation

Apart from these differences, the two discourses show similarities of narrative coherence as well: both start by introducing the actors B. and S. within a spatio-temporal framework. Both draw a line from their first contact to Mrs. B.'s death. Both refer to the process of B.'s age and illness, as well as to the process of actions and dialogues. The differences occur within these similarities. This may tempt us to suppose that DII is only a more sober or even neutral version of DI, leaving out 'irrelevant details' in the representation of what really happened. That, anyway, seems to be the court's view, as it declares itself to be reporting what Dr. S. said, reduced to its alleged 'essence'. But this account of the matter takes too short a cut. As both narratives are expected to provide what counts as a sufficiently coherent account of how B.'s death took place, they can be said to offer different values for the same variable of 'a sufficiently coherent account'. DII adds as much as it leaves out, simply by focusing on certain details which grow more important and dominant as others fade away. DII offers just one thick narrative line from the first to the last moment in the relationship between B. and S; a line, coherent in itself as it connects the various points of the same level: the sequence of requests and responses, respectively growing in urgency, diminishing in reluctancy. But DI traces several narrative lines, which are coherent with one another as they converge in one point. Thus, there are the lines of emotions (debasement, frustration on the one hand, gratefulness and honour on the other); of common deliberation (in search of the moral and legal, good and bad consequences like guilt feelings, publicity, etc.); of the doctor's professional involvement in B.'s suffering during many years; of B.'s worsening general condition; of her increasingly urgent requests. They converge narratively at precisely one point: Dr. S. giving Mrs. B. a lethal injection and, indeed, killing her.

There is some textual evidence for the difference between DI and DII on this point. We may note that ending Mrs. B.'s life is regarded in DI as the doctor's acknowledged and consciously chosen responsibility. This is manifest in the causal connectives at the end of the text; they belong to the intension of the description of what the doctor does. In DII these very connectives (with one exception) are replaced by time connectives. *Propter* is replaced by *post*. Ending Mrs. B.'s life is outside the intensional range of the description. In DII, depriving B. of her life is not recounted as the recognized destiny or responsibility of Dr. S., but as the legal meaning of what he did - a meaning which is co-referential with whatever meaning S. himself would give to what he did. That what he did was 'depriving B. of her life' is established not on the basis of his (S.'s) action but on the basis of the medical evidence from autopsy which, in this case, is of course performed under legal authority.

So, what we see here is a rather clear instantiation of what the interception hypothesis is about. Just like in the Oedipus drama, one might say that DI is about *and* produces the event of depriving Mrs. B. of her life. On the one hand it is obvious that DI presupposes this very event to be independent of its mode of representation. Of course the event of 'Dr. S. killed Mrs. B. at her request' is narrated as prior to the interpretation given to it by the litigator's discourse: 'Dr. S. saved Mrs. B. from unbearable suffering.' This is a reading according to hierarchy [H.1]. But, on the other hand, surely DI has elemcnts of the inverted hierarchy [H.2]: the killing of Mrs. B. is as much the keystone of the reality processed by the discourse as a story-independent reality referred to in the story. It is the focus that is contained in the description of all that happened. It would remain intact, even if some of the description would have been omitted. For instance, if DI would have been the script of a movie, the scene with the injections could have been cut without any spectator doubting what finally happened. This basic ambiguity - characteristic of narrative according to our hypothesis - is neutralised in DII. Here there is linear, not textual coherence. Traces of the ambiguity characteristic of narratives are erased. The story is basically a one-liner: old Mrs. B. urgently requested Dr. S. to end her life through medical intervention, he decided to do so, and on the 16th of July 1982 he did something which - on later evidence - turned out to have been 'causing B. to die'. The only hierarchy left is [H.1]. Thus, a definitive fissure between event and interpretation is wretched: there can be only 'event', if and in as much as it is independent of all signification. Apparently, when it comes to decision making, legal discourse cannot afford to leave room for doubt to the effect that what has happened is also 'only' what the story wants to be true. Everything that could possibly give rise to such doubt is denied the status of legal fact in advance.

This observation confronts us with an important question left aside until now: Why does the court believe that both succinctness and objectivity of the report on the facts of the case are served by omitting narrative elements like the history of illness and debasement, deliberation and self-chosen responsibility? When we look again carefully at the blanks in the synopsis of DI and DII, this question becomes equivalent to: Why does the court think itself justified in summarizing the depositions and records by emphasizing the explicitness and seriousness of Mrs. B.'s request on the one hand, and Dr. S.'s decision to do things which would cause her death (supplemented by medical evidence to the effect that he succeeded) on the other? The answer lies, obviously, in the concepts of article 293 of the Dutch Criminal Code, which is (still)[5] read as prohibiting euthanasia in principle:

(1) A person who takes the life of another person at that other person's express and earnest request is liable to a term of imprisonment of not more than twelve years or a fine of the fifth category.[6]

It is not too far-fetched to locate the source of the DII dominant narrative line in this article, considering the context of Dutch criminal law. Sentence (1) contains expressions which function as selection filters for descriptions of events. Only what could have happened (or not) in the terms of these filters, delineates 'what happened'. Only positive or negative references of these expressions make a story 'worth being told' as far as the law is concerned. So in this respect, that is, from the point of view of our theoretical analysis, [H. 2] reveals itself in DII all the same. 'What happened' is a construct, a focus of legal representation, however forcefully it is disguised as 'that which precedes any legal representation'.

This observation could tempt us to conclude that the law does nothing less than fabricate its own 'reality', only to subsequently try it. But that conclusion would contradict the interception hypothesis as squarely as the strategy of law itself. What we would do then is hold [H.2] for a better reading of the story than [H.1], or rather the only one possible. We would hypostatise one of the poles in the relationship between Event and Interpretation as much as the court did; only, we would opt for the other pole. And that would not be the only thing resulting from it. If such an 'alternative' account of the case is to leave the level of literary or theoretical analysis behind and acquire any legal force at all with a view to, for instance, defending the doctor, then it will come under specific pressure:

5. The present situation is The Netherlands in rather complicated, but far less 'liberal' than is sometimes thought abroad. A very brief account would be that 1) one makes a distinction between euthanasia as ending a person's life on request and abstention from useless medical treatment or suppression of pain or severe suffering in the terminal phase of the process of dying; 2) doctors are under the obligation to report actions that they deem to be euthanasia to the Prosecution Office; 3) they can be reasonably sure not to be prosecuted if they have observed a list of criteria for careful behaviour. For an overview in English see Van Kalmthout (1996).

6. ©Rijksuniversiteit Limburg/L. Rayar, S. Wadsworth, 1996.

the pressure of having to frame an 'alternative' legal doctrine. One could imagine that such a defence would prefer to concentrate on the thesis that what Dr. S. did was not 'taking somebody's life', but that he, for instance, was only instrumental to Mrs. B.'s suicide. When such an alternative doctrine is proposed in court, it usually stands no chance at all against received doctrine. This is hardly surprising. The legal system does not conceive of itself as a framework that is apt to directly absorb new experiences in particular circumstances and to express them in personal modulations. That is what it would rather leave to poetry, one could say. The systematic character of law is dependent on its conceptual coherence, suited to articulate legal norms. Of course, elasticity in the allowed values of reference is needed, for non-elastic frameworks break down rapidly. But even this elasticity and plasticity is dependent on a parsimonious conceptual regime: social complexity has to be reduced to a limited number of categories, as Luhmann observed. It is, therefore, necessary to dig into the systematicity of law, in order to try and establish which ultimate categories determine it. This is what we will see in the next chapter.

CHAPTER 3

NARRATIVE COHERENCE AND THE SYSTEM OF LEGAL NORMS

A second context in which the interception hypothesis is to be tested is offered by lawyers' frequent reference to 'the system of norms'. It is obvious that we can look at this system from different angles. From the angle of reasoning, for instance, it shows logical coherence, from the angle of genealogy, historical coherence, from the angle of social relationships, functional coherence. But what kind of coherence is reflected under a specifically legal angle? I submit that in the eyes of legal subjects, legal authorities and legal scholars, law is made into a system by virtue of the claim behind each and every decision or rule that it ultimately relates, through actual and historical social relationships, to a supreme norm of political morality.

Even if it would be true in point of fact that, in a certain political order, the law is just whatever those in power command, such commands could only be presented as would-be law through reference to a supreme norm about 'the just society'. Of course it is possible in such a case that the members of this society are not prepared to recognize these efforts and vehemently criticize the reference as a lie. But then they will in fact be saying that they are outside the would-be legal system, that they do not regard themselves as subjected to that law altogether, and they will perhaps engage in violent resistance and (civil) war. Disguising the liars, however, presupposes the very same reference to a supreme norm of justice, be it with a different content. So what I intend to concentrate on here is what the law is 'in its own eyes', so to speak. I focus on the appearance made by positive law in society. And that appearance, I submit, is always made with the claim 'to be the best it can be' from the point of view of political morality, in the terms of this society's articulation of its own identity through history.[1)]

At least since the days of the French Revolution (but in some parts of the world considerably earlier), this morality is framed in terms of in-

1. I borrow Dworkin's basic tenet in *Law's Empire* (1986).

alienable rights, inherent to the human person as a worthy and free being, and as a responsible and free citizen. Cut back to its simplest form: Whatever we enact of rules to regulate behaviour, or to mould procedures, forms and institutions, at the end of the day positive law is about respect for human dignity and the observation of human rights.[2)] Even the most arbitrary or formal decisions are supposed to bear, in the final analysis, at least some relationship to it, and that is at least part of the reason why, in the law's own perspective, law comes in systems.

So if we want our hypothesis to cut some wood on the normative side of law, it is advisable to test it on such references to human dignity and human rights. Following this advice we will have to be satisfied, for the time being, with a rather intuitive notion of 'system'. On the one hand, a conception of system derived from axiomatic calculus would be far too restrictive. With this conception in hand, not only an analysis of legal systems, but also of, for instance, ecological systems would fall short. On the other hand, systems theory in law, although it takes the 'external' rather than the 'internal' point of view on law, has made it quite clear that swift formulas about the 'open system' of law are profoundly flawed in that they forget about the system's self-defined conditions of openness.[3)] I will return to this issue at the end of this chapter. Right now, let us concentrate on the bottom line which seems to close it: reference to human rights and human dignity. We will regard it as a value of variable I in the scheme of the interception hypothesis, taking political identity as a value of E.

2. 'Respect (or: concern) for persons' is an explicit one-liner in many a discourse on the rights humans have. See, for instance, Dworkin (1977), especially the essay 'What rights do we have?', where he emphasises the point that 'equal respect' is part and parcel of respect for persons. The phrase often has a primary if implicit importance in theories of legal reasoning. For instance, MacCormick's (1984: 28) notion of 'normative coherence' as a major criterion for determining the soundness of legal arguments asks whether a certain legal norm (or set of norms) is justifiable '(...) under higher principles or values (...), provided that the higher or highest-order principles and values seem acceptable as delineating a satisfactory form of life, when taken together; one in which it would be possible for human beings, *as human beings are* to live in'.
3. Cf., for instance, Luhmann (1986).

1 Justice affronted

In order to create some initial uneasiness about this self-evident reference to rights and dignity, I will start with a short quotation from literature. Near the end of Sartre's psychological novel, *L'Enfance d'un chef* there is a passage in which the main character, Lucien Fleurier, formulates the discovery of his own existentially real identity:

> He absolutely had to find words to express this extraordinary discovery. Quietly, cautiously, he raised his hand to his forehead, like a lighted candle. He then collected himself for an instant, thoughtful and sacred; and the words came of themselves. He murmured: 'I HAVE RIGHTS!' Rights! Something in the nature of triangles and circles; it was so perfect that it didn't exist. No matter how many thousands of rings you traced with a compass you could never make a single circle. In het same way, generations of workers could scrupulously obey the commands given by Lucien but they would never exhaust his right to command. Rights were beyond existence, like mathematical objects or religious dogmas. And Lucien was precisely that: an enormous bouquet of responsibilities and rights.[4)]

As delineating a person's identity, these words should outrage us, especially when we learn that Lucien Fleurier realizes himself to be an anti-semitic *Führer*. How, we ask, can such a person frame his own fascist identity in the very terms coined in our own moral history to express law's inherent relationship to justice? Indeed, even those who are reluctant to accept Dworkin's 'rights thesis' find themselves yielding to the fundamental cultural principle that law affirms every person as being an entity with a set of inalienable and inviolable rights.[5)] Even one who is sceptical about 'law in the books' and the relevance of legal doctrine to

4. My translation.
5. Without arguing this any further, I point to three phenomena in the political penumbra of legal systems: (a) the idea of 'human rights' is referred to in political prolegomena of legal self-conception: preambles and 'declarations' of some states and the United Nations; (b) it functions as a criterion in political bargaining of international co-operation (e.g. membership of the EC; development aid); (c) it is at the basis of public goodwill of humanitarian political movements, actions and organisations (e.g. Amnesty International). The most impressive *legal* reception of this idea is probably found in the Austrian Civil Code of 1811: 'Jeder Mensch hat angeborene, schon durch die Vernunft einleuchtende Rechte, und ist daher als eine Person zu betrachten.' (art. 16).

the life of the law will agree that 'being a bearer (or a bundle) of responsibilities, rights and duties' is the primary conceptual tool lawyers use to gain access to justice within our legal systems.[6] The fact is, our own life histories, including especially our inalienable rights, are given legal recognition only through the conduit of this very concept of rights, a concept known as 'legal subjectivity' in civil law systems and, at common law, as 'legal capacity'.

In sum, both our basic understanding of the intimate relation between law and moral justice and the common and civil laws' shared doctrinal categorizing of persons as holders of rights are affronted by Lucien Fleurier. So are their implications, for instance that human persons have an inherent dignity,[7] which is the ultimate anchor both for their fundamental rights[8] and for our ascribing legal capacity to them. The moral evolution in the historical development of our Western legal systems attested to by their clear landmarks in such matters as the endorsement of bills of rights and the abolition of civil death[9] makes this clear. So

6. This is, in legal systems within the Roman law tradition, a common definition of the 'legal subject'. See classical textbooks such as, e.g., for The Netherlands, Asser-de Ruiter I, 1 (1984: 3); for Belgium, De Page I (1962: 349): 'Dans de langage courant, on appelle 'personne' un être humain, un individu. Dans le langage juridique est considéré comme une 'personne' *tout être capable d'avoir des droites et des obligations*. La notion de personne apparaît ainsi comme le *support* indispensable des phénomènes juridiques'; for Switzerland, Bucher, *Das Personenrecht*(Berner Kommentar I (2, 1976: 36). Cf. Vischer in *Schweizerisches Privatrecht* I (ed. M. Gutzwiller (1969: 556)); for Austria, see *Kommentar zum Allgemeinen bürgerlichen Gesetzbuch*, (ed. P. Rummel, I. Band, Wien (1983: 43)); for France, see P. Dupont Delestraint, *Droit Civil, Les personnes*, etc., Paris (1978: 2); for Spain, see José Castan Tobenas, *Derecho civil español, común y foral*, t. I, vol. II, (1962: 95).

7. See *Universal Declaration of Human Rights*, Preamble (1968). Cf. Benda (1983: 107ff) and references there.

8. As an *idea* it arises in the rationalist natural law tradition. Adam Smith, in his *Lectures on Jurisprudence*(Report 1762- 3:8) refers to the 'natural rights' discerned by Pufendorff - which are indeed to a large extent comparable to our classical human rights. As a *constitutional basis* they appear in the American (1776) and French (1789) Declarations. In a famous passage in the *Grundlinien der Philosophie des Rechts* (par. 258 Anm.), Hegel considers the latter event as a rebirth of politics: a nation trying to give itself a new basis in willing (though still abstractly) a specific thought content on what it means for us to be human.

9. The 'mort civile' was a sanction in France until 1854. Reference to legally permitted slavery is common place when evidence of moral growth is needed. In the meantime, however, not all political forces recognize the gain of acquiring the status of 'legal subjec-

then, Lucien Fleurier's tone of voice is worrying indeed. But should it? After all, one could say, Lucien is simply the product of fiction rather than of legal reality; and some authors for whatever reason enjoy creating the fiction of a wicked mind. Furthermore, the problem about how and to what extent the law should prevent wicked people from fabricating wicked things is, although a generally recognized legal problem, not a problem about the law itself.

Such thoughts, unfortunately, give little comfort, unless we manage to block from our minds Compagnon's insight (1979: 33) that authors creating fiction are more often than not in fact 'tinkering with the wreckages of a culture'. Thus the quote from Sartre's novel, although in itself neither a philosophical nor a legal argument, incites me to ask whether there are the sorts of fissures and flaws in our legal concept of 'person' that might eventually make it compatible with the very antipode of law and justice, with, that is, the absolute right of some to command absolute obedience. I propose in what follows to examine a legal text - the first paragraph of the German Constitution (*Grundgesetz*) - which, although short, is highly paradigmatic of what our culture endorses as a general idea of the dignity of human persons in the face of the law, and of what a legal system enforces on each and every occasion on which it renders justice. I will argue that there are two basically different ways of thinking about human dignity in constitutional law and that, further, they represent the two sides of the classical ambivalence in the metaphysical concept of 'substance'. Following Locke, I shall point out that this concept, and its ambivalence, have far-reaching politico-legal implications that can account for the outrageous paradox in Sartre's novel. I want to defend the thesis that ascribing 'human dignity' to an entity is not in itself contradictory with thinking of this entity as an enemy and that, indeed, it may be a subtle way of introducing mechanisms of power into the very heart of legal relationships. And, of course, I will show how the interception hypothesis is able to back up such an analysis.

tivity' for their organization. The Unions in Belgium, for example, have refused to accept this qualification in the context of civil law; they know that it would be too forceful a juridical restraint on their political range of action (liability in the case of strikes). Cf. Blanpain (1977: 81-82). I am indebted to my colleague René Foqué for this example. See also Broekman (1979, ch.8).

2 'What a piece of work is man'

Although the principle of human dignity is generally acknowledged to be a leading value of constitutional and international law, and although it is stated as such in some important declarations and preambles, the principle itself is rarely framed as a rule of valid *law*. One of the few exceptions is Article 1 GG, the beginning of the *Constitution of the Federal Republic of Germany*, which reads:

[1] The dignity of man is unassailable. To respect and defend it is an obligation of all state force.
[2] Therefore, the German people commits itself to inviolable and inalienable human rights as the basis of every human community, of peace and justice in the world.
[3] The following fundamental rights are binding upon the legislative, the executive and the judicative power as directly valid law.[10)]

Because of this explicit enactment and the fact that the legal order of the Federal Republic includes a constitutional court, there are, of course, a vast number of legal cases and doctrinal literature pertaining to the Constitution's first sentence:

[la] The dignity of man is unassailable (*Die Würde des Menschen ist unantastbar*).

There seems to be general agreement among legal scholars as to the meaning of [1a], or perhaps as to the point at which one ought to stop inquiring about its meaning. Absolutely central is the idea that [la] declares what the highest legal value is,[11)] and from this central but rather formal idea two lines of legal parlance have been developed. One reflects the investigation into its implications for legal techniques, in particular for the distribution of specific rights. These may range from

10. My translation and numbers.
11. See BVerfGE 45, 187 (227): '(...) den höchsten Rechtswert innerhalb der verfassungsmässige Ordnung.' BVerfGE 27, 344 (351) even qualified art. 1.1, infelicitously, as the *Grundnorm* of the legal order, obviously not in the Kelsenian sense. See also Benda (1983: 110) and references in Münch (1985: 69 f).

rather private to very public issues: from a prisoner's right to be addressed by his guards as 'sir', to the right to conditional membership of the European Union.[12] The other, which is of more interest here, reflects the attempt to articulate what constitutes human dignity and its unassailability. Needless to say that great pains are taken here to avoid definitional circles.

This second line of investigating [la] divides into two versions or strategies.[13] In the first, 'dignity' is conceived of as a metalinguistic indicator, referring to whatever people regard and act upon as their ultimate wants, desires or rights - in short, to whatever as a matter of actual fact they value most. 'Dignity' here is the name for the collection of these final human options: a core set of 'rights' such as liberty and equality in their differing respects and with their different restrictions. Because this core set constitutes for a certain community its desired self-determination, it enables the members to identify that community as 'theirs' by referring to the set in question.

In the second version 'dignity' is considered to be a specific fact about human nature, a *Faktum der Vernunft*, as Kant would call it. Maihofer, for instance,[14] articulates that fact as the principal or original or unique availability of a man's existence to himself. Framed in general terms, what he means is that a man is able to conceive of what he is and what he is looking for in the world in which he finds himself and that he can account for the choices he makes in virtue of that conception. Complementing this self-availability or 'self-hood' of man is an original non-availability of one's existence to others. Human rights, then, are a manifestation of this alleged essence of man. What constitutes his infinite dignity is not *what* some or even all actual persons happen to vote for finally, but *that* human beings are competent to make final choices about the meaning and value of human existence, virtually *everything* consid-

12. Cf. The so-called *Solange*-decisions of the *Bundesverfassungsgericht.* For an incisive analysis of the Constitutional Court's legal policy and argumentation (including its decision in the 'sir' case) see Schreckenberger (1978).

13. Both versions allow for the same opposing *political* interpretations: e.g. one may distinguish a liberal and a socialist way of handling the two strategies, or a democratic and an autocratic view on them; that depends on how one defines '*our* final choice' in the first version and '*our* self-hood' in the second. This may be a first step in explaining why, in political matters, 'les extrèmes se touchent'.

14. Maihofer (1968: 16 ff).

ered.[15)]

These two versions of man's dignity are at the basis of many incisive juridico-political debates in Germany as well as in other countries. For instance, the 'Report on euthanasia' submitted by a Dutch state commission was divided along precisely these lines of thinking in the majority's and minority's diverse opinions. The majority of the commission wanted to legalize euthanasia under certain circumstances and conditions, appealing ultimately to the actually and increasingly recognized right to put an end to one's life.[16)] The minority argued vehemently against any form of legalised euthanasia on the ground that human dignity is not identical with, but rather prior to, any specific human right and to any general human right to self-determination.[17)]

It should be stressed at this point that both versions are considered by their exponents to be tenable, even authentic, interpretations of the Kantian maxim that no one should treat any individual person as an object, as a means to an end or as a substitutable quantity. In bold terms their conflict comes down to this: on the one hand, if self-availability is not self-determination, what could it be? and on the other, if in self-determination the human self is not considered to be prior to any ascription of rights, how could there be *human* rights? These disquisitions about human dignity trigger a constant opposition between the two versions. Each is thought to fail when confronted with the challenge of the other. Nevertheless, their antagonism is productive, as I shall attempt to show by making a detour into the philosophy of knowledge and language.

3 Names, properties and substances

It is surprising how close the two versions of the concept of human dignity are to the two ways in which Western philosophy has conceived of

15. Giese (1975) presents a similar classification of two versions, but with much *a priori* sympathy for the first version, as he goes along with Luhmann's approach after rejecting the two extreme representatives of the first and second versions, namely Behrendt and Dürig.
16. See Repport van de Staatscommissie Euthanasie, 36; 43 ff.
17. *Ibid*, 243-247.

'substances' ever since Greek Antiquity. It is widely acknowledged that the term 'substance' has been the *Grundwort* of this philosophy. It stands for what is to be regarded as 'the most real', and, thus, for what philosophy is most eager to learn about: the ultimate reality that bears everything without being borne itself, i.e., the sub-stance. This concerns everything that can be said to be, ranging from, say, a white smooth stone to a grey old man. The properties white and smooth are not essential to being a stone, because, for one thing, there are many other stones and, for another, many things other than stones are white and smooth. Such properties, therefore, can be called 'accidental' rather than 'substantial'. The same holds for the properties grey and old, said of a man. These too are accidental; they are not part of what a philosopher intends to refer to when he speaks about man. This line of arguing towards ultimate realities by distinguishing accidents and substances has survived in Western thinking, in spite of severe criticism. The riddle of substances is what they are, if all properties were only accidental; and, furthermore, whether they are at all if it cannot be said what they are. I will show in due course that discourse about human dignity is a good example of that, but let me first explain one of the most forceful attacks on substances, launched by John Locke.

In his *Essay Concerning Human Understanding*, Locke analysed two ways of conceiving substances, both of which he believed to be dead ends and the results of a poor use of language.[18)] In developing his criticisms, he could not avoid appealing to metaphorical topologies (and this in spite of his well-known aversion to metaphors) in order to provide a specific focus for his treatment of the mediaeval, scholastic discussions of substance. This metaphorical topology centres on the scene of *naming*. Sometimes, he says, we pretend that our names selectively denote, out of all the properties connected to an entity, a sort of core set believed to be its 'real essence', that is, the substance itself. This is an *imperfect* use of language. At other times, however, we commit even an *abuse* of language, to wit when we talk as if some sort of substratum beyond the properties is denoted by our naming of a substance, believing that to be the 'real essence'. It is fascinating to see how Locke develops his argument in the two cases.

His example of the imperfect use of language is *gold*. Gold combines

18. This section is (in part at least, but perhaps still too possessively) based on arguments put forward by De Man (1979b) concerning Locke's *Essay*.

many properties, for example, it is of a certain colour, fusible and so on. Each of these properties can be found at quite different places and times, for example, in the tail of a peacock:

> I think all agree to make it [sc. gold] stand for a body of a certain yellow shining colour; which being the *idea* to which children have annexed that name, the shining yellow part of a peacock's tail is properly to them gold.[19)]

Not only are properties 'everywhere', they also have a habit of disappearing and making other properties disappear. Gold is not only coloured and fusible, it is also soluble. And now an epistemological predicament arises, one that spreads through the whole of social and political life: How are we to determine which properties are part and parcel of the real essence and which are not? Indeed, not just *how*, but *who* is to determine the demarcation?

> For by what right is it, that fusibility [sc. of gold] comes to be a part of the essence signified by the word *gold*, and solubility but a property of it? (...) That which I mean is this: That these being all but properties depending on its real constitution, and nothing but powers, either active or passive, in reference to other bodies; no one has authority to determine the signification of the word *gold* (as referred to such a body existing in nature) more to one collection of ideas to be found in that body than to another (...).[20)]

The imperfect use of language creates political problems of competence. But the man in authority who intends to solve them cannot legitimate his position by ontological claims on behalf of reality itself. Locke stresses the discursive character of the predicament by exploiting the topological metaphor mediating this specific way of putting the problem. It is the scheme of 'basic' and 'surface' properties. Without this or some similar (spatial or evolutionary) picture, and without the presuppositions of that picture (e.g., a point of view from which something appears as co-ordinated within these spatial or evolutionary dimensions - such as 'under', 'upper' in the one case and 'still childish', 'already adult' in the other), the predicament would not arise.

If for the sake of experiment we introduce a different metaphor, we

19. Locke, *An Essay Concerning Human Understanding*, III, 9, 17.
20. Locke, *Essay*, III, 9, 17.

can see the predicament coming into or out of focus. Let us suppose that properties constitute entities in the way in which equal hairs constitute 'someone's hair'. Now we have a purely quantitative picture and its appropriate presuppositions, as, for instance, conventions of tolerance. How tolerant should we humans be (without having much chance of finding evidence for our claim in reality) in calling someone 'bald' or in calling the three hairs on someone's head 'his hair'? In this case, the question is not which, but *how many* properties constitute a substance, and the problem of essentialism seems to vanish.[21)]

As to the other, second view of naming substances, it regards them not as the basic part of the properties but as the substrata beyond the properties, the real, immutable, individual essences of existing things upon which the properties depend.[22)] Here Locke's example is *man*, or rather, the case of

> (...) a man [asking] whether this or that thing he sees, let it be a drill or a monstrous foetus, be a man or no.[23)]

Again an epistemological predicament arises, and again it is mediated by a topological metaphor. Here it is the scheme of 'outer' (sensible) and 'inner' qualities. In virtue of this metaphor, the predicament is once again transformed into a sociopolitical, indeed a moral, problem of authority that cannot be solved by putting coins into ontological slots:

> These *leading sensible qualities* are those which make *the chief ingredients of our specific ideas*, and consequently the most observable parts in the definitions of our specific names, as attributed to sorts *of substances* coming under our knowledge. For though the sound *man*, in its own nature, be as apt to signify a complex *idea* made up of animality and rationality, united in the name subject, as to signify any other combination; yet used as a mark to stand for a sort of creature we count of our own kind, perhaps, the outward shape is as necessary to be taken into our complex *idea*, signified by the word *man*, as any other we find in it; and therefore, why Plato's *animal implume bipes latis unguibus* should not be as good a definition of the name *man*, standing for that sort of creature, will not be easy to show: for it is the shape, as the leading quality, that seems more to determine that species than a faculty of reasoning, which appears not at first

21. As it does, however, other problems arise.
22. See Locke, *Essay*, III, 10, 18.
23. Locke, *Essay*, III, 10, 21.

> and in some never. And if this be not allowed to be so, I do not know how they can be excused from murder who kill monstrous births (as we call them) because of an unordinary shape, without knowing whether they have a rational soul or no... And who is it that has informed us that a rational soul can inhabit no tenement, unless it has just such a sort of frontispiece or can join itself and inform no sort of body but one that is just of such an outward structure?[24)]

Locke's argument is powerful for several reasons. First, he challenges the ghost which had haunted the concept of substance from its very outset in Plato and Aristotle. This ghost, in fact, took the form of an unsolvable *aporia* or 'knotty problem' as Aristotle might have called it.[25)] For 'substance' is an ambiguous term, referring conjointly to the 'nature' of the thing in question and, on the other hand, to 'something which subsists independently'. These two referents exclude each other - and, one is inclined to add, necessarily so. For a core set of (non-accidental) properties is not subsistent by virtue of itself; it must be the essence *of* something. And no pure subsistence is knowable as such, since it is mere existence in singularity for which precisely the accidental properties - for example, a peculiar pattern of lines on the tip of one's index finger - are the essential ones.

Second, Locke understood both the source and the outcome of this *aporia*. The outcome in either of the two cases was totalitarianism, the governing of the dividing line between life and death by sheer authoritative decisions. The source was oblivion: We pretend that the topologies of 'under' - 'upper,' 'inner' - 'outer' are just there, forgetting that they are part and parcel of a naming scenery with its referential gestures indicating where 'there' is, with its pre-established rituals, criteria, types of occasion and qualified name-givers. Note that neither the topologies nor the scenery is ontologically warranted; the scenery has to be staged in a narrative before it can perform its founding function.

Locke has made an unorthodox move here and, to be honest, I doubt whether I am able to grasp all its implications. Had he engaged in a traditional critique of the two ways of naming substances, Locke would have used the presupposition of the second way to refute the first and vice versa. He would presumably have said, on the one hand, that 'basic and

24. Locke, *Essay*, III, 11, 20.
25. Aristotle, *Metaphysics*, 995a25 - 995b4.

accidental properties are properties all alike, at least as far as they need something existing *of which* they are properties' and, on the other hand, that 'we cannot affirm the existence of anything without some idea of a *basic* quality'. Had he done this, he would have reinforced the common bias implied by these mutual criticisms and by the two opposing conceptions of 'substance', namely, *that there are, when all is said and done, two modes of being which differ in their perfection.*

What Locke instead did was attack this very bias itself by bringing up the question of socio-political authority: Does one have the *right* to name substances and thereby demarcate grades of perfecton of being? Why did he do this? I can think of only one reason. He did it because he wanted to deny the ontological necessity of power and violence. But, again, why? The answer is contained in a rather simple law that governs the relations between metaphysics and politics: wherever reality is divided into perfect and imperfect modes of being a distinction between two sorts of people emerges: those who enact the criteria for the distinction between perfection and imperfection, and those who do not. And the important thing to see is that these two sorts of people do not just 'emerge'. They are appointed and named *authoritatively* before any authority, and even any part of reality, seem to be established.

4 Human dignity as a substance

I have just suggested that there is a parallel between the two concepts of substance Locke criticized and two concepts of human dignity. I should like to consider them now in more detail.

The first version of dignity I examined above articulates the concept by referring to a core set of rights. Now rights *are* properties, although of a special breed; for they are deontic properties or deontically qualified courses of action. As such, they can be characteristically and perspicuously formulated in the form H.-N. Castañeda (1975) proposed as:

[R] X $\text{ought}_{\text{Qly}}$ to do A,

in which 'ought' is a stand-in for various deontic operators and 'Qly' is a referring device (such as 'according to his promise' or 'according to the German Constitution') indicating some 'context of Legitimacy' that qualifies the deontic operation.[26] Such a context can be construed as a set of sets, comprising a set of agents, the ends and interests they have, facts about their situation as they define it in terms of determining factors on the one hand and possibilities for action on the other. Thus a context of Legitimacy is radically agent dependent. It can, therefore, be limited to a very relative level, e.g., limited to what is logically or naturally necessary for a certain agent to do if he is to achieve his end. But it can also be extended and become more complex, as when an agent strives to harmonize his hierarchy of ends with the hierarchy of ends of others whom he considers to be his co-persons or co-agents.

On this account of the matter, deontic properties can be found at radically different places and times, as Locke's yellow, shining gold could. For there are numerous contexts of Legitimacy, ranging from quite private wants to all-embracing harmonies of interests. Less limited contexts may override the Legitimacy of minor priorities in more limited contexts and thus make certain deontic properties disappear. For example, the child's right to corporeal integrity makes the old-fashioned paternal right to castigate one's child 'disappear' as Illegitimate in a certain context of Legitimacy. Thus the term 'human dignity' can be considered to be shorthand for an ultimate context of Legitimacy consisting of final, harmonized wants human beings have in view of the sort of life human beings should be able to live.

This first version of dignity elicits, however, a critical question which is grafted upon the second one (the 'self-hood' of man). The process of harmonization presupposes a prior common understanding and valuation of certain wants. Indeed, the respective motivational hierarchies of the agents have to be seen as comparable by reference to a common denominator in order to be susceptible of modification by the agents. To that extent, at least, the harmony of contexts must *a priori* be realized before an overriding context of Legitimacy can be negotiated. It stands in need of a 'bearer' who is *not* negotiated in the negotiations and who has, therefore, a pre-established and, in that sense, independent existence. To put this in another way, the second version stresses that we cannot *radically*

26. While refraining from giving a full list of references, I refer especially to Castañeda (1975: 185ff). For further appositions to Castañeda's view, see the article by M. Bratman and Castañeda's reply in J.E. Tomberlin (ed.), (1983). To indicate that 'Legitimacy' is used here in a specific technical sense, defined by Castañeda, I employ the capital 'L'.

negotiate who is to be co-person or co-agent, as the process of negotiation already presupposes the agreement to be co-persons in negotiating.

This explains why this second version of dignity tries to work out some difference between 'the dignity' and 'the rights' of man, such that this dignity could be said to 'underlie' those rights or, conversely, such that the rights could be said to 'derive' from the dignity. It is noteworthy in this respect that the text of the *Universal Declaration of Human Rights* (1948) in both its Preamble and its articles juxtaposes the 'inherent dignity' and the 'rights' of man as distinct categories. The question thus becomes, what is meant by this dignity *apart from* the rights?

From the same text in the *Declaration* one might gather that the inherent dignity of man is conceived of in terms of his rational and moral capacities. Though this interpretation has had its advocates, it is at present generally abandoned for obvious reasons.[27)] First of all, there are people who are not capable of any rational or moral self-conception because of, for example, their mental defectiveness. Second, criteria for what is 'rational' or 'moral' are difficult to state because they are always implied *in actu* when stated *in thesi*. That is at least part of the reason why an alternative interpretation presses itself forward, namely of human dignity as an abstract potential of self-realization of every human being. I call it 'abstract' because the predicate expressing this potential is never ascribed to any human being without restriction. It is ascribed to all men 'in principle' and to no man 'in fact'. Every human being should have the opportunity to develop not simply his own possibilities but the *best* of his possibilities. In saying this, however, we are brought back to a discussion of what counts as 'best'. If we make it a matter of negotiation, we are back to the first version of dignity; if we make it a matter of *a priori* understanding of who are to be co-persons, we beg the question.

Note that these critical points regarding the phrase 'human dignity'

27. Equalizing human dignity and rational-moral capacity can be found in rather old commentaries by, e.g., Nipperdey, Schmidt-Bleibtreu-Klein, Dürig. See also Hubmann (1967: 41ff.). Opposing this view: Benda (1983: 114): 'Wenn mann bei der Auslegung der Verfassungsnorm nicht von dem Menschen ausgeht, wie dieser in der Realität ist, sondern sich an einem sozialethischen Idealbild orientiert, dürfen sich gerade (...) besonders schützbedürftigen Personengruppen nicht auf Art. 1. Abs. 1 GG berufen.' But a few lines further on: 'Art. 1. GG gilt für jeden Menschen ohne Rücksicht auf seinen individuellen sittlichen Entwicklungsstand, weil jeder Mensch wenigstens der Idealvorstellung nach zu sittlicher Selbstverwirklichung fähig ist.'

exploit the presupposition of the first version which was criticized by the second. They all look for a set of basic properties that will enable them to escape from admitting that the only form in which human dignity is conceivable as an independent existence, prior to all rights, is the unrestricted manifold of non-identical persons in their unique singularity. If they cannot escape that admission, 'human dignity' itself would be incapable of conceptualisation. Nor would it help to retreat to outer 'leading qualities', as for instance Kriele does when he refers to

> (...) der Würde eines jeden, der Menschenantlitz trägt (...),[28)]

that is, to the dignity of all those who show a human countenance or, in Lockean terms, a 'frontispiece'; for it is impossible either to restrict *a priori* the variety of singular human faces or to agree *a posteriori* (i.e., after negotiation) on a set of basic properties of human faces.

In the meantime, one should not hide from the fact that the constant and self-propelling antagonism between the two versions of human dignity maintains and even reinforces the bias not only of a two-tiered reality, one perfect, one defective, but also its consequent bias that there are two sorts of people in the world: those who assert or enact the criteria on which the distinction is based and those who assent or subject themselves to the criteria. How does Locke's 'naming scenery' come in here?

Note first that human dignity is never discussed without a set of metaphorical topologies which are almost exactly parallel to those that allowed Locke to pose his pertinent questions about substance. In the perspective of the first version of dignity the question is which rights, which deontic properties are *basic* and which are, say, additional? As far as they are all supposed to be rights that humans have, who indeed has the *authority* to determine the meaning of human dignity? Those political powers that think they have such authority disagree vehemently about the priority of civil-political versus sociocultural rights. In fact, our text from the *Constitution of the Federal Republic of Germany* contains the very expressions 'basic' and 'fundamental' at [1] - [3]; and were one to investigate carefully the decisions of the *Bundesverfassungsgericht*, one would certainly hit

28. M. Kriele, 'Freiheit und Gleichheit', in Benda et al. (1983: 142).

upon many variations of this metaphor.[29] Not only is the spatial topology of 'under - upper' present, so are their evolutionary equivalents such as 'childish' or 'primitive' versus a more 'mature' understanding of human dignity. Again the question is posed: Who has the authority to determine such matters?

In the perspective of the second version of dignity, human rights are the *outer* sensible qualities of an *inner* independently existent human dignity. And once more we ask the question: Who has the authority to infer from the outward 'shape' of positive fundamental rights a transcendental value of human dignity? Or to determine that a specific bill of rights more or less enshrines this value? Those who think they have that authority can argue anything, because in their opinion there is always more to human dignity than is granted by any bill of rights and there is always at least something remaining of human dignity when these rights are violated. Thus, our text from the *Constitution* speaks of the dignity of man as being 'unassailable', that is, *beyond* any and all contexts of Legitimation of rights (and duties) and, in that sense, independent of them.

Let me at this point summarize a twofold provisional conclusion that may serve as a basis for further investigation: (i) 'human dignity' in both versions rests upon ascribing the name 'man' to entities; (ii) the allegedly ontological claims put forward in the attempts to define the quality referred to by the name 'man' appear to be radically parasitic on metaphorical topologies. As is briefly put in a phrase by De Man: no ontological slot without a metaphorical knot. In fact, we encounter two sets of topologies:

I	II
under - upper	inner - outer
basic - added	beyond - here
nature - childis	hunassailable - violable

29. A reliable guide would be Schreckenberger. In his book (1978: 202 ff), there is a substantial chapter on 'Die fundamentalistische Argumentation' or what he calls the 'Fundamentalrhetorik' of the *Bundesverfassungsgericht*.

5 Naming without necessity

It is almost blasphemous to say Locke stressed that metaphors matter. Indeed, he does not stress their importance; he uses their impact to introduce what I have called a 'narrative of naming'. I shall not go into the intimate connections between metaphor and narrative in general, although it is encouraging to learn from no one less than Paul Ricoeur[30)] that the connection has it roots in Aristotle's *Rhetoric* and *Poetics*, and to see the nature of the relation summarized by De Man as:

> (...) a close, though not necessarily complementary relationship between trope and, narrative, between knot and plot.[31)]

What Locke is up to is perhaps made more explicit in a narrative about naming men 'man', which Rousseau presents in his *Essai sur l'origine des langues*:

> A primitive man, on meeting other men, will first have experienced fright. His fear will make him see these men as larger and stronger than himself: he will give them the name of *giants*. After many experiences, he will discover that the supposed giants are neither larger nor stronger than himself, and that their stature did not correspond with the idea that he had originally linked to the word giant. He will then invent another name common for them and himself such as, for example, the word *man* and will retain the word giant for the false object that impressed him while he was being deluded.[32)]

The narrative presented here contains a complex discursive strategy,[33)] which amounts to the kind of 'self-denunciatory device' to be expected from the interception hypothesis. It narrates 'what happened' and yet, at the same time, cancels in the narration its ontological commitment. It does this by narrating a twofold naming scenery. The first is the introduction of the friend - enemy schema as *a priori* to any conceptualisation - in fact as an equivalent of the self - other distinction. The picture implies that in the 'original position', for any first person 'I', seeing someone as

30. See Ricoeur (1979: 141) and (1983a: 356).
31. De Man (1979b: 11; 21)
32. My translation.
33. De Man (1979a) ch. 7 On Metaphor is the basis of the following argument, though my interpretation is slightly different.

different from him makes him think that the other is a possible enemy. There is simply no other reason why 'I' should be afraid of him and express this fear by calling him a giant; for as Rousseau points out in his essay, the primitive man does not yet employ numbers to identify quantities. For him, the properties of size and strength do not in any sense refer to the world 'out there'; they are, instead, projections of fear and distrust. The name 'giant' denominates as a segment of reality the reactions of a first person to his encounter with a second.

In order to have this reaction of distrust, however, the first person must already employ a specific dualistic topology of experience. He must think that whatever he does, this second person is *basically* an enemy, or that *beyond* all the properties there is an *inner* property ('animosity') lurking, which threatens him regardless of what he hears or sees. The first person can always maintain this presupposition of an ever-imminent danger, for no matter what the second person, the alleged giant, does, it is virtually always either a sign of this inward property or a disguise of it - and, thus, a sign after all. So there is no necessity for that person to call other people 'not-giants' or 'not-enemies'. But this is only the first half of the story.

The other, second, aspect of naming scenery consists of replacing the qualitative distinctions pertaining to the friend - enemy scheme by quantitative criteria. Fear can be withdrawn and domesticated when, 'after many experiences', I (as the first person) develop a criterion from *my* guise for what counts as 'large' and 'strong' in relation to these entities. This enables me to measure the supposed giants by *my* standard or rule, and claim that in virtue of *my* standard they are *relatively equal*.

Once these transformations are completed, once I have succeeded in the attempt to reduce others to functions of my self-conception, I can safely engage in bargaining a contract.[34)] Thus, society orginates with

34. 'It is, therefore, quite understandable that the passage about naming and conceptualisation recurs in the *Second Discourse* where the origin of society is at stake, and that the discussions about the origin of language and the origin of society develop in exactly parallel terms: 'Though his similars were not for him (sc. primitive man) what they are for us, and though he had no more business with them than with the other animals, they were not forgotten in his observations. The conformities which time allowed him to mark between them, his woman and himself, made him judge of those he did not observe. And seeing that they all behaved as he would have done in similar circumstances, he inferred that their ways of thinking and feeling were quite similar to his way, and this important truth, well

the quantitative comparison of conceptual relationships[35] from the position of a first person singular. To become social, 'I' have to establish that no one is different from me in any *radical* sense. Having established this, I can recognize any of the others as another 'I-sayer'. Accomplishing this, however, does not at all imply that I have erased my attitude toward him as an enemy. I can handle my fear, suppress it, transform it into social energy without losing the idea of a possible attack from his side. Ascribing 'human dignity' to an entity is therefore not *in itself* contradictory with my thinking of him as an enemy, and indeed is compatible with, may even be a form of, treating him, in the last resort, in terms of power. Whether this ascription pertains to basic properties, including fundamental rights, or to an inner essence (self-availability) does not matter in this respect. It can only be a matter of preference for one ontological fetish rather than another.

Rousseau's narrative is, however, still more complex. It does not entail a denial that this is how men become social, but it does undermine the ontological hypostisation of what is narrated. It should be clear for anyone who reads his story that it is as much a description of the origin of our society as of our society's origin of description. I repeat: the 'primitive man' has no reason to be frightened or to measure the alleged 'giants' by 'human' standards except his political *choice* that their existence is a threat to him by virtue of the fact that it is *different* from his. Therefore, the narrative is directed against

> (...) those who explain the origin of language by means of causal categories that are themselves dependent on the generic power of the origin for which they are supposed to account. The constant warning against the mystification of adopting a privileged viewpoint that is unable to understand its own genealogy, a methodological theme that runs throughout the *Second Discourse*, also applies to the theory of language. But not selectively so. The science of language is one of the areas in which this type of fetishism (reducing history to nature) occurs, but it is not the only one. The same error prevails with regard to ethical judgment (Hobbes) or with regard to technology.[36]

established in his mind, made him follow - by a presentiment as sure as and quicker than dialectical reasoning - the best rules of behaviour for his advantage and his security that suited him to observe with them.' (p. 207) (my translation)

35. De Man (1979a: 156).
36. De Man (1979a: 142).

We are reminded here of the metaphor of perspective: we may conceive of this origin as the narrative counterpart of the vanishing-point in perspectivist pictural art. It is the virtual point in which, from the spectator's point of view, all lines of representation would come together if they were prolonged. But at the same time, this is precisely the reason why that point cannot be or contain a representation. So, the representation is dependent on, and altogether different from that point at the same time. Such is the point which a legal order calls 'human dignity'.

It should be emphasised, however, that this critique of ontological fetishism is not a *better* reading of Rousseau's story which might replace the reading of the story as an account of the origin of society. Both readings, and the opposite directions they take, are necessary for understanding that naming men 'man' is, among humans, never a question of epistemological but of political choice. A clear example of this is offered by the following piece of reasoning in political morality.[37)] In his book *Die Verfassung der Bundesrepublik in der Bewährung* (1957), Werner Weber asserts that with this 1949 constitution the obligation to respect the dignity and the freedom of the human person has become a new point of political integration, which allows each and every German to tell friends from foes. This is an astonishing interpretation of the *Bonner Grundgesetz*, as it so neatly reflects the view that the new constitution is just another value of an old variable: Carl Schmitt's theorema of politics. Schmitt defended that, ultimately, politics is to make a distinction between friends and foes, the latter being those one is prepared to kill when society is jeopardised.[38)] It is these hypostatising formulas of identity and origin which a narrative reading of law and politics aims to undermine.

6 The system of law 'after Auschwitz'

The term 'human dignity' refers to the complex grammar of naming men 'man'. Without this grammar it is hard to see how there can be any legal rights, duties, or norms at all. For the idea of the rule of law requires that the legislator and the subjects are in a position to refer to themselves and

37. Quoted by Schreckenberger (1978: 84).
38. Cf. Van Bellingen (1985) and Foqué and Van Bellingen (1985).

each other in the first person plural as 'we'.[39)]

The question now is: What brings about the reliability of this indexical reference? Adorno[40)] and, more recently, Derrida and Lyotard[41)] have pointed out that the phrase 'we, humans' as a presupposition of legal language has become suspect in our political history 'after Auschwitz'. Indeed, they say, Auschwitz has become the name for something impossible to name: that human beings are addressed by the law *as* human beings to exterminate them legally in the name of human dignity. Since Auschwitz no one knows any more whether the name 'man' gives legal access to justice or to death. Humans exist alone 'before' or 'in front of' the law, as Kafka depicted them. That is precisely how many survivors of the camps formulate their experience (if that is what it is) of surviving: of existing all *alone* ever since their stay in the camp. This surely does not mean that such a person believes himself to be 'the only human being in the world', or that, in his view, the name 'man' has turned from a generic name into a proper name. The experience is, rather, that he is no longer able to think of himself as a human being.[42)]

This is the ultimate effect of the bias mentioned in section 4, that there is an ontologically based position from which reality and, thus, humans can be divided into perfect and imperfect modes of being. It is the result of some first person plural who manages to refer to his self-conception in directing other entities as 'man', to persuade them that he did it on their behalf, in virtue of their ontologically anchored, *relative equality* as men, and to create on that basis an official historical consciousness of a social 'we'.[43)] It is also the ultimate consequence of the format which we have learned to recognize as the dominant pattern of thought in our cul-

39. Cf. Lyotard (1981: 292ff.).
40. Adorno (1966: 352-356).
41. Lyotard (1981) is, in fact, an extensive commentary on Adorno (1966: 354 ff) Rejecting Hegel's conception of dialectical philosophy. In a similar vein, Derrida (1972: 144) states: 'Ce qui est aujourd'hui difficile à penser, c'est une fin de l'homme qui ne soit organiseé par une dialectique de la verité et de la négativité, une fin de l'homme qui ne soit pas une téléologie à la première personne pluriel.'
42. In Claude Lanzmann's film *Shoah* several persons use these or similar words. So did Primo Levi. And, in my view, it is the essence of *Sophie's Choice*.
43. Cf. the analysis of Nietzsche's argument in Gerhardt (1983). The importance of 'equilibrium' as a discursive construct in legal language reflecting power is particulary stressed by Broekman, e.g. (1979, *passim*) and (1980: 42).

ture: apparently we are inclined to imagine ourselves as rooting in some pre-interpretative nature or identity which we are not responsible for, which is brought about as a pure event beyond our range of action, and which we may gradually bestow meaning upon. The interception hypothesis would say that in such cases, strategies of reversing the order from event to interpretation are also present, though perhaps suppressed; and that they are essential, though not better to the understanding of the political morality as imposed by human dignity.

7 The apex of a legal system

We are now in a position to understand better in what sense law can conceive of itself as a system - a question left unanswered at the beginning of this chapter. Surely we are not able to give a full-blooded account of the notion of a legal system, but some important points can be highlighted.

The concept of 'system' in general is at the intersection of two topological axes: the axis of 'inside - outside' and the axis of 'before - after'. We may refer to these as the spatial and the temporal axis, respectively. On the spatial axis values like 'open' and 'closed' are assigned, on the temporal axis values like 'progressive' and 'regressive' are negotiated. But both of these axes, of course, allow a very varying and differentiated use of language. Luhmann (1986: 113), for instance, holds that a legal system is normatively closed, but cognitively open.[44] We find normative closure, according to Luhmann, because it is always a *legal* norm that determines whether or not certain facts will bear legal relevance. But there is also a constant interchange of information between the legal system and its environment, such that it is tuned to subsistence (progress) under specific and changing circumstances. That is why it is cognitively open. Luhmann conceives of these two conditions as reciprocal rather than oppositional. There is no cognitive openness without normative closure, otherwise the system would not be able to select the information it is interested in. Reversely, there is no normative closure without cognitive openness, otherwise the system would have no idea how to set itself apart from its environment as something specific. Notwithstanding these

44. He follows Ashby's general theory of cybernetic systems, which are described as '(...) open to energy, but closed to information and control'.

interdependencies, the important thing is that they all circle around the possibility of determining a borderline between the system and its environment.

The question we have learned to ask now is, from which point of view this borderline is determined. The answer must be that this is a standpoint inside the system, which is, however, projected as a point outside the system. What, according to Luhmann, constitutes a precondition of normative closure, namely cognitive openness to what is outside the system, is yet, on second thoughts, the result of a quasi-cognitive act of inclusion and exclusion: the act which is constitutive of politics and by which a society closes itself, identifies itself, names itself. That is why the names of so many peoples (Inuit, Samen, Bantu) - though they sound like proper names to us - do not mean anything else but 'humans'; and it is also why other peoples have decided to name themselves 'the good people', or 'the chosen people'.

A similar problem discloses itself on the temporal axis. Here also differentiation is quite possible. Progressive and regressive movement can exist in a variety of ways, which can be interdependent. For instance, it is possible to say that too strict a legality in legal consequences of the same facts is counterproductive as far as the subjects' faith in the legal system is concerned, because it will deprive them of their belief that the law takes individual circumstances into consideration and that they will stand a chance of gaining something by going to court.[45)] But anyway, the conservation, rise and decline of a system are terms which can only be used if certain critical borderlines are set. And they will be derived from what the system is supposed to realise. Even if such an end is the conservation of the beginning, each system is teleologically defined.

And we may ask again: from which point of view is this origin or end 'a given'? Do we not recognize ourselves in the mirror of Rousseau's story on the origin of language? Can such an origin or end, which a society assigns to itself, ever be a vanishing point for that society? Or will a society always imagine a perfect reality beyond its own, to which it be-

45. I take this example from a remarkable intervention (during a TV programme) by one of the first computer experts in The Netherlands, Prof. Nielen. He pointed out that the use of computers to map fines on to alcohol permillages or personal income to social security services, so that you get the same output for the same input throughout the country, will probably go against intuitive feelings of justice in the population. He may well be right.

longs and from which it receives its legitimation? These are the questions which the interception hypothesis confronts the system of legal norms with: the set of questions that can be summarized as the challenge for each and every society to call itself a society of humans and to give an account of the self-imposed restraints of legitimacy that can prevent such name from becoming an absolute and tyrannic truth.

CHAPTER 4

ASCRIPTION OF NORMATIVE CONSEQUENCES TO FACTS

In this chapter the interception hypothesis is put to work in a third legal context, which can be generally characterized as mapping the account of facts on to the system of general norms in legal decision making. In this context, the hypothesis is supposed to elucidate the relation between (a set of) legal facts and (a set of) normative legal consequences. From here on I will refer to this relation in the present context by means of the rather Kelsenian, but not uncommon term 'ascription': what happens in legal decision making is ascribing legal consequences to legal facts. Now, can we see ascription as a value of the variable relation between Event and Interpretation? Does the former show the double hierarchy characteristic of the latter?

Some may want to argue here that ascription is performed by virtue of general legal rules, derived from statutory law or case law (*rationes decidendi*). This, I venture, is quite all right as far as juridico-political considerations are concerned. I mean, it is an important principle of legal policy to argue each and every decision on the basis of established positive law. But that does not solve the epistemological predicament inherent to legal ascription as a specific normative conditional, neither on the level of generalities nor on the level of particularities. A legal rule, on the general level, performs the same trick as does the legal decision on the individual level: it ascribes normative consequences to certain facts. For example, in the case of my individual income, the revenue office will impose a duty of payment which it derives from the general rule of a table. The table, however, consists of two columns: on the left-hand side, it shows factual taxable incomes, on the right-hand side, it shows corresponding normative payments. These duties to pay certain amounts of money as income tax are the normative consequences ascribed to the facts by the legislator. Now, what I am saying is that, from an epistemological point of view, the reasons which the revenue office or the judge have to ascribe a certain duty to pay a certain amount of tax money in my individual case, are on a par with the reasons the legislator has to ascribe such a duty in general. It is a requirement of legal policy that the former authorities derive their ascriptions in individual cases from the general ascriptions by the latter authorities. But both the former and the latter will *base* their ascriptions on similar material reasons. These reasons only emerge if they understand the rationale of the relationship which the figures in the left-hand column bear to the figures in the right-hand column, and vice versa. Such a rationale may be, for instance, the progressive line in the table, which in turn can be understood as an expression of a certain principle of tax policy that is deemed legally feasible, for instance to have the strongest shoulders bear the heaviest burden of tax. To see the rationale of a rule is, thus, as much a problem for the legislator as it is for the revenue office, the judge, or, for that matter, the ordinary citizen. Or, to put it in another way, the problem of ascription is not at all exhausted, perhaps not even mounted, by the problem of application. The latter pertains to the relation between (general) rules and (individual) decisions, the former to the relation between facts and norms, both in general and in individual cases. The problem of ascription is how the rule can be thought - which is the core of both framing and applying a rule.[1)]

Let me put the same point in a linguistically more regimented form. A legal rule is always a concatenation of facts and norms. It is, characteristically, of the form [FR]:

[FR] If A is the case, one ought to do B.

A legal decision entailing the same terms is of a form [FD]:

[FD] As A is the case, one ought to do B.

One may be inclined to think that a decision of the form [FD] is only justified if it is supported by a rule of the form [FR]. As a matter of logic, this is impeccable. It amounts to the 'practical syllogism':

1. This account of the matter explains why, basically, the problem of legal decision making is the same in common law and in civil law. In common law systems, the politico-legal demand is answered by the doctrine of precedent. The epistemological demand, however, focuses on grasping the rationale of the leading precedent, quite as the rationale of a statutory rule is the anchor for the judge in civil law.

[FrD] As {A is the case and (if A is the case, one ought_R to do B)}, one ought to do B.[2)]

But from an epistemological point of view, it seems also true that a sentence of the form [FD] provides a justification for a scheme like [FR]. It only makes sense to connect the upshot ‘to do B’ to ‘A being the case’ in the form of a rule, if A can be understood as a *reason* for doing B. Thus, [FrD] is interdependent with:

[FdR] If {A is the case and (as A is the case, one ought_R to do B)}, one ought to do B.

To put it in another way: The ‘if’ in [FR] is ambiguous or elliptic, as is the ‘as’ in [FD]. ‘If’ does not just mean ‘whenever’, and ‘as’ does not just mean ‘because’. They are mixtures of (at least) both brands; *at least* both, because each of them is ambiguous in itself. For instance, it is a tricky question what kind of ‘things’ we quantify over when we say ‘whenever’ (moments? times? situations?).[3)] And similarly, it is not obvious what we mean by ‘because’ in this context: causes? reasons? indices?[4)]

This is not, however, what interests us here most. I only introduced [FR] and [FD] in order to claim that there is an ambiguous form of both rules and decisions which involves some sort of link between their factual and normative constituents, which is surely non-inferential in terms of simple logic.[5)] Before we formalize it adequately, we have to understand its epistemological nature. The beginning of all understanding seems to be that the normative constituent is only normative if it is put in a distinctive order to the factual constituent, to wit as the interpretative upshot, more specifically the *deontic modification* of ‘what happened’. In the

2. The subscript ‘R’ attached to the first ‘ought’ stands for the ‘institution’ (sc. ‘according to school regulations’, ‘according to EC law’) in which the normative force of the ought is rooted. Castañeda’s theory of normative institutions (a.o. Castañeda, (1975)) is in the background here.
3. See Lewis (1975).
4. Compare the sentences ‘He was (definitely) dizzy, because he turned round and round’ and ‘He turned round and round, because he was (definitely) dizzy’.
5. Because of the logical gulf between ‘is’ and ‘ought’. See Castañeda (1983).

terms of the interception hypothesis: the normative part is a discursive unfolding of the facts (either a type of cases, or a singular case).

My question now is: Is this link a narrative one, in the sense which we established in the first chapter? Is it, more specifically, constituted by a similar double-bind hierarchy which we seem not to be able to transcend or synthetize by a third one? Again, in terms of chapter 1: Are the facts *also* the product of coherence in the deontic, interpretative part of the decision or the rule? Let us try to summarize the fairly rich data of a few legal processes of decision making in order to corroborate the hypothesis. We shall, thus, have to make it clear that the facts of the case at hand are supposed to be, on the one hand, prior to, and independent of the normative judgment rendered in this case; and that, on the other hand, these very facts are the focuses, indeed the products, of coherence in the normative interpretation involved. The cases I want to analyse in this respect are more or less randomly found at my doorstep. One is about squatters who committed violence when they were expelled from the premises by police force. The other is about an accident with a sawing machine, the victim being the worker least protected by labour law. The reason for digging them out had to do with the fact that I could lay hands on nearly all relevant documents of the two cases, notes of defence litigators included - which presented quite a different picture of what legal decision making is about compared to the usual method of reading the texts of the courts.

1 The violent squatters

1.1 What happens when something happens?

A Health Service Office owned several fine nineteenth-century houses next to its premises in Stationsstraat at Tilburg. By the time these houses became vacant, the health service asked permission from the City Council to demolish them in order to expand its office accommodation. Some people in that area of the town protested when they heard of the plans, as the houses, in their view, represented a value that exceeded the interest of the Health Service Office: there were scarce housing accommodation and equally scarce architectural highlights in the area. When it was rumoured that the officials were about to take a decision, these people intended to protest through a procedure of administrative law. But before they took any formal action, the City Council granted the Health Service Office permission and the alderman concerned informed the protesting citizens that legal means to have this permission withdrawn were exhausted.

In that period of rumours - while it was unclear to the public whether permission had been requested or granted - a group of six young people squatted in one of the empty houses. They had lived there for about one month when the Health Service Office received permission to demolish this house. This was on the 21st of February 1979. The Office decided to carry out the demolition without further delay. On the 5th of March, the manager of the Office had a bailiff serve a writ on the squatters (and their legal adviser), summoning them to leave the premises before the 7th of March. The legal adviser informed the squatters that this writ was not legally valid. So the squatters decided to do nothing but stay where they were.

Meanwhile, the manager went on to make preparations for the demolition. He asked the police if it would be legally permitted to start demolition knowing that there were people inside; and if so, whether the police would be prepared to stand by in order to protect the demolishers, as he had reason to believe that the squatters would offer violent resistance. The police consulted with the Public Prosecutor and with the Mayor, who are both formally responsible for public order. As a result of this deliberation, the police promised the manager that there would be protection at the time of demolition.

On the morning of the 8th of March, the demolishers and several police officers gathered in the canteen of the Health Service Office. The demolishers were instructed to demolish the house from the outside *and* to be careful as there were people in the house. So, they approached the house from the back and the dragline started its work by crashing a door and part of a wall. The squatters phoned the police for protection against unlawful entry. The answer was: 'We know what you mean.' Then the squatters started throwing bricks and striking out with iron bars. They were arrested.

It is, in fact, significant that the case is not well known.[6] From a legal point of view it is obvious why it has not attracted great attention: it is a 'clear' case, not a hard one. The defendants did not stand a chance, not before the District Court nor before the Court of Appeal, nor before the Netherlands Supreme Court (the *Hoge Raad*).[7] To each of the six arguments which the squatters' lawyers advanced against the lower courts' decisions, the *Hoge Raad* responded in the following vein: 'This Court does not have to rule on this problem, as it is a question of fact, not of law. What defending counsel brought up is so intertwined with what happened on the 8th of March 1979 in Tilburg, and with what, thus, has already been considered and determined by the lower courts, that it cannot be regarded as a question of whether any rule of Dutch law is violated. And you know very well that this is a Court of Cassation and that it does not deal with questions of fact.'

Now let us assume that the defendants' lawyers were well aware of what cassation is about. Although one may call them stubborn, they were not stupid. What the *Hoge Raad* regarded as questions of fact were, to their minds, questions of law, and very fundamental questions at that. But defending counsel and the *Hoge Raad* were bound to disagree over what counted as a question of fact, as they both stuck to rivalry, but equally hypostatized concepts of law as well as facts. Why?

Let us first face the legal problem, or rather the web of problems, as the case intersects public, criminal and private law. In order to do that, I have to give a necessarily deficient, but sufficiently informative summary of the legal situation, tracing circles of increasing circumference around the charges. When the case was before the District Court, the public prosecutor had charged six young persons with committing violence, together and in public, against police officers on 8 March 1979. The official police reports as well as the statements of several witnesses made it at least very

6. Contrary to what I have claimed in my article 'The Instituting of Brute Facts', it was published in the Dutch law reports: HR 4 May 1982, NJ 1982, 650. I owe the reference (with thanks) to Liesbeth Verkleij, my former student and present colleague - and a first-hand witness at that.

7. For the sake of the argument, which is one of legal theory and not of comparative law, I translate the Dutch hierarchy of decisional courts in terms that allow a general understanding of the case, without worrying too much about the equivalence of these terms to or the adequacy of this vocabulary for those of other countries.

likely that the six youngsters threw bricks and aimed blows at policemen and others with bars. The defendants did not deny this. They pleaded self-defence against a violent and illegal attack. They argued, that 'the law' itself, more particularly the Public Prosecutor, still more particularly the very same person representing the Prosecution Service who had brought them to trial, had provoked or elicited such an emergency situation that they had had to defend themselves by means of physical action, some of which might have exceeded reasonable proportions and had turned into effective, but non-intended violence. Therefore, they claimed, the Public Prosecutor's case should be dismissed, as the evidence he submitted had been acquired illegally and by provocation. And even if the evidence were allowed to be used, it would only prove that the defendants had done something for which they should not be punished.

To understand this argument and this claim, we need to know more about the 'facts' that are the subjects of these rivalling qualifications. Note that we feel the inclination to express this need as the need to know 'what really happened'. It will appear to be very difficult to satisfy this need.

Do we not know already what 'really' happened from the plain story? There is much more to be said, as we do not know yet what the predicaments of either the Health Service Office, or the squatters, or the police were in the eyes of the law. According to Dutch law, squatting in a house which is not in use by the owner, is not a criminal offence, though it is a tort. Article 138 of the Criminal Code states, that it is an offence to enter, without legal permission, a house *in use* by someone else.[8] In 1971[9], the *Hoge Raad* decided that this law should be interpreted restrictively: When a house is owned, but not actually used, it is not an offence to enter it. Thus, to squat in a house which is not in actual use, is not a criminal offence. It would, however, be an offence (unlawful entry) to enter a house which is actually used by squatters. If the owner of the premises wants the squatters to move out of the house, his access to justice is via civil law. He has to sue the squatters for tort, so that the judge will order them to leave.[10]

8. Cf. art. 12 of the 1983 Dutch Constitution.

9. HR 2-2-1971, NJ 1971 no. 395.

10. But to be able to sue them, in a civil lawsuit, it is crucial for the owner to know the names of the squatters. And a squatter's lesson number one is to carefully hide his name from others. This is the reason why the squatters in the case at hand did not bother to call

Though legal authorities in the Netherlands have not been altogether happy with this gap between criminal law and civil law, and have attempted, over the years, to close it in order to prevent squatting, the situation in Tilburg on 8th of March 1979 was quite clear. Notwithstanding the views of the police, the Public Prosecutor, the Mayor and the Health Service Office, the demolition of the premises, in actual use by the squatters, was illegal; at least, it could be qualified as unlawful entry. The officials knew all that. This is evident from their explicit instruction to the demolishers, gathered in the canteen, *not to enter the house, but to demolish it from the outside*. The demolition contractor declared in court that there was no technical reason whatsoever for such instructions and that he had presumed a legal reason for it.

This reason, however, was not sustained as a norm of valid Dutch law in the sentence rendered by the District Court. The Court considered that the demolition was illegal, but that the means of defence chosen by the squatters were illegal too. It argued that, immediately after they had received the writ, the squatters could have taken *legal* action (apply for interim injunction proceedings, for instance). They had the obligation to choose these means rather than chance a direct confrontation with the demolishers. Whatever the legal value of the writ would turn out to be, it should have been taken by the squatters as the adequate expression of a factual intention on the side of the owner. The proportionally justified reaction would have been to call upon the law. As the squatters deliberately chose to stay, pleas of self-defence or excessive self-defence in an (unexpected) emergency were in vain. So they were punishable.

The Court of Appeal replaced this argumentation as to the punishability of the actors by a stronger one. The writ, whatever its legal value, should have induced the squatters to defend themselves in a purely factual sense by leaving the premises in the first place, because it was clear from the start that they could not make valid any legal interest. The proportionally justified reaction would have been to show a clean pair of heels. This argumentation was upheld in cassation.

upon legal remedies after they were summoned to vacate the house: they would have had to give their names. I would like to add on account of my colleague A.C. 't Hart - Professor of Criminal Law at Leiden - that at present the courts have found a way around the name problem.

1.2 What should have happened?

It was necessary to explain at least some aspects of this case, in order to link it with the interception hypothesis presented in chapter 1, the inverted hierarchies between Event and Interpretation. I now have to show how we may see these hierarchies and their inversion at work.

The first hierarchy [H.1] E → I clearly presents itself. It is obvious that we cannot escape from reading the legal decisions in this case in the following way: whatever wide variation there may be of (i) the legal qualifications of the facts as constituting offences, (ii) the evaluations of whether the actors should be punished or not and (iii) the attributions of certain penalties, in the final analysis they present themselves as legally relevant discursive unfoldings *of and from* an event, which is itself independent of discursive signification. We may refer to this event as 'the six youngsters throwing bricks and striking out with iron bars at Tilburg on 8 March 1979'. Whatever the intentions, the context, the rules, etc., may be, *that* is what *really* happened as far as the law is concerned. We may go one step further: also the decision to offer police assistance on 8 March was a discursive, namely anticipating, unfolding of this event. The only thing is that in this very first, anticipatory legal signification of 'what was to happen', it is necessary to supply a specific 'victim' of the stones and the bars: the demolishers. Police assistance was promised because it was expected that the squatters would behave violently *against the demolishers*. This will turn out to be an important point.

Where is the second hierarchy? In order to corroborate the thesis regarding [H.2], we will have to show that this violent behaviour *against the demolishers* should not be read *only* as the point from which the normative (legal) signification unfolds itself and sets itself on stage as 'pertinent to social reality'; we will also have to show that this violent behaviour is also, and at the same time, generated as a point which derives its reality from the coherence of the normative significations. Now there is a specific sense in which it *must* have been the case in retrospect that the squatters molested (or were going to molest) the demolishers. For, remember, the police had only a legitimation for the promise of protection as well as for the promised protection, when and in so far as the squatters would exhibit violent behaviour *against the demolishers*. Otherwise the legal discourse in this case would lose its coherence and, indeed, its normative force. To put it in another way: the police had the obligation to protect the corporeal integrity of the demolishers as *individual human beings*, but they were also under the obligation *not* to protect what the demolishers were doing as *demolishers*. For the demolition was illegal.

So 'the facts of the case' - if it would come to a case at all - had to be narrated in such a way that it was beyond discussion that corporeal integrity was at stake, otherwise there would have been nothing to protect in the first place. Or rather, the police would have been obliged to protect the squatters against the demolishers. Indeed, since demolition was illegal (as the police and the authorities knew it was), there would have been little difference between throwing bricks (which the youngsters did) and throwing walls (which the demolishers did by demolishing while there were people in the house) or between striking out with iron bars and striking walls with a dragline. We may, therefore, conclude, that the second hierarchy of reading [H.2] I → E is as necessary to understand what has been going on as was the first one, although it is not in any sense a *better* reading. It is as important for the legal machinery, that its discourse is about some non-discursive acts of violence by the squatters against the demolishers such as throwing and striking out, as it is important to make discursively certain that these events involve acts of violence by the squatters against the demolishers.

Now it is interesting to note that *both* the legal authorities *and* defending counsel painfully attempted to base their argumentation on one of the hierarchies at the exclusion of the other. The authorities built their arguments on the hierarchy E → I. They could not afford the suggestion that their verdict was about a narrative *construct*, and, thus, not about 'what really happened'. So they tried to make 'the facts' unattainable by a very special strategy. I said that, in order to justify legal action against the squatters, the *datum* of (anticipated) violence from their side *against the demolishers* was essential. But however essential the irrefutability of this event may be, it could hardly be proven in court. For the police, that morning, had used undercover agents: some of them were disguised as demolishers. So the testimony of eye-witnesses would end in the swamp of an endless who was who. This constituted a serious problem as to the irrefutability of the violent behaviour. It was solved by arranging the trial in such a way that this problem could never arise. The files of the case offer interesting evidence for this thesis.

The first and most important arrangement is, that - on careful reading of the charges - violence against the demolishers *was not charged*, though

violence against police officers was. What the squatters had done to the demolishers was only obliquely implied as the reason why the police was active then and there. That was the only way to rescue the crucial basis of the whole process. The other arrangements of the trial sustained this first strategy and minimized the part played by the authorities responsible for the preparation of the demolition. Thus we may list the following set-ups:
(i) The Public Prosecutor who gave the permission to protect the demolishers, appeared in court himself to charge the squatters. In this way he was able, according to Dutch law, to avoid to be called to the witness box;
(ii) Through procedural obstruction the Public Prosecutor prevented defence counsel from questioning the Mayor of the town as a witness, so that it would remain unclear what the structure and the outcome had been of the so-called 'tripartite' deliberation between those in charge of law enforcement in a case like this (the Mayor, the chief of police and the representative of Public Prosecutions);
(iii) None of the witnesses during the trial could give unambiguous information about the identity of the person who gave instructions to the demolishers in the canteen on the morning of the clearing: the police? the Health Office? the constructor? one of the demolishers? No one seemed to have been in charge - so no one could be charged.

Defence counsel was very well aware of the possibility of an alternative reading according to the lines of [H.2], but they, too, could not afford to refrain from hypostatizing it. They were determined to prove that the facts of the case had been 'framed', and that, thus, they should be regarded by the law as 'fiction'. But they did so by formulating their intuition in the terms of received legal doctrine. They 'felt' that the event which constituted the point of departure of legal discourse was itself the product of coherence in legal discourse. It was 'framed' in the sense of 'surrounded' by legal discourse. But their defence, from the District Court up to The Netherlands Supreme Court, was based on the firm presumption that this strategy of the law can be laid bare by accusing the officials of illegal behaviour, namely 'framing the case' in the sense of fabricating evidence against the squatters. They stated 'provocation of an offence by the Public Prosecutor'. And the District Court made short work of that. For the doctrinal structure of the concept of provocation is such, that it would imply an intention on the part of the Public Prosecutor to make the squatters throw and beat. This is, of course, an implication impossible for the Court to accept.

The squatters were given a two weeks (suspended) sentence. I do not pretend to have a better solution. I do not even have an advice for a more effective strategy of argumentation, either for the courts or for the defence lawyers. In fact, the District Court makes a remarkable effort to show that it is at least sensitive to the power of narrative forces, by indicating that demolition was illegal and that the squatters should only have searched for legal ways out of their predicament. But as soon as the defendants claim the inadmissibility of the Public Prosecutor's case, the Court of Appeal and the Supreme Court take their part in making up for the facts of the case: the facts become unattainable.

2 The desperate exployee

Though not invalid, n = 1 research is usually not regarded as yielding sufficient evidence. Or in equivalent legal parlance: one witness is no witness. So I better open a second file for detailed analysis regarding the ascription of legal consequences to the facts of a case. This time, the subject matter under investigation is a set of three pleas drafted by law students in a realistic seminar on legal argumentation. These were graduate students, the case was a real case tried before the same judge who co-chaired the seminar, and who was kind enough to lend his courtroom as adequate scenery. I therefore take it that the materials are as paradigmatic of what law is about as the original trial before the court.

2.1 The facts - which facts?

Mr. Van S. took a job in the timberwork factory Uppsalan Ltd. through temporary employment agency A. When he had worked there for several days doing odd jobs, he was asked to embark on a more substantial task, as a substitute for an experienced employee who had fallen ill. Instead of taking sawn plates from the sawing machine, he now had to feed the machine with plates to saw. This steep hill in his career, however, could not prevent him from the habit of smoking. Indeed, one day he was feeding the machine while smoking a cigarette. In a moment of inattentiveness he tried to extinguish his cigarette butt on the floor while pushing a plate through the machine. His hand got pinned, and although his colleague managed to stop the saw, deceleration was so slow that some of his fingers were cut off. The Labour Inspection Office made a report on the accident and found that the machine did not meet specific standards of safe operating.

Van S. sued Uppsalan Ltd. before the Subdistrict Court, which (although it is lowest in the hierarchy) in the Netherlands has jurisdiction in all labour cases. He argued on the basis of art. 1638x Civil Code that he had a labour contract with Uppsalan Ltd., and that the latter had violated its contractual obligations, more particularly its duty of care with respect to the safety of the employees. Of course, Van S. was keen enough to refer to the Labour Inspection report.

2.2 Issues

As in the case of the squatters, it is impossible to give a picture of 'the facts' without having some knowledge of Dutch labour law as well as procedural law. From a procedural point of view, there are different levels of questions to be distinguished, which can be arranged in the following sequence.
[1] Has the judge jurisdiction in the matter?
[2] Is the plaintiff's claim admissible?
[3] Is the company liable?
[4] To what extent should the plaintiff's own fault be taken into account?
[5] Which remedies should be applaid?

In this case, the first question was as easy as it was tricky. The answer was that the plaintiff founded his claim on a labour contract, so the Subdistrict Court had jurisdiction to hear the case. But that caused a dead alley with regard to a satisfying answer to the second issue. The Subdistrict Court chose to dismiss the claim, considering that there was no labour contract between Van S. and Uppsalan in the first place. Uppsalan had hired Van S. through temporary employment agency A, so there was a contract between the latter and Uppsalan. Also, there was a contract between A and Van S, as Van S. had agreed to take on temporary jobs offered by A and to pay a small amount of money for his registration. But there was no third and direct contractual relationship between Van S. and Uppsalan according to the Court. As far as the Court was concerned, Van S. was an 'exployee' rather than an 'employee' (for the sake of clarity I will continue to use the terms of exployee and exployer in this, and only this, technical section though they are not official legal terms). In other words, he had brought his claim to the wrong court.

To understand the Court's reluctance to accept such a relationship, or at least an analogy close enough to construct a similar liability on the part of the company, one has to know that, according to Dutch law, there is a fine line between the activities of a temporary employment agency - which are legal - and the activities of recruiters - which are strictly illegal, as they are believed to create unmanageable opaqueness in labour relationships (social security, fiscal obligations, etc.). The Subdistrict Court wanted to avoid the troubled water of labour mediation in the latter sense. It believed it could only do so by refraining from a construction that would presuppose an illegal relationship between all parties involved, and thus would bring no relief to either.

So what to do? A quick survey of the prima-facie possibilities of argumentation shows that each 'solution' has its difficulties.

a) *Accept no liability at all, neither on the part of the exployer (agency), nor on the part of the employer (Uppsalan)*. This is very unsatisfying indeed, mainly because it causes unjustified and wrongful discrimination between exployees and employees in a factory.

b) *Hold the employer liable on the basis of a close analogy with cases under art. 1638x of the Civil Code.* This jeopardises the fine line discussed above, which has become part of the system of Dutch labour law.

c) *Hold exployer A liable on the basis of art. 1638x Civil Code, assuming that the agency will recover its loss from the employer, Uppsalan.* This is a rather odd construction, because the exployer would be strictly liable in situations of risks (like the production processesses in numerous factories that hire workers from A) for which it can bear no responsibility whatsoever. This would, therefore, also contradict an important principle of the system of law.

d) *Hold the employer liable in tort rather than contract, and use the analogy to contractual relationships under art. 1638x only to determine remedies*. This is a fairly safe way as far as the system of law in concerned, but like a) it is unsatisfying because it makes the burden of proof heavier for the exployee: he would then have to prove serious negligence on the part of the employer. This would introduce unjustified discrimination once again.

To sum up, solutions a) and d) conflict with the demands of equity and social acceptability, solutions b) and c) are out of line with the system of (labour) law as it presently is in the Netherlands. On the other hand, it is intuitively clear for professionals and laymen that something has to be done in favour of the exployee. So what we have here is a sort of legal vacuum, in which there is room for creative argumentations. This is where our three student lawyers came in. Their task was to find a way around these dilemmas. Let me discuss their arguments in random order, labelling them AA, BB and CC.[11)]

2.3 Three arguments

2.3.1 Using law for policy making (AA)

The first strategy we will follow is AA's, who is determined to give his argument the strongest possible juridical form. To summarize his position: he aims at holding the employer, Uppsalan, liable in contract in order to avoid unjust discrimination. His reasoning is in two stages.
1) The labour contract between the employee[12)] and the agency evolves into a labour contract between the employer and employee as soon as the employer moves to giving orders involving work that is substantially different, in particular being more dangerous, than the work the employer was hired for from the agency. For at that moment the relation of authority, characteristic of a contract of labour, changes to such an extent, that in fact the employer offers to make a contract which the employee accepts by obeying the order, thereby closing the deal.
2) Even if this were not so, it is 'reasonable' that the duty of care laid down in art. 1638x Civil Code should be called upon, as the parties (employer and employee) have anyway entered into a 'legal relationship involving labour'.

The judge was not impressed, as he refused to go along with the suggestion that there was (or arose) a labour contract. He wanted to give Van S. his due as badly as AA. But he was not prepared to stretch the language of contract so as to cover Van S's interests in the way AA advised. At first sight, one may be inclined to explain this attitude in terms of the conservative magistrate whose task it is to defend 'the system'. But I think there is more to his reluctancy than conservatism. What the judge

11. I want to thank Arno Akkermans, Ben Beljaars and Rob van Buul for permission to use their materials. The labels in the text do not correspond with their names.
12. Here I drop the use of the artificial 'exployee'.

opposes is AA's attempt to make the law subservient to a - albeit it justified - policy, excluding it from its other task of challenging such a policy. Let us take a closer look at AA's argument. The two parts of this argument are presented in an order of subsidiarity: the most pertinent thesis is put first, and if that does not work, the second one will have to do the job. This suggests that the two reasons are different in relevance, but equal in origin: they are supposed to be of the same ilk, which is the ground for ranking them subsidiarily in the first place. But this very supposition is easily contested. The reasons are not akin in the sense that the first one is a doctrinal argument, whereas the second is one of policy. What the latter says is in fact: *even in the absence of a labour contract* there can be a legally relevant relationship of labour in view of possible harm for employees. The former concludes that in such cases there *is* a contractual relationship in point of legal fact. Thus, the doctrinal argument is meant to dress up the policy argument, which is in fact the predominant one. This predominance is so strong that it takes the risk of contradiction: legal doctrine is supposed to generate a contract where legal policy concedes that there is none.

No wonder that the court did not like this line of argument. It makes too close a connection between legal policy and legal doctrine. It uses the doctrinal system as a tool to immunisz one's policy (which in itself may be a feasible one), much the same as the squatters' defence tried to do in their case by introducing the concept of provocation. But this is precisely what a system of law will not tolerate, as it is designed to assess and question the natural, i.e. political course of policies. In order to achieve this, it follows its own rules and policy in authoritatively deciding on the use of legal language, turns of legal speech and distribution of legal space and time.

2.3.2 Fluffing the system (BB and CC)

Our two other students opted for a different strategy, although for them, too, it was evident that Van S, the employee, should not be dismissed empty-handed. So their politico-legal commitment is the same as AA's. But they intend to realize it by 'fluffing' the doctrinal system. They want it to do the job for them.

BB and CC distinguish between two questions:

1) Are there contractual obligations of any kind between the employer and the employee?

2) If so, do these obligations come close to those deriving from a labour contract as laid down in art. 1637a Civil Code?

The answer to the first question is, to their minds, in the affirmative, but it requires some legal explanation. BB and CC deal with a number of doctrinal constructions that may be considered to arrive at contractual obligation. For instance, how about regarding the employer as the factual representative of the agency in the course of executing the contract between the agency and the employee, or regarding the employee as a third party entering the contract between employer and agency? But then they reject these constructions as rather artificial and propose to assume that direct rights and obligations follow from the relationships of the parties involved in labour hiring, which in itself is to be based on third-party stipulation. So the least they want to say is that there is a legal bond between employer and employee deriving from a contract. But that, they realize, is not enough to derive an equally affirmative answer to the second question. The contract involved is not a clear-cut labour contract. However, they argue, as long as the matter of agency-hired labour is not well regulated by statutory law, relevant regulations from statutory law should govern what can be constructed as sufficiently close to the matter. In this case there is not only a vague, political sense of what justice would require, but there is also legal reason, given the circumstances and obeying the doctrine of good faith in contract, to apply the regulations of art. 1638x Civil Code (liability of the employer in labour contract) although art. 1637a (labour contract) is not applicable. It looks as if what BB and CC say comes down to the same point as AA's, but their argument is legally much more sophisticated. They do not submit that there is a labour contract after all, like AA did. What they do is to construct the systemic coherence between arts 1637a and 1638x Civil Code in a number of ways, only one of which is the rather verbal inference that liability in labour contract has to be derived from a labour contract in the first place. Their point - put in its most abbreviated form - is that the coherence between the two articles is constructed in other parts of statutory law in a less derivative or 'lexical' way, for instance when it comes to two-way liability for paying social security premiums to the state. Or, in a metaphor: they are fluffing the system with bits of air in order to make Van S. and his judge live in it.

2.4 Once again: the facts of the case

The facts of this case seem totally clear, awaiting legal qualification in one way or another. There is no point in denying that Van S. lost his fingers. And it would be sheer non-sense to say that the loss of his fingers is 'nothing but' the result of narrative coherence. But then, Van S. losing his fingers is not what is directly legally relevant. If he would have lost them on a freezing night high up in the mountains, he would not have addressed the law. So there is really not much that 'awaits' legal qualification. Every tiny piece of what counts as 'fact' is as much the upshot of legal qualification as it is its triggering. Lawyers can make use of this interplay, as was demonstrated by BB and CC. This is what their craftsmanship consists of. Their strategy of defending their craftsmanship when put in jeopardy, however, does not coincide necessarily with enhancing it. Instead of 'fluffing up' the system even more, they may retreat to petrifying its basic terms. This is what AA did: he wanted a labour contract to be there when he needed one, the natural reaction to which was to oppose such wishful thinking and to acknowledge any contractual aspect of the situation. In that respect, AA resembled the opposite stand more than he would have liked to admit.

3 Conclusion

To wrap up this lengthy discussion on attributing legal consequences to facts in legal decision making, we may say that the interception hypothesis has proved to be fruitful in several respects. It clarifies the way in which lawyers work in actual legal practice and how they are implicitly aware of the two - equally tenable, but mutually opposing - hierarchies between legally relevant facts and legally feasible consequences. It explains what happens when the representatives of the legal order feel that they lose their grip on either the case or the system of norms. It even predicts (to a small extent) patterns of reaction between different strategies of legal argumentation. In particular, it sheds light on the adversative character of the legal process.

But it also deprived us from an almost sacrosanct picture of legal epistemology: the paradigm of 'interpretation'. Of course, we do not have to give up 'interpretation' as a theoretical term, as long as we have not succesfully challenged all of its possible uses. But we cannot ignore the fact that the above analyses have cast serious doubts on a certain idea of interpretation that seems paradigmatic in legal epistemology: that 'applying the law' or, for that matter, 'administering justice' is about reinflating a meaningful pattern of statutory or case law that is already there. I have no intention of questioning this picture as far as ordinary daily legal practice is concerned. I think that, for all practical purposes, lawyers should go on believing that they have to 'find' solutions (if not comfort or pleasure) in a pre-established body of law. It is better than spreading the belief that the law just does not tell anything and that it is there to be forced in one direction or another, as individual interests command. The level on which this picture has to be questioned is a theoretical one, i.e., a level which only becomes transparent in practice when the legal order as such comes under ideological or political pressure. And the question would be: If we can neither say that law is a matter of following or applying meaningful rules already there, nor be happy with the conclusion that law is simply 'invented' at the moment it is subservient to policies, what then can we say about the epistemological status of law? This is the question to be taken up in the next chapters.

CHAPTER 5

NARRATIVES, LAW AND REPRESENTATION: TOWARDS AN EPISTEMOLOGICAL ACCOUNT OF THE INTERCEPTION HYPOTHESIS

In chapter 1 we presented the basic hypothesis of this book as 'the interception hypothesis'. This hypothesis was derived from a particular branch of literary theory - the theory of narrative structure - , more specifically from a proposal by Jonathan Culler. He pointed out that this structure is based on two inversed hierarchies of reading that govern the relationship between the elementary categories of Event and Interpretation. In consecutive chapters, I offered three contexts which could support the view that a similar couple of inversed hierarchies of understanding or 'reading' is at work in legal discourse: the context of relating the facts of a case before the law, the context of constructing the system of legal rules and the context of making the system of law pertinent to the facts of a case in legal decision making. For instance, in the last chapter, I argued that the relationship between a case and a decision in a law-suit is an instance of the opposition between Event and Interpretation. By thus contextualising Culler's inversed hierarchies I carried his thesis over from literary theory to the theory of knowledge. The basic categories of Event and Interpretation became epistemological variables that could assume different values.

That the epistemological core of Culler's proposal really involves an account of narrative structure in terms of mutually intercepting referring devices, is entirely my claim. In the present chapter, I will substantiate this claim by the following lines of argument. Firstly, I intend to provide an intuitive idea of what I mean by 'interception of reference' on a more generalized level than the theory of narrative. Secondly, I shall sketch the outlines of a possible epistemological theory that may support this intuitive idea, by giving an account of the mutually refutable hierarchies [H.1] and [H.2] without tinkering with the distinction between reality and fiction. Thirdly, I want to fill out some of the open terms of this theory which will be particularly relevant for chapters 7, 8 and 9.

1 Representionalism and interception of reference

The narrative approach suggested by Culler's theory is both fascinating and easily misleading. It is fascinating, because it enables us to discover interesting data for a theory of knowledge. In the context of the law, these data may even seem tantalising, as they reveal awkward strategies of hypostatization together with massive sociopolitical consequences. But even so, we should be reluctant either to consider it as an (alternative) epistemological theory, or to reject it as the end of epistemology. It is, in point of fact, neither of the two. It provides rich materials to challenge a predominant theory of knowledge: one which tries to account for the great divide between reality and fiction in representationalist terms (an issue I shall return to shortly). It points in the direction in which to search for a more adequate understanding of this divide. But is does not, and does not intend to, offer anything in the neighbourhood of a full-blooded alternative to representationalism. Legal discourse, therefore, is right in sticking to a firm belief in the distinction between reality and fiction. But it is right for the wrong - representationalist - reasons, as I will argue more extensively in chapter 6. As long as representationalism is predominant, it cannot afford to acknowledge the nature of the two necessary but incompatible hierachies of reading as to the relation between events and facts, norms and values, facts and norms, cases and consequences, and to avoid hypostatization of either side.[1)]

In what sense, then, do narrative structures challenge a representationalist theory of knowledge? A non-sophisticated representationalist theory of knowledge departs from an opposition between thinking and being; then it proceeds to provide bridges between pieces of reality and contents of consciousness in terms of concepts, or meanings, or phenomena, or sense data, which are believed to have some sort of referential range or potential; and finally it suggests that it can test the reliability of the bridges (the 'match' between thinking and being or the actual 'hit' of the refential device). The difficulties of this account are well known, and they can be ordered in a Münchhausen trilemma pertaining to the criteria of the reliability test. These criteria are:

- either dependent on direct access of thinking to being after all; which

1. I have tried to come to grips with the political implications of representationalism in my (1988b) and (1990b), on the basis of an earlier essay in Dutch (1984).

contradicts the point of departure; or
- dependent on other bridges which in turn lack a title of being 'ultimately fundamental'; which constitutes an infinite regress; or
- the outcome of a decision, a consensus, a convention to regard some criterion as 'basic'; which leaves us with the unsatisfying notion of truth as 'legal (v. illegal) belief'.

Let us return to the epistemic stakes of narrative strategies explained in chapter 1, section 2. To narrate is, I said there, to make up for what is left out in a representationalist view of conceptual (scientific or philosophical) thinking, to wit the *singularity* of whatever singular thing one is trying to give an account of. From this point of view, it seems as if objects and events only have meanings by virtue of universal senses which re-present them to the mind. Thus, conceptual discourse may ascertain *that, how and why* something happened. But it can only do so at the cost of leaving something out: the irreducible singularity of this specific 'something'. Narratives challenge a representationalist view of concepts by attaching meanings to singular events or states of affairs in a very direct way. They stretch the limits of our world, not by using the tools of conceptual discourse and comparing the new and the old experiences by the *tertium* of general concepts and laws; rather they do so by metonymically presenting new ones that are directly, but fragmentarily, continguous to our old experiences. Narrative is, in that respect, essentially metonymic rather than metaphoric. Cleopatra's nose, for instance: how different would the appearance of the earth have been, if it would have been half an inch shorter, so Pascal says. One may be able to tell exciting and true stories about Cleopatra's nose and the meaning of that very half inch in the history of mankind, without being able to give an account of the connection of that nose to certain political enterprises in terms of general laws and concepts. If one would try to do so all the same, the constraints inherent to these alleged laws would probably contain such definite descriptions as to individuate just one singular event: the fascination caused by Cleopatra's nose.

Narratives, therefore, are justified by being about something non-discursive, something 'eventual', since *that* (I mean: telling about its contingent occurrence) is a powerful way of presenting this something in its singularity. But this is still too simple a way of putting it, as we saw in the previous chapters. When it is true that narratives are not just constituted, but *justified* by being about something non-discursive, when they take an interest in being about some non-discursive event as much as they can, they have to avoid one particular danger of their own rhetoric strategy: they should avoid the pretension of being a totally adequate *re-presentation* of the event in question as a singular event. For if they would *claim* to have the power which conceptual discourse does not have (to have found a key to the inaccessible eventuality of things after all), they would at the same time destroy the basis of their justification. At the cost of self-contradiction they would claim not only that eventuality is accessible after all, but also that they can (if only they would) give a (necessarily non-narrative!) account of what counts as adequate accessibility. They would turn into (no doubt *bad*) conceptual discourse. Narratives can go crazy,[2)] especially political ones, as nationalism proves.

Good narratives have an elegant way of coping with this danger, as Culler explained to us: they trace a sort of self-denunciatory circle around an event. They seem to intercept their own referring devices to the outward world by referring to this world as the focus of their own coherence. They are *about*, and therefore refer to, a world 'outside' the story, thus treating the story as a representation of this world. But at certain points of the narration, this world to which they refer is also, and at the same time, treated as a function that is internal to the story: the referential gesture of the story to a world 'outside' is, as it were, diverted and reflected to a world 'inside': a world posited, postulated or projected by the story to make sense as a story. But they do not replace their reference to an outside world by a projection, as this would frustrate the requirement for stories to be 'about' something prior to discourse. All they do is 'intercept' or 'suspend' the reference to an outside world by obliquely admitting that this outside world happens to be congruent with the world which they invoke in order to be coherent and which, thus, may well be an inside world from the point of view of the outside world. But as they can only afford to obliquely admit it, they also tend to erase the traces of suspension or interception by new referential devices to an outside world, which will, in turn, be intercepted again, and so on *ad infinitum*. So the story develops by enveloping itself and *vice versa*.

We may even try to go one step further. From Culler's account it follows, that 'narrative coherence' generates events as discursive upshots in

2. As one of my teachers, W. Luijpen, used to say with regard to myths.

one sense of the word, and is itself the discursive upshot of those events in another sense. What has to be conceived of as an event prior to all interpretation, turns out to be also the interpreting notion par excellence. This, now, is an important *performative* aspect of narrative texts. By mobilizing the two presuppositions mentioned above, the text succeeds in creating its own 'situation', at least in the sense of a 'cognitive' (or apprehensive?) attitude which it should be told, heard or read with. By enveloping its reference to an outside world, the story seduces its readers to wonder if *they* are the ones who are the source of the referential gestures on which it seems to rely. That is how the story pulls them into its world. It does so, not by extending or protruding its referential devices to the world of the audience, but rather by enveloping them. The effect on the audience (*de te fabula narratur*) is achieved by retreat. That is how we become 'fascinated', not because we are addressed, but because we are seduced.

2 Epistemological questions

This may be an effective and, indeed, aesthethic device to undermine representationalism, but it is philosophically uncanny. It does articulate the effects of narrative strategies, but it does not explain the epistemological mechanism that causes these effects. We saw the trick, and it was magic; now we want to know how it is done. (1) We need an exact account of the movements involved in 'interception of reference'. Precisely which movement intercepts which other movement? (2) We also need a distinction between story-dependent independence and story-independent independence of events, without giving up our previous finding that the description of the events can be 'the same' in the two instances. What would be an alternative theory which is compatible with the data of the mutually refutable hierarchies [H.1] and [H.2]? (3) Moreover, we would like to know how it all works in domains like law, where events are related to interpretations in a very specific way, namely governed by a deontic operator. Thus, we face three epistemological questions. In dealing with them, I will frankly and frequently use parts of different, but coherent theories presented by the late Hector-Neri Castañeda.[3)]

2.1 Referential transparency and referential opacity

Interception of reference can be explained rather straightforwardly by going to the roots of the inside-outside distinction regarding 'the world' related in a story. These roots have to do with the 'voices' or 'points of view' involved in story-telling. The 'voices' of the character in the story compete with the 'voices' of the narrator and the audience when it comes to referring to a story-independent world. What happens in a good, that is: a fascinating story, is that these 'voices' start interfering and intertwining in a dazzling way. But the basic mechanism is in fact rather simple, and it can be read from far simpler statements than full-blooded narratives. It works with the distinction between two sorts of transparency and opacity of so-called cognitive contexts: we have referential and propositional transparency, as well as propositional and referential opacity.[4)] Suppose the following sentence [1] is uttered by some person in the audience watching *Oedipus Rex*:

[1] Oedipus believes that he is the murderer of Laius.

We are familiar with the idea that the cognitive attitude indicated by the word 'believes' opens a context or world (rendered by the that-clause) that is not directly accessible from the world the speaker of [1] lives in. Trivially, from [1] and [2]

[2] Laius is Oedipus' father

we cannot deduce [3]:

[3] Oedipus believes that he is the murderer of his father.

3. In the period 1983-1989 I had the good fortune to discuss some of these ideas with Castañeda, but not in such a detail that I would suggest some sort of 'authorization'. I also want to stress, that here I only offer very initial expositions of his theories.

4. Cf. Castañeda [1989: 88ff], which will take the reader to a lot of other places in Castañeda's work.

The reason is that Oedipus may not know that Laius is his father, or, indeed, that he is Oedipus. The believe-dependent context is 'opaque', and it is sound philosophical advice not to quantify into opaque contexts. But note that we can take the referential device 'Laius' in two ways: it may be a referential device in the hands of this 20th century person in the audience, who knows the story of the play, who knows a lot about the king of Thebes from other myths. Then what this person does is bringing 'Laius' outside the attitude-dependent context and saying something like [4]:

[4] Oedipus believes of (someone who is in fact) Laius, that he murdered him.

This 'external' construal of [1] creates referential transparency, because now the speaker knows what he is talking about. Taken together with [2], [4] yields a perfect syllogism. But the very move that creates referential transparency, also creates propositional opacity. By transforming [1] into [4], we lose our grip on the content of what Oedipus believed. This content may well have been something like [5]:

[5] I murdered an old man at the crossroads.

Alternatively, we may understand the referential device 'Laius' as something Oedipus uses in stating his beliefs, leaving it 'inside' the that-clause. Now the attitude-dependent context becomes transparent as far as propositional content is concerned. We may say that we render what it was that Oedipus believed. But now, having created propositional transparency, we are left with referential opacity. We cannot know who Oedipus was referring to when he used the name 'Laius' to state what he believed. Oedipus may have killed two man called Laius, one of whom he knew by name, a young shepherd who once tried to steal a lamb from him; or he may have had a dog named Laius.

The explanation for the complicated phenomenon of interception of reference is that singular terms in external construal introduce some degree of propositional opacity[5)] and that propositional transparency can only be achieved by accepting some degree of referential opacity. The

5. Cf. Castañeda [1989: 95].

reference of terms in external construal (which is referentially transparent) can be intercepted by switching to propositional transparency. Narratives characteristically feature characters to which they ascribe all sorts of cognitive attitudes. Dependent on these attitudes are propositional contexts, which can be made transparent to hearers or readers by allowing referential opacity to enter. In even short stories we find already rather extensive sets of these contexts, as every singular thought of every singular character is involved. A powerful constraint on creating propositional transparency over such a large set of propositional contexts is that they must all be compatible under certain laws of consistency and coherence; e.g. whatever Oedipus refers to by 'Laius', he cannot be ascribed the belief that he did and did not murder Laius, or, for that matter, the belief that he murdered Laius twice. As all the referentially opaque uses of terms over large sets of propositional transparent contexts in narratives must be consistent and coherent, they entail the suggestion of a world 'out there'. Now (opaque, but strongly coherent) references to this story-dependent world 'out there' may intercept (transparent, but possibly weak) references to the story-independent world 'out there', and *vice versa*. This explains how interception of reference can occur.

If we briefly review some of the salient examples of inversed hierarchies of reading analyzed in the previous chapters, we will detect that, indeed, the inversion can be explained by the inversion described above, namely that of transparency and opacity with regard to references and thought contents. The tragedy of *Oedipus Rex*, from an epistemological point of view, is that finally Oedipus himself takes responsibility for identifying the internal and external construal of 'Laius': he realizes: 'By killing an old man at the crossroads, I must have killed Laius, king of Thebes, who is said to be my father'. Similarly, in the euthanasia case of the medical doctor who killed Mrs. B., construing the two hierarchies of reading was dependent on focussing on the wants, beliefs, intentions and motives, i.e. the cognitive attitudes of the persons involved. Again, when we were dealing with the squatters, picturing their behaviour both as 'what happened' and 'what must happen', we were only able to do so by concentrating on what legal authorities *believed* that would happen and what they *intended* to do. So here, also, what we really explored was a set of dependent contexts which can only be made propositionally transparent by sacrificing a certain degree of referentially transparency of singular terms.

2.2 Interception, fiction and reality

In section 1 we also asked what a non-representationalist theory would look like that could give an account of the distinction between story-dependent and story-independent independence of events, and of the sense in which these events could be 'the same' in the two instances. In terms of our paradigm example from the previous chapter we can state the question as: How do we account for the difference between 'These six squatters threw bricks and stroke out with iron bars at some demolishers at Stationsstraat 54, Tilburg on the 8th of March 1979' as a narratively posited real event (fiction) and as an event that really occured (reality)? We have to ask this question from an epistemological point of view, because - contrary to a widely held belief - the external construal of singular terms as analyzed in section 1 is neutral to existence.[6] We are not ontologically committed (in the sense that we must acknowledge the existence of) to the entities referred to by the singular terms used externally. The distinction between fiction and reality is a separate question, which we must now address.

In an article in *Poetics,*[7] Castañeda related his Guise Theory (GT) to a comparable example after a short survey of other[8] inroads. I shall continue to use my own example, following his instructive survey for a while and then, in the next subsection, turn to the merits of GT itself, especially with regard to the narrative gulf between the factual and the normative parts of legal decisions and rules.

2.2.1 Survey

There are several, prima facie promising but eventually unsatisfying approaches to make the required distinction. With Castañeda we may consider the following candidates.

[T.1] Predicate ambiguity

We may want to say that predicates have a systematic ambiguity, depending on whether they attribute properties to entities governed by the laws

6. Castañeda [1989: 95 ff].

7. Castañeda (1979); repr. in German translation by H. Pape, in Castañeda (1982) and again in English in Castañeda (1989).

8. In his view less promising, but not impossible inroads.

of physics (real) or entities that are postulated, projected, invented or hallucinated by the senses or by consciousness or by story operators (fictional). To apply this to my example: the throwing and beating in the former case is different from that in the latter. In the former case it hurts, it damages, it makes people bleed and have to go to hospitals, it urges other people to find out what blood group the victims have, etc., while in the latter case the throwing and beating of these entities does not hurt, etc.

It will be clear that the thesis here is not that blows by fictional entities do not hurt, whereas those by real entities do. The thesis is rather, that from the hurt we can tell the difference between real and fictional blows. This, however, does not seem to be a very plausible approach: some real blows do not hurt, and some fictional or hallucinated blows hurt very much (causing, in turn, sometimes very real psychic problems). So, where do we learn the systematic difference between the two sets of properties and how do we account for their apparent correspondence?

[T.2] Subject ambiguity

A second possibility is to assign different meanings to the subject expressions, dependent on whether they refer to actual or fictional entities. Now, if these subject expressions are definite descriptions, for instance, 'the only six squatters who were present on the morning of 8 March 1979 at Tilburg, Stationsstraat 54' this view perhaps boils down to [T.1]. But if the subject terms contain direct referring devices (proper names or demonstratives as in our example), [T.2] in fact means that 'the domain of fictional entities is entirely different from the domain of actual entities'.[9)]

Now, in what classical philosophy calls the *modus essendi,* this is absolutely true: the domain of actual entities is defined as the domain in which it is possible to establish, for every property P and its complement ¬P, whether it belongs to a subject S or not. In the domain of fictional entities this is (by definition) not possible. For instance, about the squatters as real entities and the property 'having red hair' it can be established whether this property or its complement 'not [having red hair]' can be attributed to the subject. Around the squatters as the products of narrative coherence there is a vacuum of properties for which one cannot decide

9. Castañeda (1979: 43).

whether or not they are attributable when the narrative does not ascribe or at least imply them.[10)] By the same token, however, we shall run into serious difficulties in the *modus cognoscendi*. As fictional entities are incomplete, it is hard to individuate them without allowing the narrative to be never-ending. To the degree that we allow for an infinite 'to be continued', the distinction between the real and the fictional entities is blurred. To the degree that the fiction is finite, we cannot establish how its subject relates to real subjects. For instance, how do we determine if the squatters who actually threw bricks at the police are *the same as* the squatters who are implicitly believed to have thrown bricks at the demolishers?

Castañeda discusses a theory built on 'story operators' as a third possibility of providing an account for both the divide and the mixture of reality and fiction. We need not discuss that here, as our entire argument can be regarded as an effort to illustrate the force of story operators. The law's discourse about 'what happened' in our example was structured in much the same way as was the fictional character Putois in Anatole France's novel - the beautiful example Castañeda refers to:

> It [the character, BvR] was invented by a (first-order) fictional character in order to refuse a boring dinner invitation: she had to await the gardener Putois. Then everybody in the story acquired the habit of blaming unexplainable events, or events not to be explained, on Putois. The situation developed in such a way that Putois was just an invisible member of the community, even more real than other members of it. (Castañeda, 1979: 45)

As in our squatters case, it is both the force of fictional referring devices and their concurrence with references to actual entities which need to be explained. In this respect, it should be stressed once again that the crucial event of the six squatters striking with bars and throwing stones is not only hypostatised by the representatives of 'the law' in the sense of 'the authorities', but also by the defence attorneys. Neither of these parties could apparently escape from treating these events

10. Which leaves, by the way, room for plenty of debates in which 'reasons never run out'. Cf. Dworkin's example of literary critics discussing whether or not David Copperfield had a homosexual affair with Steerforth. See Dworkin (1977b: 73 ff).

> (...) as having a status *outside* the stories they inhabit - *somehow* on a par with the persons who deal with them. (Castañeda 1979: 46)

Therefore, story operators are, from our point of view, to be regarded as a complex part of the data (note the 'somehow' in the quotation!) rather than as the stepping stones of an illuminating theory.

2.2.2 Copula ambiguity and narrative coherence

Castañeda's own solution to the problem starts from the ambiguity of our paradigm case as an ambiguity of the copula (resp. copulae) that links subject and predicate. To put it simply: there are neither two sorts of squatters, nor two sorts of throws and blows; but we should learn to distinguish two ways of *relating* the squatters on the one hand and the throwing and beating on the other. In still other words, I believe that Castañeda would account for Culler's opposing hierarchies of reading by two of the different ways of 'predicating' developed in his Guise Theory.

I will not discuss GT in all its comprehensiveness. Its basic tenets, however, provide an elegant way of evading the aporias of too 'narratological' an epistemology. And it should be noted that this way out is a non-representationalist one. First of all, GT starts out to offer us as rich an ontology as we can imagine, because it regards properties as 'the ultimate components of the world' (Castañeda, 1974: 10). Of all we can think of as *having* a property *f*-ness, it can be said that it *has a sort of being* qua 'the *x* such that it is *f*', i.e., as a harpooned object of thought. These thin, thinkable individuals, or 'objects,' or *guises,* are clusters of properties. They can be conceived to be of the form *c*A, where A is the *core* set or constitutive set of properties involved, and *c* is an operator on that set.[11)] Operator *c* is

> (...) the individuating structure denoted by the definite article 'the' in definite descriptions. (Castañeda, 1988: 95)

11. As to anti-representationalism, Plantinga's observation on GT is pertinent: 'It isn't just that we can *represent* or *model* the relation between concrete individuals and their properties by writing, e.g., C{A,B}; rather, the individual *really is* constituted by the properties in its core together with C.' See Plantinga (1983: 46).

For the sake of brevity we may say that, following Castañeda, 'the six squatters who were throwing bricks and striking with bars at Stationsstraat 54 Tilburg (*p*) on 8 March 1979 (*t*)' can be construed as a guise of the form [G1]

> [G1] the (six ones){being a squatter, being throwing bricks at *p,t*, being beating with bars at *p,t*}.

A second step in GT is to distinguish different *modi* in which the primitive 'existence' of these merely 'thought of' or 'thinkable' guises is differentiated. Up to this point, it was said, that for *any* set of properties, whether consistent or not (!), there is the concrete individual or guise whose core is that very set.[12)] But now, we may distinguish several types of external[13)] relations between the set in question and the guise constituted by it. They can perspicuously formulated as *sameness* relations. Thus we have:

1) Sameness in the sense of *strict identity*: the six squatters who threw bricks and beat with bars at *p,t*, are strictly identical with (are the same as) the six squatters who threw bricks and beat with bars at *p,t*. This type of 'sameness' is governed by Leibniz's law: For any individuals *x* and *y*, *x* is strictly identical with *y*, iff whatever is true of *x* is true of *y*, respectively, iff for any property *f*-ness, *x* is *f* if and only if *y* is *f*.

2) Another external mode of property possession is sameness in the sense of *consubstantiation*. Recall [G1]

> [G1] the (six ones){being a squatter, being throwing bricks at *p,t*, being beating with bars at *p,t*}.

Now let us assume that there appeared to be six defendants standing on trial at the only session of the District Court at Breda on 6 June 1979. Let us call this a second guise [G2]:

> [G2] the (six ones){being a defendant, standing on trial at *q,u*}.

We may want to say that the six squatters who threw bricks and beat with

12. Cf. Plantinga (1983: 47).
13. 'External', because operating on the *c*-operation.

bars at *p,t* were contingently (factually) the same as the six defendants standing on trial at the only session of the District Court at Breda on 6 June 1979. This can be theoretically expressed in GT - provided that certain conditions are fulfilled - as: G1 is 'consubstantiated' with G2. In a similar way we may want to say that there are indeed entities which are the same as six squatters who threw bricks and beat with bars at *p,t*. In terms of GT we then say that these entities are consubstantiated with G1. The rather barbarous word 'consubstantiation' means nothing else than that a certain set of properties is thought to be linked up with another set *in a specific way* . Specific in what sense? This type of contingent 'sameness' is governed by constraints like:

- laws of consistency: only self-consistent guises can be consubstantiated with anything[14)]; and that is why we can say, for instance, that the square circle cannot *exist*, although our thinking can gather the properties 'being a circle' and 'being square' in the same set;
- the law of completeness: what is consubstantiated with anything is consubstantiated with every property P or its complement $\neg$P we can think of. Thus, this sameness relation explains why we can articulate the existence of consubstantiated guises in terms of the laws of nature. It may well be noted that what we normally have in mind when we talk about 'the real world' is this kind of consubstantiated being.[15)]

3) A third type of sameness is *consociation*, as Castañeda wants to baptise it. In this case, the sameness relation holds between concrete guises as far as they are brought together in thought (belief, superstition, fiction, etc.). Like consubstantiation, consociation is a contingent relation. It is contingent on what a person, a social institution, a cultural tradition 'tinkers' from (partly) pieces of the real world and (partly) thinkable guises. We may, for instance, say, that the six defendants standing on trial at the only session of the District Court in Breda on 6 June are consociated *by the District Court* with the six squatters who threw bricks and beat with bars

14. Castañeda (1979: 57).

15. '(...) ordinary real objects are, like fictional characters, systems of thin thinkable objects denoted by those definite descriptions that we normally say co-refer contingently.' (Castañeda, 1979: 51)

at p,t.[16)]

There are more types of sameness which need to be distinguished if one would summarize the whole of GT[17)], and those mentioned above are only indicated in a very loose way. These indications, however, may suffice to underline that in Castañeda's view

> Real, actual, or existential contingent sameness holds an infinite set of individual guises together in one ordinary infinitely propertied object. Fictional contingent sameness holds a finite set of individual guises, grouped differently, of course, together in one fictional character. (Castañeda, 1979: 53)

Now we can return to our interception hypothesis, its challenge to representationalism and its epistemological uncanniness. I submit that an adequate translation of Culler's analysis in terms of GT would be: [H.1] (E → I) has to do with consubstantiation and [H.2] (E ← I) with consociation. Let me explain. Culler assumes, rightly, that E and I are of the same breed in the two instances of [H.1] and [H.2]. What he seems to forget about is the ambiguity of the arrow between E and I. In terms of GT: he has pointed out that in narratives the very guises that are proposed as consubstantiated are *also* proposed as consociated. As far as I can see, GT has no problems with that. GT may even admit that, in a specific case and under specific conditions, it may be very hard to tell, indeed it may be undecidable, whether the constraints on consubstantiation are acknowl-

16. It is apt to add Castañeda's stricter characterization of consubstantiation and consociation, to be found, for instance, in (1979: 57-58; see also his replies to Plantinga and especially Clark for a corrected version of consociation in Tomberlin (1983)). Let the core set of a guise *a* be /*a*/ and let *a*[F] be an individual guise whose core set is the union of a core /*a*/ and the unit set {F-ness}. The guise *a*[F] corresponding with a guise *a* is called by Castañeda: the F-protraction of A. Then we can define:

1) Internal predication: *a*(F) is true, iff F-ness ε /*a*/.

2) *a* exists = def. C*(*a*,*a*), where C* is the operator of consubstantiation.

3) C*(*a*,*b*) is true, iff *a* exists and is actually, contingently the same as *b*.

4) C**(*a*,*b*) is true, iff either (i) the guises *a* and *b* are thought to be the same object, whether a fictional object or a real one; or (ii) *b* is a protraction of the form *a*[*x* believes (thinks, supposes,... etc.) that *u* is F], where 'C**' is the operator of consociation, '*x*' is an expression referring to a person, 'F' stands for an adjectival expression, and '*u*' is a schematic letter representing a subject position.

17. Conflation, participation, transsubstantiation; not to mention the revised version of GT: Ordered Guise Theory. See the Tomberlin volume (1983).

edged. The previous subsection on referential transparency and opacity explained when and why. But that should not seduce us in thinking that there is no point in making the distinction between fiction and reality. There certainly is, as long as we do not postulate a reality which is not harpooned by thinking in the first place.

2.3 Facts and norms revisited

There is this third epistemological question to address: How could we account for the relationship between facts and norms in rules and decisions in law? I have argued that this relationship is a 'narrative' one. The previous section allows us, or so I claim, to make epistemological sense of this thesis: the very guises that are proposed as consubstantiated - the facts of the case - should also be seen as consociated. But one specific problem was swept under the carpet: if consociation is on the side of fiction and belief, then this does not entail, without further argument, that it is on the side of norms, or at least the normative upshots ascribed to certain facts. To put it in another way: Is there 'consociation' *from a normative standpoint*? It would be necessary to develop the answer in jurisprudential detail before it can be embraced as a valid account of legal phenomena. This, however, would exceed the limits of the present book.[18] I will only point to a possible explanation. And once again I shall lean heavily on Castañeda, this time on his theory of institutions.[19]

2.3.1 Castañeda on institutions

Castañeda conceives the surface profile of an institution i at a time t as an ordered quadruple $<O_i, A_i, f_i, t>$, where O_i is a set of offices, A_i is a set of officers or agents, f_i is an employment function that maps A_i on to O_i, and t is the time in question.[20] It seems quite clear that O_i, as a

18. It would entail, among other things, a full-blooded theory of conditionality in law.
19. This theory is, I think, quite close to MacCormick's and perhaps even more to Weinberger's, but I will not go into explicit comparison.
20. Cf. Castañeda (1982b), which I will summarize here, referring to other works, notably (1975), where appropriate.

set of offices, contains certain practices, to be analysed further by reference to roles and rules. That is to say: These practices will appear in the scope of deontic structures (obligations, permissions). But they probably also turn out to be part of complex hierarchies of heterogeneous deontic structures, in which, for instance, fulfilment of an obligation of type O_1 may be a factual condition for the obligatoriness of a certain type of practice O_2. Even complete institutions (in Castañeda's sense) can be functions as factual conditions for other institutions; for instance, lawyers regard foreign law as 'a fact' in applying domestic law. I should say a word on both matters.

The facts which are cited in the antecedent of either a rule or a decision, are commonly regarded as 'circumstances', as 'surroundings' in which something should be done. No doubt they are. But note that the very same actions that appear in the description of the circumstantial scenery can appear in the scope of deontic operators such as 'ought', as the italicised constituents of the following phrases prove:

[1] If someone enters a house in use by someone else without legal permission, he ought_i to *leave the premises on the request of the latter*.

[2] If such a person does not *leave the premises on request*, the police ought_i to remove him.

There is, according to Castañeda, a fundamental epistemological gulf between the action 'leave the premises on request' as the focus of a deontic operator and as part of the description of circumstances. The former regards the action as practical, as 'to be done', the latter as a matter of fact. Consequently, the logical behaviour of circumstances (propositions) is very different from that of deontic focuses (or 'practitions').[21] Examples [1] and [2] also show a peculiarity of the deontic operator: It is a compound of a pure deontic device 'ought' (which functions as a proxy for all the well-known deontic modalities) and a subscript. The subscript may be interpreted as 'by the rules of Dutch criminal law' or 'according to police instructions', etc.). These rules, in turn, have a similar structure as [1] and [2], though the subscripts may take on different values as the

21. Cf. Castañeda (1982b: 32; 1975: ch. 2, 4).

case may be. Thus, such a subscript is an institutional operator, taking pure deontic operators as arguments and qualified deontic operators as values. An institution is usually a complex hierarchy or system of deontic structures, the deontic operators of which indicate the context of legitimation for each specific action in the practical sense of 'something which is to be done'.[22)]

2.3.2 Facts as contexts of legitimation

Now my hypothesis can be framed in Castañedian terms. I believe that there is generally more to the antecedent of a normative statement than merely being a description of the relevant circumstances. However impeccable the distinction may be, this does not prevent empirical data from mixing up the terms of the distinction in an almost inextricable way. The types of facts mentioned in the antecedent of a rule or the actual facts referred to in the decision of a case do not produce their own warrant of a neat fit into the pigeonholes of our concepts. On the contrary, they can be bastards which have features of both. This can easily be the case with so-called 'brute facts' underlying legal consequences in law. Such a fact or bunch of facts is *also*, in most cases, an elliptic form of the *context of legitimation* to which the normative consequent refers in order to test its validity.

An instructive exercise on a very small scale would be a striptease test on [1]. We can reduce the antecedent to a purely circumstantial datum by deleting some elements, as the following series indicates:

[1a] If someone enters a house in use by someone else without permission, he ought to leave the premises on the request of the latter. ('legal' deleted)

[1b] If someone enters a house in use by someone else, he ought to leave the premises on the request of the latter. ('without permission' deleted)

[1c] If someone enters someone else's house, he ought to leave the premises on the request of the latter. ('in use' deleted)

22. See Castañeda (1975: ch. 5, 8).

[1d] If someone enters a house, he ought to leave the premises on request. ('someone else' deleted)
[1e] If someone enters, he ought to leave. ('a house' deleted)

I submit that deleting these respective elements diminishes our understanding of the *connection* between antecedent and consequent down to the point where it vanishes into a completely instantaneous 'as soon as ... then ...' or even into complete non-sense. We no longer understand the consequent as something that ought to be done *by virtue of* what happens to be the case. But then, apparently, 'the case' is not a mere description of circumstances; it is part of the context of legitimation, and, thus, of the institutional operator. It is, we could say, a metonymy for the context in which the norm is to be justified and not only a set of times and places in which it is to be realized.

Now, a context of legitimation is radically dependent on what a set of actors *believes*: about their identity as a group (in what respect they are co-actors), about their ends and desires, about the chains of causality in the world they find themselves in and about the openings in these chains that allow for closing by human action[23)]. In this *belief*-dependent context we find the source of what was called in the previous section 'consociation'. It allows us to determine the place where normative elements sneak into an account of facts. It is the place of the limited truth conditions we develop in order to frame a picture of the world in which we can act. If we want to engage in action, we cannot await scientific investigation[24)], which is an endless quest for causality. We rather tell ourselves or our fellow-man what the world looks like taking certain limits for granted. These limits are accepted, endorsed, enacted, or at least taken for granted as limits we do not *want* to exceed (provisionally). In this sense, they contain normative elements. The narrative data which generate 'the event' in *Oedipus Rex* are precisely of this species: the curse on Thebes, the prophecies of Theiresias, the public report of Oedipus's past, etc., they are all endorsed limits within which the practical question

23. Cf. Castañeda (1975: 131 ff).
24. And as far as we do engage in action *during* scientific investigation (for instance, in experimenting), we *normatively* limit the area in which we are going to understand what we are doing as well as to judge what we get in response and to assess the meaning and truth value of the propositions to express this.

'What should be done to Laius' murderer?' finds its factual framework. Iocaste's tactics in the play are to a large extent devoted to escaping the endorsement of these normative elements, thus enforcing their narrative force on the audience, precisely by denying them. The enactment of such limits is not something apart from the statement of fact which we make; it is a part of a narratively enacted framework. What a thing really is, Wittgenstein says, is dependent on

> (...) the poesis I surround it with (nach der *Erdichtung* mit der ich es umgebe).[25)]

What kind of 'belief' or *'Erdichtung'* would explain that the law prefers to surround its facts with bruteness? Why should social reality be thought to be 'brute' in the sense of 'being untouched (yet)' by the law? Part of the answer may be this: because that is the way the law manages, in sociopolitical problems, to pose as the answer, not as the question; as the solution, not the problem; as the effect, not the cause. In other words: that is the way law tells *itself* from politics, as the paragon of neutrality, rationality, prudence and receptiveness. It is, to conclude, the veil it uses to hide its positivity and to prevent its subjects from remembering its origin in that one moment of illegal performative occupation that Rousseau could never forget. Did he not remind us in the *Second Discourse* of that unique phrase of the one who fenced some land and fancied that he could find others stupid enough to believe him: 'This is mine.'? MacCormick says:

> If the objection is to my notion [sc. of institutional fact; BvR] that there are norm-defined facts, my reply is: find me a fact that isn't so defined. It is not 'institutional facts' which are problematic, but 'brute facts.[26)]

He could not be more right.

25. *Philos.Invest.*, p. 210.
26. Cf. MacCormick and Weinberger (1986: 102).

3 Representationalism, metaphysics and politics

Now that we have towed the interception hypothesis by epistemological ropes, we may try to explore its range in legal theory with more confidence. In particular, we may want to investigate its critical potential towards the most pervasive structures of the various contents of beliefs that can play a role in institutions. In chapters 7-9 we will turn to a few basic institutions of the law, like the democracy as a legislative institution, punishment as a law-enforcing institution, contract as an institution binding upon the agents involved in it. Of course, we will have to focus on such beliefs as are at the basis of these legal institutions, that is to say beliefs held by the agents in set A of the formal contexts of legitimation sketched in the previous section. Since, however, philosophy is interested in the most pertinent, pervasive and necessary form these beliefs may take rather than in this or that particular content or ideology, it is not too far-fetched to prepare these explorations by a brief assessment of the most general type of beliefs that are in the background of legitimation. The relevance of this exercise will become clear as soon as we discover how this general type already foreshadows certain bounds between metaphysical views regarding our awareness of reality at large, on the one hand, and political views on the other.

3.1 The metaphysics of representation and its political counterparts

I began this chapter by giving a succinct account of representationalism as an epistemological theory pertaining to the most basic relationship between thinking and being. Its scheme was that of initial opposition and eventual correlation between these two poles. Thinking is placed on the side of the subject, being on the side of the object. Knowledge, therefore, cannot be anything else but bridging the gap between subject and object, or between thinking and being. Such bridges can be constructed from different materials (essences, ideas, sense data and their ilk), which all have one thing in common: they are themselves halfway houses between thinking and being. That is to say: They are a bit of both, half reflections of reality and half projections of consciousness. They hold the place of reality in our awareness and they hold the place of our awareness in reality. And, as we saw, that is exactly why they are under suspicion. They lead into metaphysical aporias; which is to say that they deprive us of any understanding of what words like 'real' or 'true' mean in the first place. If we conceive of the intermediates as bridges that span the gap between thinking and being, we are left with the question how their reliability can be tested, i.e., how it can be established that they are what they are supposed to be, namely necessary bridges that span the gap between thinking and being. One form of the aporia is this: If our thinking is able to establish that it has succeeded in grasping reality by the use of an intermediate, it is apparently able to acknowledge reality also in another, immediate way, otherwise it could not tell the difference between success and failure of the intermediate way. But then it has to be conceded that, so to speak, the gap was already bridged before the bridge was used and, thus, that there was no need for a bridge in the first place. That, again, contradicts the initial presupposition of the gap. The other form the metaphysical aporia can take is to grant that our thinking is not able to establish the reliability of the bridge. This is, in fact, just another way of admitting that there is nothing we can recognize as a bridge. Reality will be nothing else but whatever thinking takes to be its object; thus we will have to be agnostic about what it is more than a postulate of certain ... well, it is difficult to find a word here, as even such inarticulated stuffings as 'vibrations' evoke the question whether we 'really' sense them or not. It will readily be admitted that our hypothesis tried to deal with alternative aporias, as these are just very generalized forms of the problems we encountered when preferring one of the two hierarchies [H.1] and [H.2] at the cost of the other. Preference for [H.1] will bring us to a hypostatized reality that is 'always already there', while an exclusive option for [H.2] will leave us with a reality that is 'nothing but' the shadow of our thought.

It may be objected, however, that I have made my point only by presenting a caricature of the relationship between thinking and being, and dubbing it 'representationalism'. An attentive reader may have observed that, at the beginning of this chapter, I announced to review a 'non-sophisticated' format of representationalism. I now have to confront the question if there are not more sophisticated formats of representationalism, or at least more sophisticated accounts of the relationship between thinking and being which would allow us to work our way around the rather strategic attitudes towards representationalism which the interception hypothesis seems to invite us to. Indeed, there is a metaphysical tradition in philosophy that claims to liberate us from the aporias caused by representationalism. I will discuss it as adequately as is needed here, arguing that it is a form of representationalism after all, and that it runs into the same kind of difficulties as the allegedly crude form discussed above.

The alternative metaphysical view departs from denying that there is this original opposition of thinking and being. It states: If you have to acknowledge that, apparently, there already is a bridge between the two at the moment you want to construct one, you have to draw the full consequences and admit that there was no original gap in the first place. Somehow, that is perhaps in an intuitive, unreflective or even premature way, thinking 'knows about reality' in the sense that it implies the awareness of being as independent of the process of thinking and acknowledges this mode of being as what thinking is about. To put it in a negative way: In thinking we know intuitively that what thinking achieves does not determine reality; it is finite, limited and surrounded by reality that always appears to be profounder, wider and richer with regard to our thinking. But the very acknowledgement of this limit also entails that, in a very formal and initial way, thinking has transcended it: it knows about the infinity of reality, it is 'everywhere' where reality is, and 'the whole' of reality is already present to it at this initial stage. Of course, no articulated thought content will be framed at the level of this original 'togetherness' of thinking and being. But at least we got rid of the problem of how to close the gap. Or better: If there is a gap between thinking and being, it cannot be a metaphysical one. It will be one that we ourselves, in our human condition, have to create in order to come to articulated knowledge. In order to see clear, we need the distance, but it is we who set reality at a distance if we want to take a closer look. The historical process of growing from a premature to a mature relationship towards being in thinking is what is involved here.

This second metaphysical view is, to my mind, superior to the rather Cartesian form of representationalism sketched earlier in that it asks the right questions about knowledge, reality and having 'true' thoughts. The answers, however, are far from unequivocal. Its strong point is perhaps more epistemological than metaphysical: in any account of knowledge we have to depart from the awareness that being is, with regard to thinking, that what is of a different, rather than a similar ilk, and that this difference is what thinking is most about. In other words: Reality is not just the 'other-than-thinking' instance, but more specifically the norm for thinking (that what thinking should be after). This implicit awareness of reality as 'the law' for thinking explains why there can be discussion, progress and criticism in science or, for that matter, in morals. But as far as metaphysical entailments are concerned, it should be observed that there is perhaps not too big a difference between the image of the gap between thinking and being, and the difference between the same and the other. The argument was that, if thinking knows of reality as being different from itself, it also implies the acknowledgement of its being finite in relation to this other instance. Then it was said that, in turn, this acknowledgement of finiteness implies thinking is acquainted with reality. Although initially it does not know all about reality, it knows what reality is all about. It is, in that sense, beyond finiteness and exhibits a virtual transcendence of its limits.

Now the problems arise with this word 'limit' or 'border', a notion that has haunted Western philosophy since the days of Heraclitus and Parmenides. It is all right that thinking considers itself as virtually beyond the limits of its self-sameness and acquainted with the infinite whole of reality. But that in itself means nothing more (or less) than that there is this awareness of a realm beyond what thinking presents to itself as its object. In particular, it does not mean what seems to be presupposed in the view under scrutiny, namely: (i) that beyond this border we can go on speaking of 'being' and mean more than the internal accusative of thinking; (ii) that at this side of the border we can decide that and where it is possible to cross it. This twofold presupposition is nevertheless crucial for defending the much-embracing consequences. Only one who is convinced that the order of thinking continues on the other side of the border, will allow himself to conceive of the border as a *trait d'union* linking the two realms on both sides. Such a sign, however, cannot signify but in a representing way. For the conviction mentioned above can only be the result of an ungrounded decision of a subject; the decision to attribute being-as-we-know-it-already, or, in analytical vocabulary, being as a predicate, to what presents itself as *different*, thus denying that very difference. In still other words: The difference is only allowed for within the terms of the subject-object opposition, which brings us back to the non-sophisticated form of representationalism. Indeed, we are left again with the two aporias that spring from it.

The aporias were, to repeat: either being is already present to thinking anyway (so the bridge is superfluous), or thinking is always self-enclosed anyway (so the bridge is impossible). Let us now turn to possible political strategies which are likely to be developed in front of these aporias. I do not claim, of course, that they are necessary implications; rather, they are strategies that are contingently, though paradigmatically associated with certain basic patterns of thought about our relation to reality, so as to cope with their aporetic character. The first aporia readily pushes a society to the emergency exit of totalitarianism. As it wants to make us believe that the gap is bridged in principle, it will stage society in such a way that it becomes visible that there are people who have reached the other side of the divide. It will split the members of this society into two groups: one which already belongs to the realm of truth and freedom, and thus has the right to command over the second group-those who are still in darkness and slavery, and who therefore have to obey. Whether the former is called the *Führer*, the Party, the Church, or the Sciences is of little importance: these are merely different values (and the differences may be important in everyday life) of the same variable, namely that of being an incarnation representing the real world in and to the false world.

The political escape from the second dead end of representationalist metaphysics tries to cope with the idea that thinking is self-enclosed. It will often embark on ordering societal relations as juxtapositions, each with its own truth, and equally valuable in its own right. Every truth claim will be welcomed as just another rhetoric device next to those that were already put forward. As 'reality' is whatever one says convincingly that it is, nothing really matters as long as one can have one's interests satisfied. Society becomes a marketplace to sell and buy these interests, to show them publicly, to refine, combine and exchange them. As all differences equally matter, nothing makes a difference. Its law is the law of fashion, which is basically the law of indifference in the longer run. Reference to the general interest is easily rejoined by equally shared particular interests, and the threat of deep conflicts of interests can usually be bargained about and settled by collective payments (insurances). What is respected in such a society are the fetishes that may serve to continuate indifference by way of quasi-aesthetic variations. The term 'cynicism' is perhaps the most felicitous expression of its basic attitude.

So, totalitarianism and cynicism are alternative strategies to escape from a metaphysical problem that cannot be solved in the terms in which it imposes itself on society: the problem of representationalism. Moreover, these strategies are complementary in the sense that they install each other. Political criticism of cynic behaviour often uses the bottom line of 'the strong man who will lead us (back) to real values'. Inversely, cynicism lurks in the background when totalitarian politics is criticised with reference to the relativity of all values. In modern times, these prototypical political orderings are paradigmatically embodied in two types of the welfare state: the autocratic type and the liberal type. Without indulging in too sweeping statements on actual politics, these tentative lines between a certain form of metaphysics and certain political strategies may suffice to see that they are far from innocent, and to pass on to the question how a critique of representationalism (which our narrative hypothesis claims to submit) may have its bearing on political settings.

3.2 The logic of the political

Before going any further, however, let us pay attention to the fact that the term 'representation' as used in politics and law seems at odds with its use in philosophical discourse. A candid articulation of the political connotations would render something like substitution (presenting the absent as if present) rather than repetition (presenting the present once again). For instance, the members of parliament represent the voters - some will even say 'the people' - in their absence from the political arena. The latter are 'back stage' and, apart from regular elections or irregular upheaval, they are silent. Their representatives may bind them by legislation without their consent. Such is the case also with representation in private law: if my representative (for instance, my broker) has made a deal on the stock market without my knowledge, I have to pay as if I had been present and had given my consent. The philosophical discourse, however, centres on an apparently different idea of representation. Instead of 'mimicking the presence of the absent' it rather aims (favourably or critically) at 'giving the present a new presence'. The core argument of this book is to consider narrative strategies as adequate devices for (on the one hand), getting rid of 'philosophical' overtones of representation in politics, by (on the other) laying bare the 'political' overtones of representation in philosophical discourse. Note that what is not at stake is a ban on representations (we cannot do without them), but rather on representationalism, i.e. the immunization of what we cannot do without. These distinctions may help us to search the area where the interception hypothesis will have to do its job and to focus on possible congruences and incongruences between the two meanings of representation.

Instead of going from metaphysics to politics (as we did in the previous subsection), we may also argue from the structure of political belief and work towards metaphysics. A vast number of authors have emphasised that representation is of the essence of 'the political' - if it is allowed[27)] to use the latter term for the most pervasive characteristics of political practice in general. Maurice Weyembergh (1988) has made incisive analyses of Sartre, Debray and Girard, precisely with respect to this 'logic' of the political. Following his argument for a while, we may take Régis Debray's *Critique de la raison politique* (1981) as an example. The first 'secret' of politics, Debray observes along with others, is how a group of people transforms itself from a multitude into relative unity or, if one prefers a more practical vocabulary, brings itself to a more or less regimented praxis. Such unity or core practice has to be identifiable beyond all differences in interests and positions in order for these people to gather, to order their intermingling and to solve their conflicts. But it cannot be a unity by virtue of the sole claim of unity as it is issued from one or another corner of this group; for such a claim would always, for the others, incorporate the interest of that particular corner which put it forward. So it has to be staged as deriving from 'beyond' the group, this 'beyond' being the focal point of legitimate power. That is precisely why there is a 'secret' here: something is postulated which, if it would exist, could never rise to the surface of political activities, but will always work on the level of political subconsciousness.

According to Debray, the law governing this secret is analogous to a famous law of logic, namely Gödel's theorem. The analogy would be that in politics, as in logic, no ordered system (set) can do without closure and no system can close itself by reference to elements that belong to the system. If a group wants to constitute itself as an ordered system of mutual relationships, it will have to resort to an element beyond the system. Weyembergh (1988: 99) states:

> The social needs the meta-social (p. 262), the trans-social (p. 281), the self-transcendence of the group (pp. 159, 273). Taken to its origin, there is no gradual conglomeration of the group [contrary to what Sartre thinks, BvR], no transpar-

27. Here, as elsewhere, following Lefort (1986).

ency of the group to itself (p. 267), since every group stands in need of a mediator, an Other, in order to constitute itself as *we*. Horizontal closure, constituting the *we*, is dependent upon vertical opening, transcendence, the Other, or what Debray calls the *constitutive hole*, through which the group escapes from itself.[28])

So a definition of group identity has to be brought about by inclusion that will, necessarily, be exclusion of 'other people' in virtue of this constitutive transcendence. This is in fact the bottom line in the tradition of 'political theology' ranging from Spinoza to Carl Schmitt, and acknowledged by contemporary authors like Castoriadis, Ricoeur, Lefort and many others. Political theology is a theological account of politics rather than a political account of theology. It defends the view that 'what transcends human affairs' is constitutive of 'dealing with human affairs' (as politics claims to do), whether such a transcendent element is called God, the Proletariat, the Race, the Nation, etc. The group cannot be, in its own view, its own origin, although - from another angle - it becomes it own origin precisely by postulating that it cannot be. Thus, politics is essentially heteronomous.

The phrase 'from another angle' is tricky in this respect. It is not meant to refer to the perspective of the outsider, for instance one who observes and analyses the political process from a non-political point of view. It is still the perspective that is valid for the group involved itself. What I mean is: It is not sufficient for this group to refer to an *arbitrary* point beyond itself, and it is impossible for it to refer to an *absolutely different* Other. The reference will always be a function of the particular multitude of interests and characteristics that have to be transcended. Different elements of the group - which is no group before its constitution - will have to recognize itself in such a reference. To this extent, the transcendent originates in and relates to the immanent diversity of the multitude. So perhaps Debray's picture of a *trou fondateur* is misleading in this respect: it is not a vacuum. The virtual group has to live in the awareness that transcending the group is a way (the only way, to be sure) of sustaining it.

Now Debray goes a few steps further. For one thing, he submits the thesis that 'tout ensemble social suppose une instance de représentation': a

28. My translation. References are to Debray's text.

social whole cannot do without representation. Because the 'constitutive hole' cannot be present, is has to be presented by a substitute or representative. For another, he points out that 'tout social suppose une instance de repétition': a social whole cannot do without repetition. As the exercise of political power can never conceive of itself as original, it will be inclined to think and to act as if the absence it represents used to be present 'in ancient times', 'the golden age', 'the era of the gods', etc., and that now it has to be presented anew and again. That is how, in the name of an original presence of a transcendent reality, power transforms itself into legislation, attributing normative consequences to actual conditions of social life. The constraints of such a transformational activity are themselves subject to political strategy. First of all, there are a number of rather physical instruments for the self-preservation of what is now (on the way to become) a real societal whole; this society will develop an economy and a military system. But concomitant with this is, secondly, the transition from intuitive commitment to more established and sustainable forms of 'devotion to the common cause' among the group members. This usually takes the form of orthodoxy and regimented (dogmatic) language (*fonction enseignante*). And thirdly, it appears to be important that there be some kind of group regard directed towards a corpse: the corpse of the founder (*fonction funéraire*). Note that this is not, as Girard would have it, the corpse of the scapegoat that would absorb violence among the group members. The corpse has to do, in Debray's opinion, with concrete corporeality, be it from the past, to which both the group and its centres of power can relate. If these centres would pretend to be the intermediates between the group and the realm of transcendent freedom and truth, then this corpse can always be referred to as an intermediate for these self-proclaimed intermediates. Thus, both respect for and violation of group identity become palpable matters of behaviour, to which one can refer when it comes to coercion.

This short excursion suffices to see that underneath the surface of word meaning a close resemblance may grow between the political and the epistemological account of 'representation'. As in philosophical discourse, it is quite possible, indeed evident, that the political idea of representation comes to centre on the idea of an original presence that should be presented anew and again. That explains why the category of time in politics may lose its linearity and adapt the circularity of reflecting to an origin that is to be revealed in the future. Such reflective attempts are bound to be repeated continuously, for the simple reason that they are bound to fail continuously. All incarnations of the Messiah, the Classless Society, or the Thousand-Year Reign, will be disguised after a shorter or longer period of time. Thus, the idea of realizing 'the good society' is bound up with infinite repetition. It is only within this context of repeated identification, we may add, that some awareness of linear history is kept alive. For every attempt that pretends to represent the origin has to justify itself by proving that it is not repeating the previous guise and, by implication, its failure. It has to fortify the belief that it is progress: an attempt that is successful.

This deep structure of the relation of politics with the moment of founding society is perhaps what is most regarded in the interception hypothesis. The moment of foundation is, on the one hand, the original event that has to be (re-)interpreted in the course of political practice. But at the same time it is, on the other hand, the keystone presupposed and, indeed, generated by this very interpretation. The interpreted facticity is, on the one hand, the anchor point of power to coercively enact normative consequences (by means of dogmatics, orthodoxy and symbolic fixation), while, on the other hand, these consequences find their origin in the death that was instrumental to the foundation. The alterity bound up with this moment of death and which is the warrant of the group's political unity, is transcendent to the group on the one hand, and immanently determined by the group on the other, for instance by topological metaphors as seen in chapter 3. So the three contexts in which we have tested our hypothesis (those of events and facts, norms and values, facts and norms) find their place in this all-embracing double hierarchy between the origin and the end of history itself: proton and eschaton. By maintaining that there is a double bind between these poles we may prohibit representationalist accounts of politics to become part of our Context of Legitimation (in the sense of the formal scheme developed in the previous section). Or, in other words, we may criticise accounts that acknowledge only one of the arrows between the poles. In chapters 7 to 9, I will address some problems in jurisprudence with this critical intention.

CHAPTER 6

THE GUISES OF LEGALISM

My intentions in the remainder of this book are directed towards demonstrating in what sense a narrative understanding of law is important. In later chapters I will go into specific issues of different areas of law. Here, my concern is on a more general level. My thesis will be that the interception hypothesis is important not just to refute legalism, but especially to refute proclaimed refutations of legalism that are in fact guises of legalism.[1)] This main thesis will allow us to develop, in the chapters to follow, a more precise view on the critical potential of the notion of 'narrative coherence'.

1 Guises of legalism

Legalism is commonly attacked by pointing out that law is never a *straightforward* application of an (allegedly properly established) general rule to the (allegedly brute) facts of a case in sociopolitical life. It is, rather, a complicated judgment, a creative decision, constituted by the mutually dependent processes of building a decidable case and shaping an applicable rule. There are many sophisticated accounts of this complexity.

The view that rule-governed law is not mechanical law was already clearly expressed by those who are believed to have given birth to legalism: the founding fathers of the *Code civil* in France. General rules, says Portalis in his *Discours préliminaire* to the *Code civil*, necessarily leave gaps, as they cannot provide for an infinite variety of cases in the future. These gaps ought to be filled by the decisions of judges, based on common usage, received doctrine, or natural law principles.[2)]

1. Thus, this chapter is, basically, arguing a thesis put forward by Jan M. Broekman. See his (1982: 145), where it is stated that 'someone's legal theory is some other's legalism'.
2. It is, by the way, interesting from a Dworkinian point of view, to note that Portalis's term 'natural law' is not equivalent to a set of eternal, universal and necessarily affirmed values, but rather to historical, political and partly institutionalised beliefs about what is, in

But the emphasis that rules are not to be applied mechanically, that they always leave gaps, that they always need a *supplement* of interpretation, is not in itself either a corroboration or a refutation of legalism. It is, in fact, deeply ambiguous. To put it in another way: the device 'rules are never enough' *may* be just a variant of the device 'there are never enough rules'. Why can this be the case, and when can it be the case? The answer to the former question is not so difficult. When a judge appeals to common usage, received doctrine or (natural law) principles, he does so to fill gaps in a (system of) rules. So, whatever he selects from usage, etc., is conceived of in advance as a *part* of the (system of) rules, as far as it has to *fit* within a blank which is governed by rules in at least two senses: (a) it is left open, surrounded by rules; (b) it is moulded by the parameters of these surrounding rules. The appeal to rules as such is never a symptom of legalism; the appeal to the interpretative 'supplement' of rules is never a symptom of the refutation of legalism.

The crucial question here is, in my view, a Wittgensteinian one: if we want to distinguish between a legalistic and a non-legalistic interpretation of rules, assuming that neither of them is mechanical, it is important to know what we mean by this word 'fit' in the relationship between a rule and its interpretation, especially '*what* fits *what* here?'[3] We may conceive of the interpretation of rules in a number of ways, which all boil down to this idea: that it is the rule which governs the interpretation (or, for that matter, the action), not vice versa, and that it does so by virtue of the *fact that it is epistemologically possible* (though cognitively difficult) *to formulate a set of truth conditions or assertion conditions* on 'fitting'. The idea is, that the judgment whether a particular interpretation or action is in accordance with the rule or not, whether it 'continues' the rule or not, whether it is a step already foreseen by the rule or not, has its epistemological basis in such a set of truth conditions or assertion conditions.

the final analysis, implied in the efforts of a specific society to give itself a political identity. And this idea of society could very well be mechanical indeed, as Foqué analyses in his (1987) with reference to the preparatory works to the *Code civil.*

3. *Philos. Invest.*, § 537: 'So we have somehow read courage into the face. Now, once more, one might say, courage fits this face. But what fits what here?' Cf. §§ 136-138; § 216; p. 183.

It is well known[4] that Wittgenstein rejects this idea with all his philosophical and rhetorical vigour. He shows that it leads into a paradox:

> (...) no course of action could be determined by a rule, because every course of action can be made out to accord with the rule. The answer was: if everything can be made out to accord with the rule, then it can also be made out to conflict with it. And so there would be neither accord nor conflict here.[5]

The answer Wittgenstein mentions in his quotation is not the solution to the paradox, but its consequence. The solution is much more difficult to formulate, since it goes against the grain of conceptual and propositional thinking as it is commonly conceived of. This common conception is *representationalism*. The wayward antagonist in the *Philosophical Investigations* is, in many cases, the representative of representationalism, beginning with Augustine in Par. 1. Baker and Hacker summarise this position very lucidly:

> It is very tempting to conceive of a sign as standing in a projective relation to what it represents. This conception may be variously realized. Frege conceived the *senses* associated with words as determining a reference. The *Tractatus* conceived of the proposition as a logical picture representing a state of affairs. The representing picture, the proposition, was held to include the pictorial relationship, 'the correlation of the picture's element with things' *(Tractatus* 2.1514). *In a like manner*, if one conceives of the meaning of an expression as constituted by the rules, one may think that *the rule* must, in some sense, contain a 'picture' or 'representation' of what complies with it. For understanding an expression must constitute knowing, grasping, the rules that constitute its meaning. Those rules stipulate how the expression is to be used. So by grasping the rules one must grasp how to use, how to apply the expression. But that would only be possible, it seems, if the rule determines independently of us what accords with it. Otherwise, how could I, by grasping the rule, know what to do with the expression the meaning of which is given by the rule (Precisely analogous is the thought that an intention, expectation, or order must contain a 'picture' of its fulfilment). (...) A second great confusion is closely connected with the first. We are inclined to think that it is the mind that infuses symbols with their meaning.

4. Especially from the Wittgenstein renaissance since 1980. For an overview I refer to Parret (1983) and to *Synthese* 58, 1984, no. 3.
5. *Philos. Invest.*, § 201. Kripke (1982) offers a detailed elaboration of why there is such a paradox. Whether his solution has anything to do with Wittgenstein's philosophical *Anliegen* is doubted by Baker and Hacker (1984), on the basis of strong arguments.

And when we realize that there is indeed a gap between an explanation of the meaning of an expression and the use of the expression, it is altogether natural to think that it is the mind that bridges that gap, that effects the connection between a rule and its application. (...) Pricking the bubble of these philosophical flights of fancy is one of the tasks Wittgenstein undertakes in the *Investigations*' discussion of rule-following.[6]

In a legal context, this twofold conception of infusing symbols with meaning bears the name of legalism. Legalism, therefore, is not so much dependent on the idea that rules govern interpretation or actions, as it depends on the idea that they do so in a specific way, or in a very specific relationship with other concepts such as 'sameness', or 'agreement', or 'usage'. Each of these other concepts may therefore function as the apex of a legalistic framework, even if its role is announced as the definite refutation of legalism. To rephrase this framework briefly: it presupposes (a) that there is some picture of facts (about the world, about our cognitive attitude, about social conventions of assertability) with reference to which we can make out whether some action is or is not in accordance with the rule; and (b) that the mind of the legislator, or the judge, or the citizen is the agent that maps the features of this picture on to the action he has to regulate, to evaluate or to generate.

I shall demonstrate, using three examples from contemporary legal theory, that key concepts like 'sameness of type' (Larenz), 'agreement' (Esser) and 'praxis' (Aarnio) are on the edge of a representationalist (and, thus, legalistic) conception of legal interpretation. In each of these cases I shall take my cue from a text by Wittgenstein and point out how a representationalist reading of these quotes is exactly what Wittgenstein attempted to avoid.

2 Sameness, similarity and type

In par. 225 of *Philosophical Investigations* we read:

The use of the word 'rule' and the use of the word 'same' are interwoven. (As are the use of 'proposition' and the use of 'true').

6. Baker and Hacker (1984: 442).

Indeed, it is a maxim of practical rationality (rather than 'formal' justice), to do the same thing in (essentially) similar cases. But how do we get hold of this sameness and similarity, given that cases are never identical? To solve this question, Larenz proposed a theory of types in his *Methodenlehre der Rechtswissenschaft*, referring in the early editions to Hegel, in later editions also to Gadamer's hermeneutic philosophy in *Wahrheit und Methode*, although with certain restrictions.[7)]

These restrictions are actually what is interesting, because they are indicative of the fact that Larenz only accepts the view on interpretation in *Wahrheit und Methode* if it is stripped of its anti-representationalist sting. Gadamer's view on interpretation comes quite close to Wittgenstein's;[8)] curiously enough, it has the application of a legal rule as its paradigm. Gadamer infers from an analysis of this paradigm that the interpretation of rule always means 'creating the rule anew, making it a new rule'. Rules do not stay the same under interpretation or application. So they do not 'guide' us in the sense of representing a picture with projective lines which our minds can lengthen until they 'hit' the facts of the case at hand. Larenz is not willing to accept this radical consequence. If it would really be true, he says, that the normative content of a rule becomes a different one in every case of its application, then it is impossible to treat like cases alike. Larenz concludes that Gadamer has jettisoned not only the concept of sameness and the concept of rule, but also, and more inportantly, the concept of justice.[9)] He believes that, in consequence, his own theory of types remains a necessary element in a reflection on legal method, however much he sympathises with Gadamer's view.

7. The 1st (1960) and 2nd (1969) editions are considerably modified by the 3rd (1975). It contains an interesting post-script.

8. As Gadamer confessed to me in a personal conversation on 9th April 1984, he was very much in sympathy with Wittgenstein's views on interpretation.

9. 'Eine Maßstab verlangt, daß er auf alle an ihm zu messende Fälle in gleicher Weise angewandt werden. Das scheint nicht möglich zu sein, wenn sein Inhalt, was Gadamer ausdrücklich auch für die juristische Auslegung in Anspruch nimmt, 'in jeder konkreten Situation' - d.h. für jeden einzelnen Fall - neu und anders verstanden werden muß. Zwar ist es richtig, daß kein Fall einem anderen in jeder Hinsicht gleicht. Soll dennoch der 'gleiche' Maßstab angelegt werden, so darf jedenfalls nicht jede Veränderung der Fallkonstellation auch schon eine neue und andere Auslegung der Maßstab nach sich ziehen. Dann wäre der Gedanke des 'gleichen Maßes', ein Grundelement der Gerechtigkeit, reine Illusion.' Cf. Larenz (1979: 191).

Frankly, I doubt if Larenz sympathises with Gadamer's hermeneutic tenet at all. I would rather be inclined to hold that Larenz's notion of 'type' is anything but hermeneutic.[10)] According to Larenz, a 'type' is a half-way house between, on the one hand, the individual, empirical and concrete object (or state of affairs), and, on the other hand, the abstract concept.[11)] It is more concrete than a 'concept', as he declares with reverent reference to Hegel. But the reference is tricky, notwithstanding the reverence. Indeed, Hegel distinguished between an *abstract concept* and a *philosophical concept* of factual reality.[12)] The former is restricted to the construction of a scheme or list of *common features* from a necessarily limited number of particular phenomena. This is an *abstract* concept, because it neglects altogether the questions that are most urgent to answer and which the latter sort of concept aims to address: Why is it that we see these features as *belonging* together, when it is always possible to refer to exceptions where some features are missing? Why is it that we see them as belonging to a certain spatio-temporal framework in history, without which 'features' could not even be formulated? And from what point of view could it be said that such a set of features *develops* in time and that such a development is, for instance, growth, or desintegration, or war, or entropy? These are the questions of philosophy. To answer them, philosophical concepts should be conceived of, according to Hegel, as aiming at the historical coherence of reality and even as being themselves part of this historical process in which coherence in reality comes to light.

This very brief and inadequate summary of the Hegelian notion of 'concept' may suffice to show that Larenz's notion of type is of quite a different breed. He suggests that we distinguish two 'phases' of type building. In a first phase, we would select from concrete particular 'Gebilde' (forms) a set of relevant features (general properties, relations, proportions). In a second phase, these selected features would be used

10. I defended this thesis at a seminar law and hermeneutics (Tilburg, December 1982), unaware of even better arguments in Frommel (1981), which I read afterwards.

11. A 'type' '... stehe gleichsam in der Mitte zwischen dem Individuellen, Anschaulichen und Konkreten auf der einen und dem 'abstrakten Begriff' auf der anderen Seite; er sei Konkreter als der Begriff' Larenz (1979: 445).

12. *Enzyklopädie*, §§ 160-162; 163 (and Zusätze, especially the second one).

> (...) in order to describe the type as a whole of features.[13)]

Larenz calls it a 'phenomenal picture' (*Erscheinungsbild*;[14)] it is, thus, not the aim of philosophical understanding, but a carefully prefabricated *paradigm* of data which legal doctrine, rather than philosophy, allegedly has to deal with. This 'whole of features', however, is far from equivalent to Hegel's notion of a philosophical concept. It is a construct from *abstract* features. These features do not become more concrete by virtue of the fact that they are put together and baptised a 'type'. For this is only a second step of abstract thinking about abstract thought. So 'ownership' of a watch and 'ownership' of a multi-national company are, at some level of abstraction, to be grasped as 'similar' in the sense that they are supposed to share a common 'ratio legis'. The 'type' holds a projective relation to this shared 'ratio legis', and legal doctrine is nothing else than the sustained effort to protrude, and thus to represent, this already established relationship. Precisely because 'types' are considered to be describable rather than definable, they presuppose that history has come to a full stop and that we can now gather the salient features of certain phenomena in the light of the law. Law is the light, not history. The latter is brute facticity', the former pure 'validity'. The notion of 'type', therefore, is deeply ahistorical. Such a hypostatized thought occupies the place that is, in Hegel's philosophy, reserved for full-blooded historical phenomena and their inherent partial reasonableness. In this specific sense, it functions as a *representation* of history. This representation is allowed to 'interpret', for instance, a rule of law, and it is not the case at hand that is allowed to do that, as Gadamer would have it. Larenz again:

> In the plenitude of the particular features the 'nature of things' is mirrored. For they are nothing else than the specific, legal aspects of concrete, human relationships which realize themselves again and again in the life of the law.[15)]

Let us note how this kind of representationalism urges Larenz to copy

13. '(...) zum Zwecke der Beschreibung des Types als eines Merkmals-Ganzen'. Larenz (1979: 445 cf. 200 f).

14. Larenz (1979: 448; cf. 500).

15. 'In der Fülle der Einzelzüge spiegelt sich die 'Natur der Sache'. Denn sie sind nichts anderes als die besonderen rechtlichen Aspekte von in der Realität des Rechtslebens immer wieder verwirklichten konkreten zwischenmenschlichen Beziehungen.' Larenz (1979: 456).

almost the whole of *possible* cases in terms of 'types' of cases: we need not just 'types', but also 'normal types' (p. 450f.), 'exceptional types' (p. 451), 'atypical configurations' (pp. 451-452), 'transitional types' and 'mixed types' (p. 456). So, in the end, nothing is gained or ventured, but one thing: that nothing counts as 'following a rule', unless an act of mind has judged that it is a feature of an, albeit exceptional(!), type. And as there can, apparently, be (at least virtually) as many types as cases, this judgment is sheer decision.[16)]

It is, indeed, Wittgenstein who has pointed out that this is not interpreting a rule in any practical sense of the word. It is, at the most, substituting the rule by another one.

> It is no act of insight, or intuition, which makes us use the rule as we do at the particular point of the series. It would be less confusing to call it an act of decision, though this too is misleading, for nothing like an act of decision must take place, but possibly just an act of writing and speaking. And the mistake which we here and in a thousand similar cases are inclined to make is labelled by the word 'to make' as we have used it in the sentence 'It is no act of insight which makes us use the rule as we do', because there is an idea that 'something must make us' do what we do. And this again joins on to the confusion between cause and reason. *We need have no reason to follow the rule as we do.* The chain of reasons has an end.[17)]

What Wittgenstein does *not* mean here is, of course, that one could not have (good) reasons to follow a specific rule; he means, rather, that in case we decide, on the balance of reasons, to follow a specific rule, we are not guided by reasons which function as rules about following the rule we follow.

But now we are left with a serious difficulty: if the chain of reasons has an end, where does it find its end? The hypothesis of this book entails that narratives are ways of ending a chain of reasons without hypostatizing the end. But let us first pay attention to a more candid and common

16. Krawietz (1984: 39) on Larenz: 'Wer so argumentiert, kann nach Belieben eigentliche und uneigentliche Auslegung gegen einander ausspielen.'
17. *The Blue and Brown Books*, p. 143 (Brown, II, 5). Let me emphasise that I do not quote this text to illustrate the thesis that all (legal) reasoning is in the end arbitrary. It is important to relate 'an act of writing and speaking' to *Philos. Invest.* § 208 ff. and compare it to the function belonging to, e.g., the expression '... and so on', or a gesture, or examples and practice, which are all narratively ('teaching'!) determined.

answer: the chain of reason has an end in human agreement.

3 Consensus as representation

It is tempting to read this candid answer from another well-known paragraph of the *Philosophical Investigations*:

> The word 'agreement' and the word 'rule' are related to one another, they are cousins. If I teach anyone the use of the one word, he learns the use of the other with it.[18)]

One is inclined to believe that agreement or 'consensus' among the members of society constitutes the rock-bottom one is looking for, when it is asked how a rule determines the steps that should be taken in order to follow that rule; or that it is, in the final analysis, a particular opinion agreed upon by many (or outstanding) people which determines what counts as 'doing the same as the rule says', or 'doing the same as in similar cases', or 'doing the same as in this *type* of case'. Such an opinion is presumed to be the place where the chain of reasons ends, where we give up justifying what we do, for instance because we cannot avoid using this opinion in whatever we justify, even the opinion itself or even the opinion about justifying opinions.

Although Wittgenstein warned his readers that this is the representational idea of 'agreement' which he wants to refute,[19)] the idea is tempting indeed for certain theories of legal interpretation. This seems especially so for those theories that venture a form of non-cognitivism towards ontological natural law principles or values. Granted that there are no such principles, it is nevertheless a fact, they hold, that

> Every individual and every society recognize certain normative principles as intuitively evident,[20)]

and that there is, in this sense, a 'minimum content of natural law', to

18. § 224.
19. Cf. § 241, which is discussed in the next section.
20. MacCormick and Weinberger (1986: 122; cf. 166-167).

misuse Hart's famous phrase. These shared convictions would have the form of, for example, 'Thou shalt not kill' or 'No one should profit from his own wrongdoing', or 'Quid pro quo', etc.

It is not so much the question whether these convictions are in fact 'shared', given the amount of violence and theft in the world, as it is the question if they are really convictions, beliefs or opinions. When it comes to *opinions*, very *few* people believe that 'one should not kill', in this unconditioned form. Most people are of the opinion that there are exceptions. A few examples will illustrate this. If one should not kill, under no 'circumstances', one should perhaps kill no vegetables, micro-organisms, ants, wasps, rabbits or chickens, or cows, or horses, or humans. Of course (as a matter of course[21)]) what is meant is, that people should not kill human beings. But is that, in this unconditioned form, a shared opinion? It certainly is not. That is precisely the reason why a rule of this kind is not a part of any system of criminal law which I am familiar with. Most people believe, that there are *many* exceptions. For instance, they believe that one is allowed to kill humans if one is involved in a violent attack and is forced to defend oneself; or if one faces the duty to protect others, or to prevent someone from killing; or if you are ordered to do so by your captain in a war situation; or if someone suffers terrible pain and it is certain that he is going to die within two hours (days? weeks?); or if people getting killed can be regarded as the result of an anonymous act, or a side-effect of it, or as the result of the functioning of an economic system, a strategy, or a tactics; or if it concerns the execution of a legal death sentence; or if people kill themselves; or .... etc. Does this lead to the conclusion that we do not agree that one should not kill? We obviously do agree, no doubt about that; but not as a matter of *opinion*.

There is, as a matter of fact, most often agreement on some point (for instance, the formulae of a bill of rights) *in spite of* the differences in opinion about it. And as a matter of value: agreement is valuable, because there is virtually always this 'in spite of' in socio-political matters. For instance, we do not strive for consensus where opinions in the sense of justifiable beliefs are silly (e.g. concerning the quality of the weather in the Netherlands), or factually unanimous (e.g. that the earth is round or that the principle of not to kill does not imply that one should not eat

21. Indeed, the expression is far from innocent. Cf. *Philos. Invest.* § 238, where Wittgenstein adds: '(Criteria for the fact that something is 'a matter of course' for me)'.

vegetables). We may even doubt whether, as a matter of conceptual geography, we would know what we would mean by consensus in *opinion* on these matters. Agreeing on each other's *opinion* is a relatively rare and perhaps even boring form of agreeing with each other. We value consensus, because it enables us to live with differences of opinion and heterogeneity of views. Primarily, consensus embodies the promise and evokes the hope that there is a way back when processes of justification, debates between opinions tend to become hopelessly endless, a way to a common place where we are no longer expected to think, but to join a flag, to mutter a wise saw, to nod assent to 'the law'.

This is not to say, that a flag, a saw or a law cannot be the objects of consensus of opinions. They obviously can. This is the case when they are seen as representations of truths about the world, or as Ricoeur prefers to call them, 'ideologies'. Ricoeur was among the first contemporary authors to remind us of a valid pre-Marxian semantics of the word 'ideology'[22)], and to point out that an ideology is, in the first instance, to be seen as the effort of a social group to stage (in the theatrical sense of the word) its identity, for instance in a narrative about its origin or about its desire with regard to 'the', i.e., their world. Thus, it becomes possible for such a group to remember this identity collectively by commemoration of what, by definition, no one has witnessed.[23)] But this remembrance, says Ricoeur, is just a first incitement:

> (...) for this domestication by remembrance may be the beginning of consensus, it is also the beginning of convention and rationalisation. (...) It is for social praxis what a motive is for an individual plan: it justifies and prompts to actions.[24)]

Ricoeur reveals that this dynamic, generative potential of an ideology tends to take the form of a code, a grid, a framework of simplification and schematisation, which enables the social group to envisage not only itself, but also history and, in the end, the whole world.

> This code character is immanent to the justifying function of an ideology. Its capacity to change things is only kept intact on condition that the ideas which it

22. The orthodox Marxist conception being 'false awareness'.
23. Ricoeur (1977: 198 ff).
24. Ricoeur (1977: 198); my translation.

> submits, are transformed into opinions and thinking loses some of its austerity to enforce its social efficacy[25])

Ricoeur adds, that, although this third aspect of an ideology is a matter of opinion (*doxa*) and, thus, of maxims, slogans and proverbs, of likelihood and persuasion, it is by no means in itself deceptive, or pathological. We should bear in mind that this is the price we pay for social efficacy. And I would like to add on my own account: We should bear this in mind, particularly when we observe a legal theory appealing to an 'open' or 'topic' way of legal reasoning, which should eventually burst the rigid concepts of legal doctrines ('dogmatics') or legal rules. To call upon 'topoi' is not in itself a refutation of legalism, because such a call may forget that it has paid the price of consensus. This is the sort of oblivion we call representationalism.

It is interesting to see how Esser's theory of legal interpretation tries to come to grips with this form of legalism. As is well known, his key term for criteria of rational legal decisions is *Konsensfähigkeit*, their 'consensual potential'.[26]) This entails two things: the decision should, to a certain extent, arise from agreement, but it should also be apt to raise agreement in society. This is only possible, according to Esser, when the argumentation for the decision gives ear both to the established and systematized conceptual apparatus of legal doctrine, and to case-dependent, not (yet) integrated, evaluative points of view (topoi). These two aspects are in constant interplay. It is obvious that one should ask for evaluative viewpoints, not only for those which are at stake in a specific case, but also for those which are embodied in the more or less traditional concepts of the doctrine. We are not able to understand the normative meaning of a traditional concept like 'real property' unless we are prepared to account for the present economic and socio-political meaning of (for instance) 'having a house'. But in the meantime, it is also obvious that we are not able to account for legally *relevant* viewpoints of evaluation unless we are guided by a tradition of judgments on what is legally relevant, a tradition that cannot but give itself the form of conceptual coherence: a systematis-

25. Ricoeur (1977: 200): my translation.
26. Cf. Esser (1979: 10) and (1970: 9; 24; 84; 115).

ed truth or theory about legal relevance.[27]

Esser is convinced that legal doctrines become irrational if they forget that their concepts are, in the final analysis, sedimented evaluations of socio-political life. He is also convinced, however, that legal decisions would become irrational if courtrooms would turn into theatres for philosophical debates about the essence, or the possible existence, of the evaluations of socio-political life by the parties involved in a trial. The same argument that Dworkin brought up against positivism (to wit, that it embraces an 'all or nothing' way of thinking only to find itself forced into decisionism), is brought up by Esser against the suggestion that a lawsuit can be extended to a Socratic dialogue (the paradigm of philosophical discourse on final values): it leads to 'all or nothing' world views, endless antagonisms, decisionism and, thus, alienation.[28] He points out that it is of the essence of legal institutions to establish reasonable ways to solve socio-political problems *provisionally*. And in order to arrive at provisional solutions, it is important that social actors are not allowed to discuss a blueprint for an ideal society before they are safe to give up their conflict and embark on 'applying' what they agreed upon. That would be representationalism *par excellence*. Most problems of socio-political life are provisionally solved along the way: by the praxis of trying to solve them and not by a meta-level discussion on what this praxis should be like. They ask for what Wittgenstein called 'an act of writing and speaking,' which is not an act of reasoning on what counts as following a rule. It is perhaps comparable to the experience which every author has: some parts of a paper, for instance, are only discovered by actually starting to write the paper, and they would remain in the dark if one were to imagine what to write before actually writing it.

So in this respect, Esser attacks representationalism by showing that doctrinal concepts are not just descriptions of the world 'out there'; they are, primarily, articulations of how we evaluate our acting in the world. Moreover, he resists representationalism by showing that consensus is not a matter of theory which can be put into praxis. But in another respect one may wonder whether Esser does not commit himself to the bias he tries to circumvent. Notwithstanding the theses summarized above, he

27. Cf. Esser (1972) and (1974). Esser avoids the simple binary scheme in which 'law in action' is expected to force open the 'law in the books'.
28. Cf. Esser (1974: 536) and (1979: 18-19).

also asserts explicitly that the concept of consensus itself has to be understood as a *Meinungskonsens*[29], an agreement in opinion, if not on the solution of a problem, then on what viewpoints, evidence, procedures, etc. bear on the effort to find a solution.

This is not just a verbal coincidence. Esser really situates consensus primarily on the level of categories, concepts and classifications, propositions and truths. When he speaks of 'griffige Konsensformeln' he means formulae which candidly express what people agree on as shared opinions; he does not, in any way, underline or imply that consensus itself has already the character of agreeing candidly on certain formulae as formulae, not as propositions; as symbols, not as truths.[30] He seems not to take into account that forming and exchanging opinions about how to act in the world presupposes a *currency* (a counterpart of money or the standard of money: *precious* metal, or *beautiful* shells) for what is to count as 'the world', and *to what extent*. This symbolic dimension, when something is *named* 'the world' without a guarantee that there is already something which we can designate as the bearer of this name apart from the name, is rarely accounted for in legal theory.

4 'Form of life' as representation

The idea of consensus as representation of a shared opinion necessarily prompts a careful reading of *Philosophical Investigations*, par. 241, where Wittgenstein answers an imagined objection from the representationalist:

> So you are saying that human agreement decides what is true and false?' - It is what human beings *say* that is true and false, and they agree in the language they use. That is not agreement in opinion but in form of life.

Wittgenstein situates consensus in a realm that is already *presupposed* by

29. Esser (1979: 14).

30. Esser knows, of course, perfectly well that propositions about norms in legal doctrine have a peculiar status, because the value 'truth' has a peculiar semantic ring here: '(...) daß es sich als kognitiv erfaßbar ausgibt und doch die argumentativ erhärtenden Aufstellung von brauchbaren, d.h. akzeptabelen Wertungsgesichtspunkten erlangt.' (1979: 7) But the point is that this 'Aufstellung' of evaluative viewpoints or 'Gerechtigkeitsentscheidungen' (1974: 537) already requires a sign adhered to by a community.

the propositional structures of *doxa*, a realm which he designates by the words 'form of life', or sometimes 'attitude' or 'picture of the world'.[31] It is not difficult to see how these kinds of terms can be misunderstood along the lines of representationalism, thus giving way, in the context of law, to yet another guise of legalism. If we would assume that a form of life is a pre-legal, but nevertheless institutional praxis of a certain social group, we do precisely that. Kripke's challenging exegesis of Wittgenstein circles around the very misunderstanding that following a rule is tantamount to 'being judged by a community to have shown (in enough cases) to respond to a situation in the same way as most of its members do'.[32]

Baker and Hacker (1984) are pertinent in their argument that this view is precisely the opposite of what Wittgenstein had in mind:

> For Wittgenstein, agreement is a framework condition for the existence of language-games, but it is not constitutive of any game. (...) It is not surprising that if one tries to go beyond rule-following into the framework that makes it possible, one will, in the process, lose the very concept of normativity one is trying to clarify; and with it too the distinction between correct and incorrect.[33]

Nevertheless, they also hold that

> It is *acting* to a rule, a *practice* of normative behaviour that lies at the bottom of our language-games. (...) It is no coincidence that Wittgenstein often quoted the line from Goethe: Im Anfang war die Tat.[34]

It is important to note that, according to Baker and Hacker, Wittgenstein does not invite us to a conception of 'form of life,' which boils down to 'informal institutions', e.g. patriotism, paternal love, respect for professors, bargaining on the market, etc., nor to 'the customs of every-day life'[35]. 'Following a rule' does not mean being guided by a picture of

31. The phrase 'form of life' is to be found at only five places in *Philos. Invest.*: §§ 19, 23, 241, p. 174 and p. 226, and at two places in *On Certainty* (358 and 359).
32. Kripke (1982: 286-289).
33. Baker and Hacker (1984: 438).
34. Baker and Hacker (1984: 444).
35. Aarnio (1981: 48): 'The basis of consensus lies in our *forms of life*, and therefore consensus is brought about in life practice.'

these institutions or customs rather than by the rule itself.

In recent publications, professor Aarnio submitted a view on legal science and interpretation which departs explicitly from reference to the Wittgensteinian concept of 'form of life'. His clarifications of the concept seem to match neatly Baker and Hacker's. Referring to *On Certainty*, par. 204, he states:

> The form of life is a matter of action, it is a matter of acts (cf. with 402). We shape our form of life with our action, and in our action ultimately are shown the things we trust (7 and 358).[36)]

According to Aarnio, language-games are built on this 'praxis', which consists of diverse, fuzzy-edged, 'sub-praxes'. Participating in a form of life is a precondition for being able to take part in any of the language-games that *manifest* a specific form of life. There is no *rational* transition from one form of life to another; one may only be *persuaded* to change one's form of life.

I am, however, not quite sure if, on closer examination, Aarnio shares Wittgenstein's argument when it comes to avoiding the pitfalls of representationalism. I list some evidence for my doubt.

1) Aarnio regards the form of life as a 'multi-layered phenomenon'[37)]. But one may ask if not, rather, the relationship between 'phenomenon' and 'noumenon' is part of our form of life.

2) Aarnio appears to conceive of a form life as 'in a way' an object of interpretation,[38)] where Wittgenstein maintains that it is '(...) so anchored that I cannot touch it.'[39)] Or, at another place: '(...) as it were, a dream of our language.'[40)] Therefore, it is, by definition, not an object of interpretation, but the 'grammar' of interpretation itself. The metaphor of a dream is forceful here. Although we speak of 'interpreting' dreams, what we really do is interpret narratives with a specific accidental:

36. Aarnio (1979b: 34). References in the quotation are to *On Certainty*.

37. Aarnio (1979b: 34).

38. And the interpreters (the 'auditory') '(...) transmit into legal-dogmatic interpretations the foundations of the consensuses they have created' Aarnio (1979: 35).

39. *On Certainty*, § 103.

40. *Philos. Invest.* § 358. I personally think that Max Black is right when he argues that the concepts 'form of life' and 'grammar' intermingle in Wittgenstein's later works (after *Philos. Invest.*). See Black (1980: 329).

'dream'. The *concept* of 'dream' itself, however, is tied up with unconscious labour (Freud) on certain aspects of our lives, which is not accessible to conscious interpretation.
3) Aarnio holds that a form of life is not an object of *rational* interpretation, but of persuasive interpretation. The success of this persuasive effort is determined by the acceptability of proposed ways of acting for a certain audience or 'auditory': '(...) the auditory is the "human side" of the form of life'.[41)] But here again, we should ask if Wittgenstein did not also block this road to presenting 'the human character' of our actions as 'representation'. In *On Certainty* § 475 (and a few other places as well) he qualifies the form of life as something *animal*, something which has, thus, by definition no human side. Or better perhaps: *something which is not human by virtue of the authority of humans to call it human.*

Here Von Wright's remark is pertinent, that Wittgenstein did not have in mind 'full-fledged action' but 'pre-praxis', which precedes intentional action.[42)] It is, therefore, perfectly all right to say that a change in forms of life is not a matter of rational interpretation, but rather of rhetorical persuasion in action. But what is to count as 'human' does not *precede* - least of all in the form of philosophical prolegomena - the praxis of 'counting something human'. So I am inclined to believe, that - unless I misread Aarnio - his appeal to Wittgenstein does not imply a commitment to Wittgenstein's concern to refute representationalism. To that extent, Aarnio's highly sophisticated account of legal thinking remains indebted to legalism.

5 Summary and prospect

This chapter has been chasing what was called representationalism in legal theory. I have tried to show that this almost innate mode of 'thinking' in our culture materializes particularly in the different nodal points which together determine 'following a rule'. If my argument is sound, it implies that each of these points - 'rule', 'similar type of case', 'consensus', 'praxis' or 'form of life' - can be the cornerstone of a legalistic view on legal thinking. For legalism is nothing else but representationalism in the

41. Aarnio (1979: 35).
42. Von Wright (1982: 179).

context of the law. It holds that there is some picture of facts (about the world, about our cognitive attitude, about social conventions of assertability), with reference to which we can make out whether some action is or is not in accordance with the rule; and that the mind (of the legislator, the judge, or the citizen) is the agent which projects the features of this picture on to the action it has to regulate or evaluate. In this respect, legalism is a variant of the general idea of representationalism I sketched at the beginning of section 1.

Now it is intuitively clear that we *are* able to tell if some action accords with a legal rule. Wittgenstein (but also Gadamer, and more recently even Derrida) has made this ability the paradigm case to argue against representationalism. His claim could be rephrased, therefore, as: the practice of law, as far as it is a practice of rule following and rule endorsing, is not adequately understood by representationalism, or, for that matter, legalistic theories of law. But then, of course, the question arises: How should it be understood? To answer this question, the notion of narrativity could play a central role, although this notion, too, runs the risk of being incorporated in the representationalist framework.

In the course of the argument in this chapter it was said that the interception hypothesis submits the notion of narrativity to refer to a way of making the edifice of justifying reasons come to an end without hypostatizing the ground we let it rest on. Indeed, that is the idea of rule following which is at the heart of a non-representationalist account of law. I cannot clarify its force on the meta-level of pure philosophy. Specific analyses, like the ones I am about to embark on, are needed. Nevertheless, it may be useful to indicate the general direction in which these analyses will go.

It is characteristic of narrativity, remember, to oppose two ultimately structuring hierarchies of understanding such that they correct each other. Not unlike our riding a bike, constantly correcting our steering to the right as well as to the left by going to the left and to the right, thus going in at least *a* direction by going astray constantly, we understand the texture of the world without an a priori warrant for the correctness of our understanding, But, as it seems, we are perfectly able to correct our understandings on a piecemeal basis, and even to correct our corrections, if only we are prepared to acknowledge the provisional and, indeed, global character of what we call 'correct'. What we need is not an a priori warrant of correctness of our understanding, but rather an a priori recognition of radical difference in understanding. 'Radical' here means that there is no necessarily shared background or *esprit commun* to which the difference can be traced back, and which would, therefore, be prior to the difference. It means that unity (or 'ground', or 'form of life', or 'consensus') will always be seen as something to be achieved in bridging the difference rather than making abstractions from it. It also means that such bridging, as it has to start from the pole of whoever articulates the difference, i.e. from a first-person point of view to a third person (the other),[43)] amounts to the a priori cognitive attitude of letting the third-person point of view count against the I's (first-person) point of view. To put it in a similar way: There is no truth that can ground our understanding in advance, which in itself is a truth we understand, though not a grounding one.

43. I expressly use the index third person, rather than second, in order to emphasize (in line with Levinas) that, in the final analysis, the other is the one who does not enter the first-person's world, so that it is impossible for the 'I' to meet the other.

CHAPTER 7

DEMOCRACY AND REPRESENTATION

Democracy as parliamentary representation is the first of three hot issues in contemporary legal debate which I want to address in order to test the interception hypothesis as part of a critical theory of law. At the very heart of this issue lies the question what is represented in parliamentary representation, such that it can be called a (form of) democracy. Indeed, the basic problem of parliamentary democracy is a referential one: in what sense does this institution refer to 'the people'? Both the usual defense and the usual critique of parliamentarism revolve around one specific interpretation of this reference: parliament is supposed to represent some entity (the people) which is already existent in virtue of certain characteristics which precede such institutional representation. The advocates of the system will point out that it more or less does, while the critics will try and prove that it does not to any reasonable extent. Morover, parliament's authority as a legislator largely depends on the the belief in society that parliament is what it is supposed to be: a mirror image, or at least a small-scale model, of society. Whether the debate is about nationalism and separatist movements, collective rights of cultural minorities, or the democracy deficit in the European Union, reference to a 'real' people is what is at stake. The interception hypothesis will allow us to discover that democracy is as much about challenging such political closure than it is about reinforcing it. We will use it to propose two readings of a famous characterization of democracy, namely as the political organisation of a 'fatherless society'.

To introduce the problem, two attacks on the received view are discussed: Rousseau's and Kelsen's. The notion of political representation will then be central in three sections. First I will return to the question I embarked upon already in chapter 5: Why and in what senses is it necessary for a social group to conceive of itself as a (limited) whole, in order to act politically and be 'a people'? Secondly, I want to investigate the logic of representation from the angle of the interception hypothesis, and defend the view that representation in a democracy can only be meaningful if it represents the identity of a group as one that infinitely postpones (rather than repeats) definite representation of political power. Thirdly, it is asked how the two can be reconciled: democracy seems to be the representation of irrepresentability. This is not a contradiction, but an incongruence of what is said *in thesi* and what is done *in actu*. This incongruence is the core of both the vulnerability and the strength of democracy. But how can it be brought out in political acting?[1)]

1 The received view and two of its critics

In a democracy, a received view says, 'the people' is in charge of the legislative arm of government. First, the people determines its will *expressis verbis*, and subsequently obeys its own will. It can do what it most determinedly wants to do. Being able to do what one really wants to do amounts to freedom. Thus, the people is free.

The above view is much more than etymology. It is the official ideology of democracy, often ascribed to Rousseau and his Social Contract. The supporters of this view welcome Rousseau's name most graciously. His fame as a frantic romanticist allows them to carry their argument one step further. The dream of self-government - so they say *pace* Kant's *Gemeinspruch* - may be right in theory, but is of little use in practice. Its setting has to be transformed from the spontaneity of a simple, small-scale community into the management of contemporary complicated society. The hard facts of practical political life make it necessary to develop a system of representation: the people will have to elect a representative body called parliament. To this body legislative power (or at least part of it) is to be conferred. Parliament is said to exercise this power on behalf of the people. Political parties - rejected by Rousseau as breeding nests of antagonisms in society - are necessary as catalysts to mobilise different political

1. The paper on which this chapter is based started out as a critique of Habermasian thought, and made several detours in political philosophy before receiving Habermas's most appreciated and illuminating direct reply at the 1994 Tilburg symposium on *Faktizität und Geltung*. Parts of it were already submitted on prior occasions, in particular at the meeting of the working group on Critical Theory (Utrecht, 19-4-1991), at a seminar on Carl Schmitt (Leiden, 15-12-1992), at a public lecture on the Claude Lefort's ideas at the eve of his honorary doctorate (Tilburg, 18-9-1992) and at the 1993 IVR World Congress in Reykjavik. I thank all who made comments and asked questions. I am also indebted to my colleague Dr. Mogobe Ramose at Tilburg for his incisive remarks.

viewpoints and to form an élite of candidates for election. At regular points in time, fixed in advance, legislative power is restored to the people in the most direct manner so that the people may judge whether or not parliament has represented its will. Such a judgement is complemented by the people's decision to prolong the service of the same members of parliament or to replace them with other parliamentary representatives. This manner of restoring power directly to the people at regular intervals is called elections. Free and fair elections, then, are part of parliamentary representation.

As an ideology, the above doctrine including its amendments may be quite acceptable. The point is that this doctrine is supposed to hold both as an ideology and as a philosophy. With regard to philosophy, this is all the more surprising, as the doctrine has been criticized severely by at least two powerful philosophical arguments. It is hard to imagine that they would have been forgotten, as they are related to particularly memorable periods in European history. A short reminder will therefore do.

(i) On the eve of the French Revolution Rousseau himself, the alleged godfather of modern democratic ideology, explicitly *denies* that legislative power, as an attribute of the sovereignty of the citizens, can ever be represented at all. In his view, the claim to such a representation is conceptually inconsistent. Moreover, Rousseau is at pains to argue against the claim that 'practice' prompts to representation in matters legislative. The heydays of the Roman Republic were a paradigm of political complexity, he comments in the extensive chapter IV, 4 of his *Du Contract Social*; but the citizens themselves remained in charge, and no representation of legislative power was ever needed. Representation, Rousseau points out, is in its place only where executive power is involved. In other words: where the Romans made use of forms of representation, it concerned executive rather than legislative power.

(ii) Kelsen, the defender of parliamentarism on the eve of the most vehement assault on democracy in Europe (nazism), condemns the received view as a 'totemistic mask' - an explicit reference to his fellow Viennese, Freud.[2)] Apart from its nineteenth-century function as a lightning rod for primitive manifestations of a political morality of freedom, he says, this view is of little value when it comes to the philosophical justification

2. Kelsen (1927).

of democracy. Kelsen's argument is not that in a democracy 'the people' cannot be represented in its legislative power, but that there is no such thing as 'the people' to represent in the first place. What the term 'the people' does is to present a bunch of different, partially even conflicting interests as a unity. This is fine for certain political reasons. But it does not amount to the existence of some entity identical with this unity, that can be re-presented in the political arena. Such an idea can only arise if one is eager to project one's constructions into the order of reality and conceal its hypostatic character. In this vein, Kelsen vehemently criticizes Carl Schmitt, who had defined democracy as a political order in which the governors and the governed are identical.[3)]

For Kelsen, there is first of all a functional justification of democracy. As all forms of government, it emerges from the division of political labour (cf. Durkheim). Every society at some advanced level of complexity will develop forms of differentiation between the governors and the governed in order to sustain its very existence. In a democracy, however, the said division of labour is based upon a principle of political morality. This principle is that every 'I', being a member of a given society, must allow an equal amount of freedom enjoyed by itself to other 'I's', who are members of the same society, while 'the I perceives the You as of the same essence'.[4)] This principle or 'world view' (as Kelsen prefers to call it) does not attain the force of social necessities like the division of labour. It is just a way of understanding and shaping such a division, for instance in the following sense. Those who are elected to take part in exercising public authority do so on condition that they respect the right of the temporary minority to become an alternative majority in the future. If and when the temporary minority becomes the actual alternative majority, then the incumbent majority must relinquish the exercise of public authority because it has lost title to it by becoming the new minority. Representatives will step back after a set period of time to return to the ranks from which they were elected, thus expressing the temporary character of their mandate. Democracy, says the liberal Kelsen, is a system of government in which no one has an ontologically substantiated right to power. Democracy is the government of a society 'without a father', as he frames it - again with clear reference, but also in clear contradistinc-

3. See Schmitt (1928).
4. See Kelsen (1933).

tion to Freud's myth of the original tribe in *Totem und Tabu*.

To summarize: both Rousseau and Kelsen state that it is contradictory to say that in a democracy 'the people' is represented as a legislator; the first because its legislative power is inalienable from the people as the set of citizens, the second because the people is a political hypostasis. Rousseau anticipates Kelsen's objection in that he concedes the, by definition, premature and hypostatic character of the notion of the people. The social contract can never have an ontological warrant, he says, as this would presuppose 'that men would be already before the laws what they have still to become by the laws'.[5] On the other hand, Kelsen acknowledges and enforces Rousseau's insight by stressing that ruling by majority vote (either electoral or legislative) can never be justified as 'on behalf of' the people.

Though there would be a lot more to say about Rousseau and Kelsen, we leave it at this, as it has led us already to the heart of the problem of political representation in democracy: to imagine a political self without there being a subject which this self reflects.

2 Habermas's account of democracy

I regard this question as pointing to a predicament in modern political philosophy which is not fully acknowledged. It goes, for instance, unnoticed in the basic idea of Habermas's *Faktizität und Geltung*. Habermas states his Principle of Discussion[6], which governs the political account of morality, law and politics in terms of validity, as follows:

> [D*] Valid are those and only those norms of action which *all virtually involved* could agree on as participants in a rational discussion. (my translation; my italics; BvR)[7]

This principle D* harbours, in my view, a classic Münchhausen trilemma

5. *Contract social* II, 7.
6. I am reluctant to call it a principle of *discourse*, as, for one thing, *discourse* and *Diskurs* are far from identical in meaning and, for another, I am not sure whether or not Habermas's principle is meant to serve both meanings.
7. Habermas (1992: 138).

regarding norms that are to decide the political question *who is to be virtually involved?* - and who is not? Either the answer is simply decided upon (so that the phrase refers to the normative force of the factual), or it leads to infinite regression (who is to decide, who is to decide, ... etc.), or it is based on *petitio principii* (who is involved is decided by who is involved in the first place). It seems to me that this problem should be addressed and resolved in order to set our hopes on what I regard as the most beautiful phrase of *Faktizität und Geltung*: democracy as establishing

> [P*] (...) a solidarity among foreigners - foreigners who have renounced violence and who - while co-operatively regulating their living together - reserve to themselves the right to remain foreigners for one another.[8)]

I name [P*] the Principle of Pluralism, since - in my reading of the book at least - it formulates the ultimate Habermasian perspective of law as the institutional sediment of deliberative politics in a radically pluralistic and inclusive society. I am in almost complete agreement with this principle P*. What I doubt, however, is if D* can lend sufficient support to it. And as the latter is the very basis of Habermas theory of democracy, I must confess that my question sounds very pedantic indeed. In its philosophically crudest form, however, it is a question which is familiar to us from a long tradition: the question as to whether justice in social relationships can have any meaning over and above rationality. And if so, how positive law could account for that.

On p. 138 of *Faktizität und Geltung,* Habermas comments on the term 'those involved' (Betroffenen) of D*, in the following vein:[9)] 'By "those involved" I mean everyone affected in his or her interest by the foreseeable consequences of a general practice governed by norms.' This commentary brings out what is the problem with D*. Take the phrase 'foreseeable consequences' and savour its normative flavours: Foreseeable in

8. '(...) eine Solidarität unter Fremden - unter Fremden die auf Gewalt verzichten und die sich, bei der kooperativen Regelung ihres Zusammenlebens, auch das Recht zugestehen, für einander Fremden zu *bleiben*.' (my translation, offered with the caveat that 'Fremden' is ambiguous between 'strangers' and 'foreigners'. I chose the more political term. The italics are Habermas's.) Cf. Habermas (1992: 374).
9. Refraining, though, from clarifying 'virtually' (möglicherweise).

what time frame? By what method? At what costs? Without a standard of normality, which in turn refers to what a certain group values as 'normal' in the light of *its own* beliefs and preferences, the formula will not work. So the act of a group uniting oneself to one group is already presupposed in D*. This is the very reason why the well-known trick with the foresight of a reasonable man in tort law can be done in the first place. A similar argument applies to the phrase 'affected in his or her interests'. Whether or not a certain practice affects my interests, is - in the context of justifying norms - an inherently normative question. In answering such questions we rapidly reach the point where it becomes all-important to know if the norm is to harm or to further my interests, if it does so considerably or marginally, etc. Here, as in the case of foreseeability, we cannot escape from reference to the beliefs and preferences of a group which is already identifiable for itself as a specific unity. To put this in another, more generalized and shorter way: The phrase 'those involved' in the principle D* is an indexical device to be used by a group which has already constituted itself as a limited whole. Justification of norms cannot be accounted for in an abstract principle, which can be applied in a variety of ways, one of which being a political way. The presupposition of 'le politique' (as distinct from 'la politique', in Claude Lefort's terms) is at the heart of the principle of validity. To put it in another way: There is a lot more 'facticity' in D* than Habermas is ready to believe.

I said I am in *almost* complete agreement with P* as the ultimate perspective of law being '(...) eine Solidarität unter Fremden'. The hesitation concerns the choice we seem to have when translating the phrase into English. 'Der Fremde' is both the *stranger* and the *foreigner*. The stranger is the one who is outside our community as a cultural whole. The foreigner is the one who is outside our community as a political whole. The former is the one we are not used to, the latter is the one who is not where he belongs. I choose to translate 'Fremden' by 'foreigners', thus deliberately challenging the quote from *Faktizität und Geltung,* p. 374 and its contextual meaning. What worries me is how principle D* can give an account of the position of 'foreigners' in the philosophical sense of the term. This philosophical sense is, in my view, 'those who are "the others" with respect to some first person plural posing as a political entity', i.e. the relationship between a first person plural and those excluded from its indexical political reference.[10)] Can they be included in the expression 'all virtually involved'? Either they cannot - but then indeed P* is not compatible with D*. Or they can - but then we should revise the idea of democracy as self-legislation by a first person plural. The latter will turn out to be the case, as we now proceed to analyse the problems of representation.

3 Politics and representation

I am going to argue that representation in a democracy is not a 'second-best' option compared to 'direct democracy'. It is (conceptually) the only feasible way of expressing the irrepresentability of the people. I will, thus, have to defend the thesis that this expression of irrepresentability of the people still requires (conceptually) representation of the people, as every political enterprise does.

3.1 Politics requires representation

There is at least one very good reason why even the political expression of the irrepresentability of the people - if there were such a thing to express in democracy - requires representation. This reason is that political acting in general requires representation. Since it will hardly be denied that democratic acting is a species of political acting, we will proceed by a simple syllogism to the thesis announced. What is to be demonstrated, then, is that political acting requires representation, and the sense(s) in which it does so. The following is to show that there is a threefold conceptual sense in which this requirement comes to the fore.

10. Though it is quite conceivable to 'intersubjectively enlarge' this first person plural (Habermas (1992: 280)), the enlarged 'we' will still be a 'we' distinct from 'others'. In order to ground that distinction, this 'we' will have to refer to a realm that transcends what is, for that 'we', social reality. By hypothesis it cannot find such a point of reference, in social reality itself, since reference to this point is what constitutes social reality in the first place.

3.1.1 Representation as reflexivity

Let me start where we left the discussion of political representation towards the end of chapter 5. The first problem of any political enterprise, indeed of the political enterprise as such, is to present an image of society as related to this society *itself*, as present to *itself*, as recognising *its identity*, that is: to become transparent to itself and to speak of itself as a limited whole.[11] This has to do with the special character of political power. Not every exercise of power is a political exercise of power or an exercise of political power. Machiavelli's greatness as a political philosopher and advisor is completely based on that discovery. The political enterprise cannot even conceive of itself as the sheer exercise of power (and, ultimately, violence), unless it acknowledges, perhaps tacitly and 'counterfactually', that it exercises this power on behalf of, in the name of, to the benefit of, a social group that recognises itself in this project, name or benefit. This is clearly a reflexive relationship: a second presence, or a second order presence of the social group to itself. That is why we may call it re-presentation. Not that there is first society, and then along comes politics which relates it to itself. If politics is to be conceived of as the shaping of society, we have to concede that, conceptually speaking, there 'is' no society prior to politics. In order to give an account of society we have to appeal already to the concept of politics. On the other hand, politics cannot be conceived of, nor can it conceive of itself, without presupposing society as already related to itself in the form of some unity or whole. This whole can only be a whole *by virtue of* being limited, that is to include some and exclude others. Though it may come to embrace the whole of mankind (as distinct from extra-terrestrial life), it usually refers to an enclosed segment of humankind. Such a segment considers itself to be a special and self-contained whole distinct from other segments of humankind.[12] On this basis it then proceeds to claim a certain degree of exclusiveness. It is of the essence of politics to make this distinction between *we* and *others*, between who are *in* and who

11. This section is indebted to both Weyembergh's (1988) and Claude Lefort's insights, to which I shall turn within a few paragraphs.

12. Cf. Rousseau in the first chapter of the *Manuscript de Génève,* where he turns down the notion of 'le genre humain' as a philosophically viable point of departure for his theory.

are *out*.[13)] Note, that this distinction is a purely indexical and formal one: It does not presuppose any psychological or anthropological account of a corporate identity, a common feeling, or a republican (communitarian) ideal. Note also that this necessity does not bring about the deontic implication that it is *right* to do so. That is a question which we will have to deal with later on. The problem at hand now is: How does this 'we' emerge *for itself* as the subject of politics, as its reflexivity has to be brought about by politics in the first place?[14)]

To be sure, this is not a problem of empirical theory of whatever brand. For historians, sociologists, anthropologists, political scientists and their ilk it is pretty clear how a society becomes for itself a limited whole, although it might be very difficult to find out how it happened in fact in a certain case. For a particular society it may be this particular language, this common enemy, this shared want or interest: these are the kinds of factors that may turn out to be important. But here we are concerned with the conceptual logic of politics; consequently, we have to face other diffi-

13. Carl Schmitt has argued that this distinction is to be characterized more specifically as one between friends and foes: politics begins were you are prepared to kill someone because - in spite of his being your neighbour or your economic partner - he belongs to the foe. Though the wars in Lebanon and Yugoslavia lend considerable empirical support to this thesis, as a conceptual analysis it seems overstated: the rather formal distinction between we and others is a sufficient basis for the political framework to build upon. No doubt it contains enough hierarchical overtones (of who is the first person) to explain why in some cases it takes the form of friends v. foes.

14. This twofold insight is not a purely philosophical deduction. It has to do with what everyday political experience tells us. When you want to start a new political party, or to launch a new political programme, or to comment on the government's recent policy, or to organise firm opposition, the first thing you have to attend to is: how to assure that the social group in which you act sees itself as one? Otherwise there is no way to what you have to do next: to develop the typical logic of the political discourse in referring to the *common* good, the *general* interest or in using first person plural pronouns like *we* or *our*. And if there is no reference to or use of these expressions, you can never expect to do what politics is supposed to be about: the formation and management of 'a society'. Even if you have a one-issue party or even if you relentlessly seek your private interest, you have to dress your language in this form and, thus, to presuppose or to pretend that there is some one determinable social group to which anyone can be said to belong to or not. We may remark that here lies the ground for the strong appeal of nowadays right-wing nationalism in Western countries. Its challenge is: Why open our borders for political and economic refugees when you know in advance that you will have to close them at some point in order to maintain a political attitude, and, thus, a society, in the first place?

culties. Of course, in ordinary language we distinguish between the political on the one hand, and the social, the economic, the private, the religious, etc., on the other, all being commonly said to be 'aspects' or 'spheres' of societal life. But from a philosophical point of view it is to be recognized that the very concept of society presupposes that these or similar 'aspects' are already determined, organised or structured in one way or another by virtue of some self-image which any society must have acknowledged prior to its structuring. The very idea of a society already entails the idea of a structured unity. Thus, the instance of politics (as Claude Lefort has pointed out[15)]) presupposes what it has to bring about in the first place. By this I am in fact - with Lefort - stating two things. One is that a society has to 'stage' itself an an entity externally *different* from other entities. Another is that a society has to 'stage' itself as an internally *structured* unity.

3.1.2 Representation as substitution

So, in order to understand the core of politics, we have to understand how this identification can be made from the point of view of those actually making it. *It is part of the grammar of political discourse that the gesture by which a social group closes itself into a limited whole requires reference to a realm that transcends what is for that group social reality.* The argument is, in my view, quite compelling. Since any place within society is, by definition, a particular place from which you cannot identify the whole of society in a credible way, the only other way to acquire credibility for your identification is to make reference to some point connected to, but outside society. The first and foremost implication of this conception is that, in the final analysis, the group is just a substitute of its transcendent counterpart. This is not to say that, from any point of view, political thinking requires religious belief. It is to say that, from its own point of view, political thinking must acknowledge the trans-social in order to establish the social as its substitute. Indeed, as an empirical matter of fact, many peoples of the world pay tribute to this general thesis by referring in their anthems and in their foundational history to their 'creator'. But in the context of this chapter the relevant fact is that even in

15. See especially the essay 'Permanence du théologico-politique' in Lefort (1986: 251-300); cf. 255 ff.

a politically secular age, this creator is created by the social group in order to enable the group to enter into a relationship with itself, while at the same time the group will renounce or disclaim that it is, itself, the creator of its creator and cherish the belief in a trans-social reality.

3.1.3 Representation as repetition

We may say that there is something deeply contradictory in the very roots of the political enterprise: society has to make itself present to itself by reference to a reality that is by definition absent, and never present. Hence the need, from the internal viewpoint of politics, to format representation as repetition. The substitute can never become identical or establish direct contact with 'the real transcendent thing' without destroying the transcendent character of the latter. Accordingly, the only form the substitute can take in making reference to the transcendent reality is to repeat the act of referring to itself. Here repetition represents itself by claiming to represent the transcendent reality to which it refers. This is why political representation entailes repetition, as explained in chapter 5.

Strategies of repetition take on different forms. Repeated violent repression is only the most primitive and, in the long run, ineffective one, and therefore hardly a strategy in the proper sense.[16) To sustain the substitution mentioned before, to ensure its reference to the trans-social, to stage it effectively in social reality, more sophisticated strategies of repetition or *mimesis* will be developed. What is needed is a tale to tell (the era of the founding fathers), a song to sing (the anthem), a place to come to (the monument), a horizon to disclose (the dream). These basic things gradually turn into societal functions and institutions. Firstly, the symbolic instituting of power is, at the same time, the instituting of doctrine, of canons and of orthodoxy, of training and examination. Thus, the primordial intuitive belief of the members of society is tranformed into a system of knowledge. Foucault's writing is, among many other things, an extensive analysis of these mechanisms. Secondly, it is important that the group is dressed to look at a corpse: the dead body of him (her, those) who died for the group, whose death they can narrate and commemorate

16. 'Cf. Machiavelli, *The Prince*. Also Rousseau, *Contract social,* I, 3: The strongest will not be the strongest for long, unless he transforms his power into law and obedience into duty.

periodically. This body is the intermediary for the intermediary representatives of power. In other words, to be belief-worthy in their claim that their power is only a derived one, being intermediary between the absent (since transcendent) origin of power and the present society, the representatives themselves need to give way to an intermediary in a concrete form. Each representative is like Kafka's guardian at the door of the Law: the guardian is only a guardian in a whole series or hierarchy of mightier guardians, however absent they factually are.[17)] Thirdly, (and enforcing the last thesis) society needs institutions to cope with the inevitable eventual failure of any representation. The staging of representation is a circular, perhaps even viciously circular enterprise: as soon as one setting which claims to be the true intermediary is disguised, there comes the other, claiming that it will do better (which, by the way, presupposes criteria of its own).

To sum up, I have submitted three law-like ideas of what could be called the grammar of political representation:
- the law of (symbolic) exteriority (to install reflexivity);
- the law of substitution (to establish exteriority);
- the law of repetition (to sustain substitution), which takes into account functions like educating the members, commemorating the founders and excusing the governors of society.

I do not claim that this picture exhausts the analysis of political representation. But it is sufficiently detailed to question the Habermasian idea that democracy, as a political system, is about discourse and debate. It also suffices to show what is special about democracy.

3.2 Democracy questions representation

Now I want to argue that, conceptually, democracy is a form of political acting having a special relation with representation in the threefold sense discussed above. Claude Lefort describes the process in which a commu-

17. I would like to think that perhaps there is some connection here between Debray's guess, Lefort's (1992) idea of the 'corps interposé' and with Girards scapegoat: the former as one in the row of guardians to protect one's own body from death, the latter as the same picture in the negative (as with the corpse of Louis XVI becoming the founding body of the Revolutionary Era).

nity's identity becomes transparant to itself as the 'staging' *(mise-en-scène)* of the place 'outside' where the source of power resides and with reference to which social relationships come into existence.[18)] 'Outside' - that is beyond all that depends on determination by the group. God, Reason, Tradition, Man, Market, the Working Class, the Race - these are all, I submit, alternative namings of this exterior place where, in the final analysis, power in society is believed to stem from, to reach for, to reside in. Lefort stresses that this 'outside' is a *symbolic* place - an exterior place which in its exteriority is imagined from the interior of the society itself. But it would be too simple to call it a projection and think that that will do to indicate that its transcendent character is 'really' immanent. Not only the society involved would not accept that, but even the critic would not know what to say when asked against what kind of reality he would test his allegedly unmasking statement that the image is 'only' a projection. Symbolic does not mean unreal, to the extent that 'virtual reality' is as real as the actual one. Quite to the contrary, the symbolic means the very cement which 'holds together' discrete segments of our dealings with 'reality', as we never come even close to the whole of reality as such. The reference is to a 'transcendence from within' - to borrow Habermas's phrase. There is however, in my view, a radical difference between his use of the term and mine: the transcendence in question is not a necessary and universal (though counterfactual) presupposition of established communication, but a regional, though necessary presupposition to establish communication (or, for that matter, socialisation). Exclusion seems to be at the heart of communication. Those who 'we' appear not to understand, the barbarians as the ancient Greeks called them, are rather those we have chosen not to understand in the first place. Communication as based on exclusion is something which has to be philosophically accounted for, especially in a philosophy of law.[19)]

Now there are different ways in which a society can institute itself by reference to this symbolic 'outside' and preserve this reference in its very acting as a social entity. The first distinction will be that between a society that can contextualise this reference in religious belief, like in pre-

18. Lefort (1981: 123 f); (1986: 112; 264 ff).

19. Or, to put it in another way, there is a philosophy of law presupposed in Searle's pre-condition of constitutive rules in speech act theory: 'Normal input and output conditions obtain.'

revolutionary Europe, and a society which cannot, as it has accepted a fissure between the basis of its political existence and religion. The latter is, generally speaking, the case in post-revolutionary Europe. But that does not mean that in secular society there is an unequivocal way of referring to the symbolic exterior. Here Lefort situates the distinction between totalitarianism and democracy.[20] A totalitarian regime is characterized by obliterating the symbolic character of its outside focus, and turning it into something that is incorporated by a special human being or organization, the Führer or the Party. In a democracy, on the other hand, the symbolic character of the exterior place of power is acknowledged, not in the sense that it is constantly disguised as a fiction, but in the sense that this place is preserved in its constitutive function of making social life possible, since imaginable, interpretable, corrigible and organisable, *but always up to a certain point, and never to the end of a definitive truth.*

That is why Lefort can assert that in a democracy the place of power is empty.[21] That does not just mean that no one has a natural right to power (so one has to compete for it). It means, even more, that there is no definitive structure of society by virtue of which power can be exercised (so there is no reason to compete for it in a life-or-death, i.e. a definitive, struggle). As to what will be the provisional structure of society, all men are called upon to speak out and, thus, to participate in articulating the common wealth, on condition that they do not monopolize it. This is, for Lefort, the deep sense of human rights in democratic society[22]: postponing every definitive description of man, which, in turn, entails postponing every definitive legitimation of the limits a society has set itself in order to become 'one'. To that extent Rousseau was right: In the end we are all involved as citizens in determining what kind of society we would want to call ours. For in that sense, the citizens have inalienable legislative (constitutional) power that cannot be represented. This also seems to be the only sense we can attribute, in a political context, to the notion of 'the People' as a political subject. Habermas (1992) seems to conceive of his procedural theory of law and democracy in a similar

20. Lefort (1981: 111 ff); (1986: 276).
21. Lefort (1986: 27; 265; 268f.; 273 f).
22. Lefort (1981: 45-86; 68); (1986: 31-38).

vein.[23] But it should be stressed, as Lefort does in fact, that the underdetermination of the nature of society and the involvement of all citizens in the determination of its provisional organisation, is not a ground for saying that we can do away with representation. Leaving the place of power really empty amounts to an open invitation to a type of power which needs no legitimation as it is staged in advance as the saviour of society. Representation is inevitable, not only factually, but also conceptually.

4 The incongruence of representation

Representation is needed to present the irrepresentable character of the legislative power of all citizens. This is not logically contradictory, as the two tokens of 'representation' appear in logically different parts of the conclusion. It is not even much of a paradox. All we say is, that in democracy there is an incongruence of what is done *in thesi* and what is said *in actu*. One cannot legislate that legislative power shall be irrepresentable but in a speech act uttered by a representative body. That is probable the reason why the phrase 'legislative power shall be irrepresentable' is in fact never a legislative phrase, while 'legislative power resides with the people' is. The former is rather a 'theoretical' statement. To put it in another way - a way derived from speech act theory: in a democracy, 'the people' only appears at the place of the political subject in a phrase which cannot be uttered by this political subject itself, i.e., in a phrase that is the object or content phrase of a speech act and never the speech act itself, as it is to be performed by the representative legislative body.

[SAD] $\underline{\text{The representatives:}}$ $\underline{\text{(We, the irrepresentable people, decide to } \chi]}$

act content

23. Cf. Habermas (1992: 534), where Habermas refers indirectly (via U. Rödel) to Lefort's famous dictum: 'Im demokratischen Rechtsstaat als der Behausung einer sich selbst organisierenden Rechtsgemeinschaft, bleibt (...) der symbolischen Ort der diskursiv verflüssigten Souveränität leer.'

Therefore, there is an unbridgeable chasm between the political subject in the content of legislative utterances in a democracy and the political subject making these utterances. So what we say is that democracy can never have the form of a performative. It can never be moulded as a speech act in which there is a perfect congruence between what is said and what is done, between language and the world. A performative - as J.L. Austin has pointed out in a way that was profoundly trivialized by some of his fans - is a speech act in which one does what one says in saying what one does. Democracy is far from that in that it has nothing of the immediacy, the sacramentality, the innocence or the almost animist character of a performative.

This is the problem which the received view on democracy as 'the sovereignty of the people' does not account for. The crucial problem pertains more to the concept of politics which makes direct democracy a contradiction *in adiecto* and less to the fact that the complicated nature of contemporary society renders direct democracy impossible. This problem is solved once we acknowledge that there is a logical gulf between the places where the subject of politics appears: the subject of the speech act requires the act of representation, while the subject of the content phrase requires the language of irrepresentability. The consequences of this distinction are, I believe, rewarding. We may now appreciate that in a democracy parliamentary representation is not 'second best' compared to the ideal of no representation at all. Its quality is dependent on how convincingly the irrepresentability of the people is institutionalised in political, socio-economic and cultural forms. It is, I believe, also a solution that makes Habermas's recent phrase on democracy as based on the identity of the authors and the addressees of legal norms, less ambiguous and more perspicuous. There is, indeed, this identity if the content of democracy is considered. But it vanishes once both the content and the act of democracy are taken into account. Would that not be the case, then Habermas's phrase bears a rather uneasy resemblance to Carl Schmitt's characterisation of democracy as the identity of governors and governed.[24)]

24. Habermas (1992: 141): 'Das Demokratieprinzip erklärt (...) den performativen Sinn der Selbstbestimmungspraxis von Rechtsgenossen, die einander als freie und gleiche Mitglieder einer freiwillig eingegangenen Assoziation anerkennen.' This is to be read in connection with (1992: 153): 'Die Idee der Selbstgesetzgebung *von Bürgern* fordert nämlich, daß sich diejenigen, die als Adressaten dem Recht unterworfen sind, zugleich als Autoren

But that is by no means the end of the argument. For although the insight into the incongruence might bring some relief for those who take a theoretical interest in political praxis, philosophically we are now left with an even bigger problem. A very general way of putting it this is. It may well be the case that, from a philosophical point of view, we have to make the distinction between act and thesis, as well as to bring out the incongruence. But what is 'bringing out the incongruence' supposed to mean from the political point of view itself? Note that there is no point in assigning to politics the task to answer the question of how we can overcome the incongruence. We cannot. Democracy can only be a way of living it. But how should philosophy account for what this means on the level of democratic politics itself?

In order to answer the latter question it seems apt to begin by contemplating more seriously what is implied by the deceivingly simple insight into the incongruence of thesis and act in the case of democracy. The obvious thing it implies is that, least of all, the democratic speech act is candid first person language - whatever the received view may say. This is so in spite of periodical 'general' elections. Instituting elections already presupposes that some people, representing 'the whole before the whole is constituted', have decided who belong to those (virtually) involved and who do not. As these elections presuppose membership of the legal community, the latter cannot hide from and must be aware of the fact that its subject ('we' - the good people) has been constituted by exclusion. Others have been left unaccounted for. Democracy, therefore, seems to be the politics of guilt after all: the guilt of having done something equally unavoidable as unjustifiable, to wit, the closing of society by reference to transcendent reality without questioning its premature ontological commitment. So, how could it ever be celebrated as the politics of freedom?

This, I presume, is what lies behind Rousseau's much forgotten sigh

des Rechts verstehen können.' The immediately following phrases (154) make it clear that this 'zugleich' is to be understood as 'identical'. This also appears to be the idea of the fourth principle (156) on public autonomy, whereby '(...) Rechtssubjekte auch die Rolle von *Autoren* ihrer Rechtsordnung (erwerben) (...).' Cf. the explanation on (160 f) and (162): 'In den verfassungsgebenden Akten einer rechtsverbindlichen Auslegung des Systems der Rechte machen die Bürger einer originären Gebrauch von einer politischen Autonomie, die sich damit auf eine performativ selbstbezügliche Weise konstituiert.' See also p. 492. (All italics are Habermas's.)

that, at the end of the day, also his construction of the 'droit politique' will fall apart.[25] It can only moderate and slow down the process of civilisation, which is, to his mind, a process of decline. But in the end he acknowledges that democracy is part of this process. He even grants, in plain language, that his construction is an impossible one, because it assumes that men are already before the laws what they still have to become by the laws.[26] That is the point where Rousseau has come full circle; and it is also the point where he gives in, quits his project of political thinking and indulges in autobiographical projects, continuing political discourse with other means.[27] In order to understand what 'to live the incongruence' means, we may rather turn to the master of law and guilt, who, like Rousseau, placed democracy in the context of the civilisation process: Freud.

5 Democracy as the government of a 'fatherless society'

Freud himself uses the word 'democratic' in a context in which we also find the phrase of the fatherless society[28]. It is where he attempts to picture the origins of civilisation through the myth of the original tribe. In fact, it refers to the state in which the sons/brothers of the original tribe live just after they have murdered the father: '(...) an originally democratic equality'.[29] One will recall, however, that this stage is a transitory one, as it is one of unfulfilled desire. 'Nobody could or should reach anymore to the perfection of the father's power, which they earlier wanted so badly.'[30] It therefore gradually develops into another stage, and in which the omnipotence of the father is projected unto a human being or man-made institution: the father-gods, the patriarchs, the kings. So, finally, the fatherless society is one in which the father is more present than

25. Rousseau, *Contract social* III, 2: 11; 15.

26. *Contract social* II, 7.

27. The autobiographical works have the political intention to defeat in advance whatever law will come and find him guilty.

28. A phrase which Kelsen will use later to characterise democracy.

29. '(...) eine ursprüngliche demokratische Gleichstellung.'

30. 'Es konnte und durfte niemand mehr die Machtvollkommenheit des Vaters erreichen, nach der sie doch alle gestrebt haben.' (my translation). Freud, *Totem und Tabu* (1913: 179-180).

ever. Is that what democracy boils down to? Is it the continuation of first person authority by other means? Is the critique of subject philosophy a blow-up of subject philosophy, grounded in the belief that 'we', the participants in rational discussion, are the subject? Is the metaphysics of power still at work in the 'post-metaphysical era' (Habermas)? It surely looks that way often when it comes to empirical matters of fact. It is the dangerous situation in which, according to Lefort, the place of power is empty in the ontic rather than the symbolic sense of the word: vacant. Then there is infinite discussion, political hesitation and eventually the inevitable appeal to 'a strong man'.

What Freud tried to express in his myth of the original tribe is that our culture is, in its core, a process of civilisation that sees itself as placed under the father, i.e., under an authority which posits the law; and, thus, it is placed under the instance from which guilt - as falling short of the law - originates. Some are inclined to think that modern society is modern, precisely in as far as it is enlightened about the source of its guilt and replaces it by reason. But if we see civilisation as a growth in rationality or, for that matter, reasonableness, we do not escape from that picture. We are actually making it happen.

I want to illustrate this by seeing what happens when we give the following, specific interpretation to the most democratic account of rationality available today, which is, indeed, Habermas's paradigm of the pragmatic presuppositions of the ideal dialogue. Does it escape from Freud's critique? It does not necessarily. It means only that the 'assembly' of discussing participants takes the chair of the father and that, from that moment on, *it* generates the phenomenon of guilt *in them*. In a rather obvious sense, they can never do what is the right thing to do according to their own standards of reasonableness. To ground that claim, we must distinguish between different points of view, from which different arguments are accessible. Let us suppose that, for a philosophical spectator, the result of a discussion under ideal conditions is tantamount to a rational result. He even formulates these conditions, as Habermas does, in a more specific way: without any authoritative pressure from outside, the participants in the ideal dialogue relate their communications, if challenged, to the criteria of the truth of their assertions, the sincerity of their intentions and the validity of their norms. Factual discussion is rational to the extent that these ideal conditions obtain, although they will always remain imperfectly reflected in everyday life. Suppose he tells all that to those participants in whatever discussion there might be, who want to have some idea of what would be a rational outcome of their debate. So now they know the law of rationality. But that does not entail that they can obey it. They are in a sort of double bind. Their first option is to decide at a certain moment that the ideal conditions are *sufficiently* fulfilled to call the outcome of this particular discussion a reasonable one. But that is a decision which requires criteria of what is *sufficiently rational*, while, by assumption, there were no other criteria than those of the ideal dialogue. So they should conclude that they in fact set themselves (as empirical subjects) the criteria of rationality - which is the very thing which any idea of rationality would exclude. This is a good ground for guilt. The alternative option is an equally good one. In the alternative, they infinitely postpone the decision that the consensus they seem to reach is a reasonable one, as they concede at the same time that one can always do better. But then the discussion will never end in the justified belief that it had a rational outcome. For either it will not end at all (as the history of philosophy exemplifies), or it will end (as we have to do with empirical subjects) because of other reasons than reasonableness: It is becoming late, one is getting hungry, the other bored, two are falling in love and three are realizing that they will need one another in the future. In all cases there is the guilt about the debt towards the Law of Rationality which remains open. Without embarking on too much folk psychology, one might even imagine that the participants will experience a certain frustration, realising that what they reach by discussion could also have been reached by other, equally peaceful means. Indeed, in some cultures social problems are solved peacefully in ways quite different from discussion.[31)]

But there is something puzzling in what *Totem und Tabu* holds about the fatherless society. Before Freud concludes his argument about the convergence of the history of Western culture and psychoanalysis - the major issue of his book - he notifies his readers of two difficulties which should be explained before the convergence thesis can be deemed to be sufficiently justified. It is the second one which is of interest to us here. It gets its specific character from the title of this part of the book: 'Die infantile Wiederkehr des Totemismus'. The difficulty is this: How is it pos-

31. There is the story of the Inuits who are said to solve some kinds of conflict by letting the antagonists (verbally) make jokes at the expense of one another. The one who gets most of the audience's laughter wins.

sible that the whole of culture can be the result of an original act of which we cannot find a single historical trace? Well, says Freud, that is precisely the core of infantilism to be found in neurotic people. The guilty consciousness can 'stage' the original act to present itself such that the original scene is the product of the guilt ascription and not the other way round.[32] In other words, it might have been quite possible that the sons never killed the father, but that they projected their guilt before the law into the murdering scene. And although Freud cannot resist the temptation to submit that there is in 'primitive man' such an immediacy between thinking and doing that the original act would have come first and the guilt ascription afterwards, ('Im Anfang war der Tat'[33]), he concedes that there is, in principle, a double relationship between the Law and Guilt: the Law is not merely the source, but can also be the focus or the vanishing point of Guilt, just as Guilt is not merely the source, but also the focus of the Law.

This double relationship, if not hierarchy, between Law and Guilt could be read as a second, and deeper, meaning of the phrase of the fatherless society. Indeed, there are textual incentives to look for a dual meaning.[34] Freud himself stresses the fact that the figure of the father appears twice in the scene of totemistic sacrifice: firstly as the god, secondly as the animal sacrificed. That is to say: firstly as the father *interpretandus* (the one who should always be asked for norms, i.e., a categorical part of the legislative 'grammar'); secondly as the father *interpretans* (the one who has decided for one rather than another of possible norms, and is therefore a legislative actor, not just part of a legislative grammar). Freud warns us that there is no superficial allegory here; that there is a real dual reading without any mediation. But if the father appears twice in the sacrifice scene, and if one appearance is not an allegory for the other, then there is reason to think that there are also two radically distinct conceptions of the fatherless society. The first is one of a petrified order between *interpretandum* and *interpretans;* that is one in which the balance of power between the brothers obstructs seizure of power by any of them,

32. Freud allows for the same possibility in the case of the wolfman. I was brought to these lines of the argument by Culler (1981), the chapter on story and discourse.

33. *Totem und Tabu* (1913: 194).

34. Although the phrase itself appears clearly only in the context which was already mentioned at the beginning of this section.

and which gradually evolves into religiously and socially authoritative institutions. The second is one in which the order between *interpretandum* and *interpretans* is liquified or rather constantly reversed; that is one in which the brothers regard their idea of the fatherly power as a contingent articulation of what binds them together and in which, therefore, authority may become something different from legitimate power.[35)] But what?

6 Authority and rationality in politics

The common idea of authority is, indeed, that it can be defined as legitimate power. Within that conceptual framework the question of democracy becomes one of how political power can be (made) legitimate. That, I would think, is only a paradigm of the first sense of a fatherless society.[36)] It is of tremendous significance, but only if read in its opposition to a paradigm derived from the second sense. The second sense, in which the very idea of a father-legislator becomes a function of a form of life, allows us to contrast this question with the reversed one: How can authority be made powerful? This presupposes that the core of authority can be conceived of as at first independent of power. I think that, indeed, we can and should conceive of it that way. Here I can give only a short version of an argument I developed elsewhere.[37)] But let me stress, again, that this second reading is not a better one than the first; it is a necessarily complementary one, if we do not want the concept of authority to dissolve in a corrosive dilemma.

The dilemma to face is this. Either we grant that, conceptually, the law can only be the product of authoritative politics. But then we cannot define authority as legitimate power, since this would be circular in as far as the concept of law is implied in the word 'legitimate'. Or we do claim that authority is legitimate power. But then we have to develop a concept

35. It may be relevant to note that the only society compatible with the Freudian idea of liberating psycho-analytic therapy is the second one. Otherwise psychoanalysis would be the seizure of power in disguise, and Freud a new father.
36. It is also, I submit, the idea of power proclaimed by the prototype of Arnheim in Musil's *Der Mann ohne Eigenschaften*, who holds that you need to have power in order to have the power to improve things.
37. Roermund (1990b), ch. 3.

of law which is - for the conception of its factual existence - independent of politics. The escape from this dilemma is, in my view, to discover a third way. We may try to avoid the consequences of the first horn by arguing (i) that it is possible to define authority in political terms, independent of the concept of law in as far as the meaning of 'legitimate' is concerned, as well as independent of 'power' where it comes to its law-making capacity, but (ii) that it is impossible to define the concept of law without referring to that kind of political authority. Here is my definition: *Political authority has any instance that appears able to show the actors in a particular society the vanishing point of this society's existence*. That is to say: An authority in the strict sense is capable of disclosing to a society the focus of its coherence while at the same time suppressing the idea that at this point there is some definite picture of the limits of its wholeness in the double sense of their positive validity and their relativity (or openness to change).[38)] So where, on this account, authority does not derive from is some hypostatized transcendent realm that sanctions whoever is able to make the decisions in the conflict between the first person and 'others'. This latter, Schmittian idea, is an reification of the second reading of the Freudian phrase, which is as massive as the one we encountered in interpreting the first.

By calling democracy a political practice in which the place of power is supposed to be empty (not vacant, but empty; not non-existent, but empty), Claude Lefort has suggested that this is precisely what democracy is about: the empty place cannot be but the vanishing point of a society's self-conception. By calling the place of power vacant rather than empty, Lefort would have implied that democracy is the equilibrium of powers held by the sons in competition for what is still the father's power. In this model of thought, the father would be more present and potent than ever. But most other interpretations lead to the same point, especially those who - in the tradition of the Enlightenment - give the place of power to an instance whose role it is to enact what is rational. This instance may be called, alternatively, Science, Philosophy, The Ideal Communicative Dialogue. All of these instances are values of the one conceptual variable 'the father', 'the legislator'. So this strategy also exemplifies the same model of thought, which conceives of the place of power as being vacant rather

38. I also believe, pedantically enough, that this definition holds for authority in the sense of the scholarly expert.

than empty. And it produces the same awareness of guilt, which is the ultimate source from which a legitimation of the primary distinction between 'we' and 'other' seems to flow. This is why I submit a different account of 'the empty place of power' in a democracy. My account is that it means the practice of construing the place of power as the vanishing point of a certain society: a point where all its lines of legitimation converge in, but which is nothing more than a point, i.e. a place where no meaning is articulated, no image presented, no work done. I would like to think of law as the product of such a democratic practice.

Now this is exactly what parliamentary democracy is (again: conceptually) supposed to do: both to confirm and to challenge the identity of a particular society, acknowledging the incongruence of what it does and what it says. It requires withholding the political act from the extreme: if you have to exclude (and you will have to), you do not have to exclude once and for all, under all circumstances, whatever the needs of those outside, the aliens, the refugees, the workers from abroad. If you have to appoint substitutes (and you will have to), you do not have to appoint them once and for all: as a master body, one and united, which one cannot approach. If you have to endlessly repeat the instauration of authority (and you will have to), you do not have, by the same token, to educate in blind worship instead of critical respect, to commemorate a hero in every founder, to apologise in defence rather than remorse. So, in the end, there may be restored at least some congruence between the thesis and the act of democracy: the act can gain some credibility for the thesis after all. Democracy is, one could say, a politics of shame in a culture of guilt. This, I would like to submit, is the vertigo of Habermas's phrase about democracy as establishing solidarity among foreigners. It is precisely from the presentation of this virtual reality - the exclusion of the predicate 'foreigner' from our political vocabulary - that democracy can derive authority. Democracy as an ideal, to summarize, is not self-legislation *tout court*, but self-legislation with an in-built account of what the self does not represent.

CHAPTER 8

LAW AS PUNISHMENT - PUNISHMENT AS LAW

A second debate selected for the purpose of testing our hypothesis, one that is central to contemporary legal practice and theory, concerns 'the war against crime' and the sustained effort to make criminal law the most powerful weaponry in this war. Indeed, the debate goes to the very meaning of 'the rule of law' in criminal law or, what comes down to the same point, to the role of power and violent coercion in investigating, prosecuting and punishing crime. There are those who say that, if it is to obey the rule of law, criminal law should conceive of itself first and foremost as a set of constraints on state power in crime fighting, so as to protect citizens from sovereign arbitrariness even in the case that they have become criminals. The most orthodox among them go as far as to forbid any 'fighting', i.e. any method or tactics, that is not explicitly permitted by law. There are others who want to reverse this order by saying that if criminal law is supposed to be law enforcement, we should enable it to use means effective to that end in the first place. Protecting law abiding citizens against the harmful effects of crime should, according to them, be prior to protecting criminals against state power. The rule of law can only function if it respects and integrates this order of things.

To rephrase the question: the debate is about whether punishment is, in the final analysis, part and parcel of the concept of law, thus making law participate in the exercise of public power, or whether the concept of law can only form a constraint on punishment, which in itself remains an extra-legal, political practice. Is punishing not just characteristic of law's appearance in society, but is it also part of law's justification? In still other words: is it primarily reasonable of law to punish certain wrongdoings in the name of society (and secondarily punish it as mildly as possible), or is it primarily reasonable of law to restrain punishments that a society imposes on what it deems to be wrongdoing (and secondarily fight criminal behaviour in a decent way)? No lawyer would be prepared to choose either horn of this alleged dilemma, and most of them would go for some sort of unity between the two. But how to conceive of such unity? Asserting that the 'either ... or' is to be replaced by a 'both ...

and' is a purely verbal strategy as long as the link is not conceptually articulated. So are other phrases in which 'mediation' or 'intertwinement' are supposed to do a lot of work. The interception hypothesis will have to prove itself by offering a better insight into the complexity envisaged by these formulas.

Let us begin by sharpening our awareness about the problems of reference and representationalism involved in this debate, as the interception hypothesis is designed to operate in contexts that feature such problems. In fact we will meet them in different modes as we briefly review the main questions of criminal law. After that, we will discuss, on the basis of the interception hypothesis, how we may conceive of punishment as part and parcel of the twofold relationship between state and law. As is the case of democracy, it will be important - last but not least - to distinguish a philosophical account of this relationship and a philosophical account of how this relationship is brought out in practice. We will be careful not to transfer immediate 'application' of philosophical insight to agents who have to act from the point of view of either political efficacy or legal accountability.

1 Reference and representation in criminal law

The basic questions of criminal law are rather well known, which is not to say that they are easy to answer. If we overlook them, we may arrive at the following five sets, which are, admittedly, not exhaustive but surely of primary importance. As we will see, they all embody a view on punishing that is heavily dependent on representational discourse.

1) *Why punish anyway?* What sense is there in legal punishment and what justification can be given for it? There are two rivalling answers, equally keen on pointing out that punishment refers to a pre-existing order which it represents. One says that legal punishment is about retributing wrongdoing and restoring the balance of justice. The other holds that it is about preventing wrongdoing, either the perpetrator from a specific crime or any legal subject from a certain type of crime. In these types of answers, the pre-existing order in question may differ as far as its ontological status is concerned. In particular we may want to distinguish reference to a transcendent and to an immanent order of values: some will say that there are universal, pre-legal, moral standards of retribution or, for that matter,

protection which transcend the contingent preferences in particular societies; others will point out that the 'wrong' in wrongdoing is equivalent to what a certain society does not want to happen, although it may be contingently true that a lot of societies disapprove of a few things that are rather similar. But whatever the differences - restoring or protecting an order, a transcendent or an immanent order - the sense of punishment seems to be linked up with the possiblity to refer to a pre-established world endorsed by a certain society as one that 'should be' the case. Such references materialise when it is asked how to map crime and punishment: How serious the infringement is that should be restored or how massive the means of protection should be?

2) *Who is to punish?* The readily given answer to this question is: the state, and only the state. Although this is in accordance with the traditional doctrine of the state having the 'monopoly of the sword', i.e. the exclusive right to exercise violent coercion, it is by no means self-evident. Historical reasons for hesitation come to mind: it is not just imaginable that legal punishment is a part of private law, in point of fact it has been private law for ages. Contemporary efforts to reconsider the position of the victim in Western criminal law bear testimony to the fact that even our own age is not insensitive to the awareness that there is a thoroughly private aspect to society's dealings with crime. The tension between public and private aspects of criminal law is surely not something we have left behind. Moreover, as both the concept and the appearance of the state seem to have begun 'to die the death of a thousand qualifications' (now that regionalism and supra-nationalism regain strength), the exclusive role of the state in legal punishment becomes increasingly elusive. However, all these historical or sociological considerations cannot obliterate the awareness that the answer to the question Who is to punish? harbours a deeply representationalist picture: the state as representing, at the same time, the integral sum as well as the apex of all private interests, whether they are group interests or individual interests. The old - Rousseauist - statement that in a state 'everyone' refers to 'each of us' and that general interest and private interests are mutually dependent in a rigid sense, accounts for the state being the one to act if and when private interests are harmed by crime.

3) *Under what conditions is legal punishment to be applied?* Official doctrine holds that no punishment should be applied in the absence of a legal rule that specifically qualifies certain facts as 'a crime'. A certain course

of action is not a crime if there is no law against it. From this deceivingly simple 'nullum crimen' principle, two types of problems seem to persistently emerge in legal practice, and they are both about reference and representation. One is about the extension of the description which qualifies certain facts as 'a crime': does the wording of 'stealing' refer to the case in which I use electricity someone else is paying for without his permission and for my strictly private interests? Also when I plug in my coffee machine at my university office to make myself a nice cup? Or, to take a different problem of the same type: How to react as a government, when a certain course of action comes close to preparing a crime, but in itself is not criminal at all, for instance buying certain equipment?[1)] Can it be regarded as already within the range of events the law is referring to? In what sense is the law offering a 'picture' of a crime which then can be 'recognized' in ordinary life? The other type of problems derives from a different interpretation of the question: for what kind of policies is legal punishment the appropriate instrument? A government, in the name of the welfare state, is often keen on regulating ever more areas of social life by legal sanctions, thus making administrative law the twin-brother of criminal law and vice versa. In other words: punishment policies often represent administrative programmes. The justification in the background is the upshot of what was explained in the previous paragraph: to the extent that in administrative law the government represents the state and, by the same token, the public interest, not complying with administrative regulations amounts to committing a crime. Farmers, for instance, often complain about being 'treated as criminals' by the administrative agencies of environmental law. This is of course not to say that environmental law is unjustified or too strict; it only indicates that the picture of state power representing the exclusive threat of forceful coercion in the case of crime works in two directions: 'if no crime, then no punishment' logically compels to 'if punishment, then crime.'

4) *Who is to be punished?* The wrongdoer, of course, since he did wrong. But here again, there are problems of reference and representation. It is one thing to establish 'who-did-it', but it is quite another and more complicated thing to establish whether or not he is guilty of what he has done, and still another thing to decide whether he who, strictly spoken, is guilty

1. Cf. The interesting discussion on a Dutch legislative proposal to sanction 'preparing to commit a crime', with contributions by, e.g., De Waard [1992], Mols and De Roos [1992].

of committing a certain crime should be punished given the specific circumstances of the case. In other words, not always the wrongdoer represents the wrong that is done in a sufficiently direct way. That this is really a problem of representation, and that we develop various parameters to determine who can pose as wrongdoer in function of our policies, can be learned from legal history. Not too long ago, most legal communities in Western culture were convinced that, for instance, animals could be perpetrators of crimes and consequently be punished. At present, we witness the rise of corporate entities receiving punishment in criminal law, like polluting companies, while only individual persons employed by such a company would have been hold criminally responsible just one decade ago.

5) *What should be the standards of punishment in law?* The most important principle that is supposed to govern the answer shows a clear inclination towards the discourse of representation: there should be proportionality between the severeness of the crime and the severeness of punishment, as well as between the severeness of punishment and the personal characteristics determining the agent's behaviour. Inversely, the principle of proportionality allows us to make inferences from the sanction to the type of person who has committed the crime as well as the kind of crime committed. But then, not surprisingly, also the difficulties of proportionality take their cue from representionalist discourse: apart from the problem how one can establish proportions between such multiples, can there ever be any reasonable proportion between crime (or guilt) and punishment when it comes to serious harm done? And how does one account for the fact that the severeness of certain 'crimes' is judged differently, not only in different countries, but in different parts of the same country? For instance, nuclear pollution is believed to be worse than homosexual behaviour in some (parts of) countries, but not in others.

6) *Which modes of punishment are to be applied?* The common forms of punishment are, without exception, hopelessly problematic. Apart from the demands imposed by the rule of law, there are the demands of effectivity and efficiency. The death penalty is a case in point, but similar doubts can be raised against the effects and costs of prisons, fines and 'alternative sanctions' (e.g. social services).[2)] A more profound ques-

2. Cf. the Introduction to the extensive research in Van Kalmthout and Tak [1988/1992].

tion, one to which we were made sensitive by Foucault [1975], is if we are aware how 'common forms' of punishment relate to other disciplinary regimes imposed on us by society? The transition from corporeal punishment, via incarceration and fines, to services and trainings is perhaps too easily booked as 'humanisation' of criminal law. Without denying this moral qualification, we may ask, at the same time, what shifts in functional mechanisms, as so many modes to picture 'suffering', 'confessing' and 'adapting', are tacitly taken into account by these transitions.

The overall picture that seems to emerge from these brief characterizations is that of criminal law authorities pursuing a political programme of protection in virtue of a pre-established order of sociopolitical life, by retreating, albeit in the last ressort, to allegedly appropriate means of coercion, framed in descriptively adequate textual mappings of crimes and sanctions. The meaning of the text mirrors the actual facts, the sanction mirrors the crime restoring the balance of interests, the modes of coercion mirror the functional distortions as far as they are brought about by the perpetrator, the protection of citizens (criminals included) mirrors the pre-established order. In the background is a clear-cut double dualism: one between state power and law: in the case of crime, law is there to justify political coercive power and political power is there to realise law; the other is between the ideology of pre-established order and law: in punitive action, law enforces a pre-established order of society and this order, in turn, sanctions the action. On this basis of this twofold dualism we may pick either one of two conclusions which are equally underpinned by the representational relationships involved: either law enforcement seems to be the only way to legal protection, or legal protection seems to be the only way to law enforcement. These two positions are exactly those which form the opposite camps in the debate which I referred to at the beginning of this chapter.

2 Legal punishment and interception

Legal theory takes the conceptual furniture of law as its point of departure, but it does not take it for granted. Therefore, from a theoretical point of view, we may well ask about the credentials of criminal law's reference to a justifying 'pre-established order' and to a realizsing 'punitive power'. What does it mean for power to be 'punitive'? What is it about sociopolitical order that could be characterized as 'pre-established'?

2.1 Punishing

It is not uncommon to believe that courses of action like punishing, revenging and raging are more or less of the same ilk, or at least on the same conceptual scale. Especially when punishment is analysed in terms of retribution, such kinship becomes an attractive frame of reference. With critical overtones either present or absent, as the case may be, it is asserted that when retribution is the bottom line of punishment, the latter boils down to 'an eye for an eye, a tooth for a tooth' and, thus, revenge and raging with anger. Critics will often hold the additional belief that such a view of punishment as retribution, once put to work in sociopolitical practice, will spiral into increasing violence. But let us pause to ask if there really is such a phenomenological link between punishment and other forms of repressive reaction?

I will not deny that certain practices of punishment are tantamount to revenge or rage as far as matters of fact are concerned. But the very fact that we are able to establish that they conflate in certain cases indicates that, on a conceptual level, we are familiar with their differences. These differences will probably originate in the perception of different phenomena. I also do not want to deny that punishing, revenging and raging have nothing in common on this conceptual level, for it is hard to miss the point that they are, all three, vital reactions of violence against (possible) infringements of an existing (order of) power.

But punishing differs characteristically from either revenge or rage.[3)] Rage is primarily an emotional reaction that can burst out against whatever is experienced as unacceptable. It can come down on everything and everyone in its way, sometimes blind to its self-destruction. Revenge, on the other hand, is a much more calculating, thus rational reaction. Although it can be wide-ranging in destruction, it will invariably try and detect the limits where its violence becomes counterproductive. It will keep the risk of self-destruction at a distance. The mafia, which has pol-

3. Scheler [1966: 363ff.] has presented an incisive phenomenological account of these differences.

ished the practices of revenge to perfection, acknowledges, as few other organisations do, the importance of a precise calculation that can determine where extreme violence will lose contact with the laws of revenge and be fed by sheer anger, to its own detriment. Indeed, rage can be restrained and transformed into revenge.

When it comes to punishment, a new plunge is taken. No longer are the ground and the limit of the reaction to be found in the subjective interests of the punisher, as in the case of revenge, but in an order of interests that is *deemed* to be independent of him, and in that sense objective. To put it in another way: Punishment comes in weights and measures. It is, like revenge, calculating, but it pretends to calculate not from the subjective point of view of the punisher himself. Whether the order of weights is believed to derive its alleged objectivity from being willed by God, or from being favoured by an impartial spectator, or from being identical with what a certain society values most, these are all various ways of substantiating one and the same thing: punishment occurs in the name of an order that is thought to transcend the punisher's subjective ideas and choices. Thus it is characteristic of punishment that it cannot do without symbolically staging the presence of such an order and refer to it. In this regard, punishment is part and parcel, indeed the paragon, of what the previous chapter has proposed to take as the core of 'the political'.

Now if we accept the differences between rage, revenge and punishment, and appreciate that the latter is committed to objectivity although it can only warrant its claims in a limited way, we are able to see what law can have to do with punishment: it will, in some way or other, be involved in this warranting process. But, more importantly, we may also recognize that punishment conceptually requires or postulates a warranting order as instrumental to its efficacy. This brings us to the question about the pre-established character of the sociopolitical order that criminal law is supposed to refer to.

2.2 Punishment and the order of freedom

Philosophers like Rousseau, Kant and Hegel have argued - in rather differing ways, to be sure - that there is more to be said about the character of the order that should be at stake for punishment to become legal. In other words, they hold that there is something pertinent conceptually linked up with the parameters of objectivity intended in punishing. They claim that the ground of the punitive act can be nothing else but the belief that the crime which it seeks to punish is an unjustified infringement of *freedom*. In a basic sense, freedom is not just one of the countless contingent preferences people may have; it is, rather, tantamount to the very idea of having preferences (choices rather than inclinations) and being able to pursue them. In as much as a certain political order is believed to be an order of freedom, punishing infringements of this order is tantamount to restoring freedom. This specification is important for various reasons.

First of all, it can account for the fact that there is punishment outside the area of politics, for instance in pedagogical situations where infringements of freedom in the social order are not at stake. Consequently, there is no question of the idea of 'legal punishment' here. It sounds rather absurd to make a close analogy between grounding your son for disobeying domestic rules and punishing a criminal for disobeying the rules of society. But then, the distinction is a relative one: There are connections between domestic rules and the rules of society (e.g. the importance of family values), while on the other hand the rules of society are always the rules of a particular society and, in that sense, domestic. So reference to freedom in the social order points to a distinction that is all but ready-made, but that is important to constantly try to make.

Secondly, to bring legal punishment in connection with the political project of society as an order of freedom, clarifies a certain grammar of punishment. If legal punishment countervails attacks of freedom, then it may conceive of itself as countervailing countervailances of freedom. The former are thought to 'undo' the latter. Hegel, in a similar vein, speaks of punishment as a 'negation' of crime, while crime in itself is a 'negation' of freedom in society.[4)] Not all philosophers would be prepared to use the same idiolect, but it is not too difficult to see what Hegel had in mind. It is obvious that no punitive act could negate the *fact* of a crime, neither in the sense that it could be denied to have taken place, nor in the sense that it could be ignored as far as its social impact is concerned. Criminal

4. Hegel, *Grundlinien*, § 101: 'Das Aufheben des Verbrechens ist insofern *Wiedervergeltung* als sie dem Begriffe nach Verletzung der Verletzung ist und dem Dasein nach das Verbrechen einen bestimmten, qualitativen und quantitativen Umfang, hiermit auch dessen Negation als Dasein ebensolchen hat.' Cf. § 104.

law goes to great pains to establish the facts as well as the impacts of crimes that have been committed. But if 'negation' has nothing to do with denying or ignoring the factual occurrence of a crime, it neither comes down to verbally disapproving of it by virtue of legal norms. It is not tantamount to the simple reproach: 'X, what you did was legally wrong.' Surely upholding a legal norm against a criminal act is what the law is. But it is of the essence of law to 'uphold' by doing something, not just saying something,[5] and this to such an degree, that in legal contexts saying something often amounts to doing something.[6] Legal norms are not only 'positive' in the sense of being enacted but also of being enforced. Law, that is, is upholding norms by interfering in social relationships, thus by the exercise of coercive power. 'Negation' in Hegel's sense amounts to what some interpreters have called 'practical negation', i.e. resistance. And so legal punishment in his view is: to resist *in actu* infringement of freedom in society.[7]

But does that not mean that punishment replaces one wrongdoing by another? The Hegelian answer is: No; there is a clear-cut distinction between the evil punished and the evil punishing. The former is locked up in the agent's own particular frame of reference, without considering the feasibility of his act in terms of good and bad. If he is asked: 'Why did you do it?' answers may come up like: 'I didn't think about it', 'I needed the money', 'I wanted to have fun', 'I was outraged', 'Plenty of others have done it', etc. The latter, the punishing evil, is committed to a process of objectification or justification or universalization, in which it has to be accounted for in terms of what we are to allow if we want to respect one another's freedom in this specific society.[8] So 'practical negation' is not just resistance, but accountable resistance against wrongdoing.

5. Hegel, *Grundlinien*, § 104: 'So *ist* und *gilt* das Recht, gegen den *bloß für sich seienden* Willen bewährt, als durch seine Notwendigkeit *wirklich*.'

6. Cf. J.L. Austin's [1962] references to law in the presentation of his theory on performative language, in particular his initial label 'operative'.

7. Cf. Hegel, *Grundlinien*, § 101.

8. I do not assert that the criminal acts in an arbitrary way. What we see, especially in organized crime, is sharp calculation of interests: self-interest against opposing interests of others. This indicates, anyway, the awareness of difference between 'smart' and 'stupid' as a species of the genus 'right' and 'wrong'. So the criminal cannot retreat to ignorance when society demands that these distinctions should mean something in the area of social freedom. See Hegel, *Grundlinien*, § 100.

Moreover, the account has to derive from not just any pre-established order of preferences, but from a society's conception of a specific overriding value: freedom. But note that these accounts cannot be made but in the process of political discourse. They do not descend from philosophical heaven to be 'applied' in the realm of politics. The order of freedom is not pre-established in the sense that it precedes politics; rather, it is set by politics *as* an order that precedes politics. So it does not precede politics from what could perhaps be called 'an external point of view'. And although such point of view is not irrelevant (it is the point of view of the present argument), it is not the point of view that allows direct political claims about the order of society. We are left with the inversed hierarchies between a pre-established order of values and a political order that claims to realise them.

In chapters 5 and 7 I have argued that law in general is nothing more or less than politics under self-imposed and institutionalised self-restraint. So, in as far as punitive behaviour is one of the manifestations of 'setting society in order'[9], i.e. of politics in modernity, it will become part of a legal order to the extent that it engages in self-imposed self-restraint. Given the idea of law being politics with a proviso about its very ground, and legal punishment being an expression of this core trait of law, we may add an essential element to the grammar of punishment that Hegel proposed. Punishment in the sense of legal punishment not only requires practical negation of the negation intended in crime. It should also bear testimony to the legal order's awareness of the provisional character of its own ground. In other words, it should also (practically) negate its being (definitely) in the right. If we were to borrow Hegel's idiolect, we might even frame the succinct thesis that legal punishment is negation (proviso) of the negation (punishment) of the negation (crime). But in a more transparent, though also more shocking vocabulary, we may express the same by saying that it is of the essence of legal punishment to hold the crime in favour of the criminal, though not on his own but on the legal order's accord. This is not to say that the latter approves of his crime; it means that the legal order recognizes that there is only a relative, not an absolute distinction between the particularity of the crime and the particularity of the order in the name of which the crime is punished. A legal order is

9. The phrase derives from Lindahl [1995].

precisely particular (rather than universal) in the sense that it has always dubbed *itself* to be a just order and has, therefore, prematurely proclaimed its rights to punish. Law is always posited, and therefore never definitively justified law. Postponement of its own pretension of rightness, indeed righteousness, is what has to become evident in the practice of law enforcement. The ancient Jewish penal law, we learn, knew the punishment of beating: forty strokes minus one.[10)] This institution symbolically expresses the above. To put it bluntly, forty strokes would have been punishment, forty minus one is legal punishment. In the 'minus one' the proviso of the legal order regarding the rightness of its own choices and beliefs becomes manifest, not only during the executionary stage of the punishment (the executioners may make mistakes in counting the strokes) but already in the stage of criminal law enactment.

It will be objected that this view is flawed by the argument of infinite regress. If a proviso is in place regarding the rightness of punishing interference with a crime, then a proviso is in place regarding the rightness of the first proviso, and so on *ad infinitum*. Well, this is indeed what I have in mind, but I do not regard it as a flaw. I have explained that the proviso is a practical one, i.e. one that manifests itself in acting. To put it simply: It will manifest itself in acting prudently, with a constant eye for making no irreparable mistakes. Now, in acting, a proviso on a proviso, if it is to mean anything at all, does not mean a renouncement of the latter, but a reinforcement. It means that there will always be more things to attend to than you have thought of when you decided to be prudent. So in fact the argument that the provisos go on infinitively once they have come into an account of legal punishment, is a welcome one: it underlines that law is a historically permanent caveat of politics.[11)]

So punishing in the legal sense will imply at least three things:

1) Legal punishment will not escape from participating in what is generally at the core of politics, to wit, to realize the identity of a particular society, its wants and beliefs.

2) Legal punishment will (institutionally) acknowledge that the allegedly objective order of weights and measures presupposed in punishing generally, can be improved on: it is always possible to better justify this order

10. The example, but not the thesis it aims at, is Hegel's.

11. For an extensive account of history as an element in the definition of law, see Van Roermund [1990d], ch. 3.

and reduce the residue of pure self-interest.
3) Legal punishment will (institutionally) acknowledge that this process of refinement is uncompleted at any moment that crime has to be sanctioned. It will, on its own accord, let its provisional character count against itself.

Note that, in this view, according to the first characteristic, society itself remains the judge of what it can afford to impose on itself as self-restraint. The difference law makes is that society is committed to making such a judgment, and to corroborate it as much as possible, while at the same time upholding that this is an infinite process.

2.3 Interception - once more

The first section of this chapter brought out that criminal law tends to get involved in a double relationship of representation. Conceiving of itself as being at the crossroads of political power and a pre-established order of values, it functions as both the justification of power and the realisation of order. The previous section investigated the former bond by asking in what sense punitive law could relate to the conception of an order of freedom as pre-established. The present section deals with the same issues deriving from the latter one: the relation of punitive law to the exercise of power, in particular state power.

Especially in criminal law, there is a strong temptation to believe that law holds the place which, during the Inquisition, the Church assigned to itself: it does not 'thirst after blood', it it only disposes those that are found guilty to the power of the state. The presupposition carrying this belief is that there is dualism between state as the representative of political power, and law as the representative of public reason. This dualism, like the previous one, is far from neutral: it has to be understood as an hierarchy of terms. Law is supposed to be the dominant term of the relationship. Law is supposed to provide the norm for the exercise of political power, which is incorporated by the state. Now, let me recall from the previous chapter that Kelsen vehemently denied a dualistic relationship between law and power. He did not want the state to incorporate the latter pole so as to give law predominance over it.[12)] Kelsen understood the

12. See for an extensive account my [1990b] and chapter 7 of this book.

danger of drawing political consequences from philosophical insight. The dualism he attacked was a political one, too eagerly drawn from the philosophical fissure mentioned. His argument was that such dualism may look like a morally welcome prevalence of law over power, but that in factual practice its logic will work the opposite way, namely as an ideology for power to dominate law. It offers politics, being the instance of law enactment, a legitimating device to interfere as soon as law is endangered, in the name of 'higher law'. The emergency state of law will be called upon to set positive legal orderings aside and let those in power decide what to do on behalf of law - but without it. Dualism between law and state thus subjects law unrestrictedly to power, pretending that it subjects power unrestrictedly to law.

What such dualism, as criticized by Kelsen, tries to conceal is that law is not simply 'there', but that it is always to be made, posited, enacted and enforced, and that it is, thus, intrinsically linked up with power anyway. In other words, such dualism denies that law is, like political exercise of power, a practice. It can only form a conception of itself in such a practice from the point of view of acting with regard to, indeed in, a specific, i.e. identified and limited society. That is why this practice stands in need of what this books calls 'narrativity' or 'interception of reference': a form of knowing that opens up and challenges the politically determined conceptual framework that a society invests itself with.

From a philosophical view on law and power this limitation does not work in the same way, although it does work. For philosophy, politics is a practice that is linked up with society, but as a variable, not as a value. It wishes to establish the relationship between 'the political' and 'society' in terms of much more structural and, in fact, theoretical parameters than are available in politico-legal life itself. Thus, it is able to distinguish between law and politics on a level of pertinence and abstraction where neither of the two themselves can operate. More specifically, it can conceive of an opposition between law and power which cannot be immediately transformed by either positive law or actual politics in their respective accounts of historical facts. To put it in another, more technical philosophical vocabulary: the differential dualism between law and politics discovered by philosophy is not equivalent to the ontological dualism that would assign law and politics to a dualistic opposition of orders of being. There is no ontological opposition between positive law and politics.

The difference between the philosophical point of view on the one hand, and the viewpoints of law and politics on the other, works both ways. For one thing, philosophical insight in the primacy of law over power cannot inflate a political preference for the practice of legal protection (law as a 'warrant') over and above the practice of law enforcement (law as a 'tool'). Speaking from the philosophical standpoint and defending the primacy of law over power, we cannot transform this to the legal stance that criminal law is primarily about protecting citizens from a powerful government, leaving it a secondary concern to enable the government to enforce the law against more or less powerful perpetrators. For another thing, if we acknowledge that legal protection and law enforcement form a double hierarchy in the sense of our interception hypothesis, we cannot infer from that the philosophical thesis that there is no distinction between them. Though philosophy can determine law as primarily a norm for, not an instrument of political engineering, the two have to tango together when it comes to doing either law or politics. The one pole of the relationship has to leave it to the other to realize its most pertinent aim.

3 Some consequences

3.1 The (non)sense of legal punishment

It follows from the above that legal punishment cannot aim at definitive destruction or submission of the criminal without losing its prima facie claim of being a part of law. But it should be added straightaway that this is a conceptual pointer, not a legal norm. It indicates in what direction those involved in a particular political order should think if they are to justify their norms. But different political orders can frame very different ideas about what constitutes (definitive) destruction and submission, depending on varying ideologies. Contrary to what one might think at first sight, this in itself does lend support to a primitive form of practical relativism, to the effect that any punitive policy can eventually be defended with reference to a suitable ideology. It only follows that one cannot circumvent the political process of a certain society in determining what the pointer points to. But precisely the supposition that there can be different ideas about that has to be accounted for in the punitive policy of any society, and it will in itself be a ground for relativising, rather than hypostatizing, one's own idea. If legal punishment bears testimony to the law's postponement of a self-proclaimed order of righteousness, it should use this postponement to make all those involved (victim, official, criminal) deal with the perpetrator's life in this particular society, not to exclude him from it. Now, does this mean that there is a philosophical argument against, for instance, capital punishment? I think there is not, although I find it appalling in all cases and morally wrong in democratic legal systems. In other words, I have emotions that have little philosophical value pertaining to all cases in which the death penalty is the ultimate legal decision, but I think I do have arguments against it in *some* cases depending on the social and cultural characteristics of a specific political order. Let me explain.

I can just imagine that a society is in favour of capital punishment and can give an account of its belief that the death of the criminal would not amount to total and definitive destruction of the individual. This could be the case, for instance, where the legal order of that society is situated in a religious context in which it is generally believed that there is life after death and that the criminal is not deprived of this life, but only put at the mercy of those who reign in this realm, God or the gods. Now secular democratic societies flourish by allowing such a belief to be a matter of individual preference: its cement is not so much belief as it is meta-belief, i.e., a belief about beliefs, namely the belief that no beliefs about the good society has a privileged access to truth. It is hard to see why bringing an individual to death would not mean, in a such a society, definitively wasting his life in the name of self-proclaimed justice without any proviso. So I think it conflicts, in such circumstances, with the account of legal punishment as advocated by this chapter. But so do other forms of legal punishment if, depending on circumstances and social values, they run counter to the core idea of law as self-restrained politics. For instance, if a legal order disposes of statistically corroborated materials showing that imprisonment is likely to ruin people's life, it should doubt, on its own accord, the legal feasibility of this form of punishment. An administration that goes on to apply a form of punishment that is known to be ineffective, or one that undermines the positive effects of its legal policy by policies in other areas, such an administration is putting its legal order in jeopardy. It does not what it professes to do: to allow something to count against it even it is not forced to do so.[13] Even if it remains true that societies may differ widely in the way in which they conceive of themselves and in what they think they can afford to self-impose restraints on this conception, a society should be open to what counts against it if it is to be a legal order at all.

3.2 Retribution, prevention, reconciliation

I stated that legal punishment makes a proviso to its own legitimacy, indeed a proviso to this proviso, *ad infinitum*. This does not entail the suspension of punishment, but the suspension of definitive monopolies of legitimation in criminal law. In that sense, legal punishment should not be 'definitive'; it should use this suspension to hold the crime 'in favour' of the criminal. This, again, does not entail that he should not be punished for the wrong he did, but rather that the sanction should harbour the opportunity for a new relationship between the criminal and society. Which sanctions are the most useful to attain that goal, is a question that criminology and criminal law should answer, not philosophy. These disciplines have to wrestle with the fact that, for instance, in Western societies it has been doubted already since Von Liszt whether (short) imprisonment can be very effective in this regard.

Anyway, how such a new relationship could be furthered is a much more interesting debate for lawyers than the obsolete question what should be the primary purpose of legal punishment: retribution, general prevention, or special prevention (resocialisation). The dilemma becomes nonsensical as soon as we realize that legal punishment is not just a species of the genus punishing (justified punishment), but the question mark behind the justification of punishing as a political practice of retribution. It amounts to self-imposed self-restraint of retribution, remaining retribution all over. It is not very illuminating to say that general prevention rather than retribution is the keyword in this formula. What else could constitute the standard of what is to be a crime and what is to be its proper sanction than the values that the society involved deems to be endangered and that it wants to defend? Retribution and prevention are the two sides of the

13. This key description of law as the openness of politics is derived from Gadamer, as is explained in my [1990d].

same coin: if retribution is the sense (or 'intension') of punishment, prevention is its reference (or 'extension'). The element that really challenges both of these is the awareness and the will to hold them within certain limits so as to bring the criminal, his victim and society at large into a new relationship. If there is a keyword for that, it would be the somewhat archaic word 'reconciliation' - a term hardly used in criminal law. So retribution and reconciliation do not exclude each other. On the contrary: the interception hypothesis, applied to legal punishment, reveals them as opposing in terms in mutual interpellation. This means that sanctions which block any kind of reconciliation, for instance because they are massively perceived by their subjects as sheer revenge from the side of society, are to be questioned as forms of doing justice in criminal legal policy. But it also means that sanctions which promise reconciliation in advance, betraying their roots in self-protection (thus retribution) of society, are questionable as parts of a criminal legal system.

That does not say very much about the kind of sanctions that should be applied; it should remain a matter of public debate (and, thus, of state authority) what is needed to exercise retribution *and* to restrain its claim to an absolute right in one fell swoop. And there can be different standpoints involved in this debate: the community may demand imprisonment of the criminal, the victim may demand compensation of losses, the criminal or his representative may demand that something be done about his social deprivation. There is no criterion to establish in advance what would be a provisionally justifiable outcome. But there can be no doubt that these are the perspectives that really count.

A useful side-effect of all this is that in criminal policy making we can do away with infelicitous notions like 'resocialisation' and 'deterrence'. As for resocialisation, the noun 'reconciliation' is better in all relevant respects. For criminal law is not a one-way street. It is not based on the sole assumption that society is in the right and the perpetrator has to adapt until he is an impeccable member of this allegedly homogeneous body. Reconciliation implies a commitment on both sides to work on a new relationship between the criminal and society. It requires the authorities in a society to ask (and not only to ask *themselves*) whether the crime under investigation has causes rooting in the structure of the society itself. If that is the case, it does not justify crime, but it does justify reluctance in trying to 'resocialise' the criminal, indeed in establishing his guilt and the appropriate penalty. Moreover, even if there are no such causes found, society will have to be prepared to prevent lifelong stigmatisation as it prohibits the criminal from entering into a new relationship with society. It also seems to me that only reconciliation, not resocialisation, can provide a conceptual framework for contemporary efforts to re-assess the position of the victim in criminal law.

How about deterrence? The answer is not too difficult. In as far as deterrence is nothing more or less than prospective retribution within the framework of certain values deemed endangered, everything is already said. Of course there will be an element of deterrence in legal punishment, as it is a vital reaction by society to what it regards as an infringement of its identity, i.e. its subsistence. But that element falls under the proviso that we have discovered as being at the core of law. For that very reason deterrence cannot be the ultimate goal of imposing and executing penalties in law. If it could, the proviso would lose its force. Then the criminal would be used as a mere instrument for political engineering, a policy that Kant strongly disapproved of in his philosophy of ethics and law. If crime *prevention* is to be effective, it is well advised not to lean too heavily upon imposing and executing penalties, as Rousseau already knew: increasing severeness of sanctions is a sure sign that the state is on the verge of subsistence.

3.3 State authority and criminal law

This brings us to the question if putting state authority in charge of legal punishment contributes to the legal quality of punishment. It is in this respect that rereading Kant may help us a great deal. It is often thought that Kant has little more to say on punishment than that it finds its basis in retribution. A more accurate reading[14)], however, will reveal a far more sophisticated account of the matter in his works. In fact the idea of retribution plays hardly any role in his answer to the question what would be, in principle, the justification for punitive action by state authority. Rather, it enters the scene when it is asked who is to be punished and according to what standards. If the latter questions are asked, Kant's view is that guilt should be the anchorage of punishment and proportionality its

14. One like, for instance, Mertens [1991].

rule. But if it is asked why, as a matter of principle, state authority may be justified in applying punitive sanctions, Kant argues that the reasonableness of punishment as an action of law and the reasonableness of state authority being the subject of punishing in law are two distinct questions. To the former, he answers in a similar vein as I explained in the previous section: the ground for punishing in law is the infringement of freedom in the social order through criminal activity. Law should countervail this infringement by effective action. To the latter, his response is a corrollary of the former: State authority should be in charge of legal punishment, because and in as far as the state is the only political form of social relationships in which the external freedom, i.e., the freedom of pursuing one's prefer- ences, of one individual is made compatible with the external freedom of another by virtue of general laws. Of course, his theory of the social contract (mainly deriving from Rousseau, in Kant's case) is in the background here. It is included in this conception of the state that the latter is never a means towards an end, but a goal in itself.[15)]

Note that this argument is about principle, not about facts. It does not follow that some factual state regime cannot be criticized for the way it exercises its punitive policy, nor does this line of thought imply that some particular form of state authority, for instance the nation state, is the exclusive or privileged body to be in charge of legal punishment. What Kant wants to highlight is that (external) freedom for everyone can only be understood as a matter of law from a very specific politico-philosophical presupposition concerning the organization ('Verfassung') of civil society. We can read this quite clearly in the heading of the *Metaphysische Anfangsgründe der Rechtslehre*, section 9:

> 'To hold something external as one's own is only possible in a legal state of affairs, under a publicly legislating authority, i.e., in the civil state.'[16)]

And more explicitly on the state in section 45:

15. Cf. Mertens [1991: 42].

16. 'Etwas äusseres als das Seine zu haben, ist nur in einem rechtlichen Zustande, unter einem öffentlich gesetzgebenden Gewalt, d.i. im bürgerlichen Zustande, möglich.' (AB, 72; my translation)

> 'A state is the association of a group of people under legal rules. To the extent that these rules are a priori necessary, i.e., that they follow directly from concepts of external law as such rather than being authoritatively enacted, its form is the form of a state as such, i.e. the state idea as it should be according to pure, legal principles, which serves as a guideline (norma) for any actual association to a collective body (thus, internally).[17)]

From Kant's thesis that there can be no law without 'the idea' of a state it does not follow that the state is conceived of as instrumental to the ultimate goal of realizing law as mutual external freedom. Such an interpretation would forget that the core of the thesis is its reversibility: there can be no state without law, no more than that there can be law without state. Law and state are *reciprocal* conditions, which in itself runs counter to the idea of instrumentality. For the concept of law as aiming at mutual external freedom is not, in Kant's view, a wish, an ideal or a value; it is a norm for action: something that ought to be realized in social life the mode of which we can only conceive reasonably by the model of the social contract as constitutive of the state. Therefore, as much as the state has law quality, the law has state quality. We cannot 'tell the dancer from the dance', to put it in the words of the poet.

So the ultimate justification of state authority being in charge of legal punishment lies with the principle that only a body politic that can call itself 'state' has the right to countervail by action infringement of mutual external freedom. But that is certainly not all there is to it. And the problem is not that such a principle is in itself fairly formal, but rather that, as a principle, it is incomplete. What it lacks is not just the recognition of the fact that all material interpretations of what external freedom, infringement and countervailance amount to will be matters of concrete legal policies, but mainly that these concretisations will be principally contingent on political interpretations of societal wants and facts, and thus provisional. No actual state or state goverment can, therefore, pretend to have a necessary and universal definition of freedom, etc. It will always

17. 'Ein Staat ist die Vereinigung einer Menge von Menschen unter Rechtsgesetzen. So fern diese als Gesetze a priori notwendig, d.i. aus Begriffen des äusseren Rechts überhaupt von selbst folgend (nicht statuarisch) sind, ist seine Form die Form eines Staates überhaupt, d.i. der Staat *in der Idee*, wie er nach reinen Rechtsprinzipien sein soll, welche jeder wirklichen Vereinigung zu einem gemeinen Wesen (also im Inneren) zur Richtschnur (norma) dient.' (A 164-165; B 194-195; my translation)

be a questionable idea for which it claims to use coercion justifiedly. For instance, even if it grants its citizens the right to life and claims to protect them from murder, it may be unable to respond to challenges regarding its poor policies in other areas (health, environment) that have to do with 'right to life'. And it is this questionability which has to be accounted for in law enforcement. On the other hand, however, the principled character of law as a provisional restraint on politics should encourage us to show a certain leniency when it comes to understanding ancient or foreign law rather than to set it aside as 'exotic'. It is important for understanding our legal system to appreciate why Ancient Europe used to punish those who (succesfully) committed suicide, their kinship and heirs.[18)] It is equally important to be aware that we may find it evident to prosecute a mother who kills her illegal child, while Kant, in spite of the Enlightenment, would be much more hesitant of such a policy. All such concretisations of 'mutual external freedom' are resumptions of a political group's own (rather: owned) identity through history. Thus, punitive policy will always hold an element of 'social defence' that may be historically 'necessary' but will never exhaust neither the claim nor the call for freedom. Otherwise retribution becomes the keyword not only in applying punitive sanctions but also in justifying the practice of legal punishment itself.

3.4 Making the rule of law rule

Our question was whether punishment should primarily be conceived of as a matter of power rather than law. It seems that the answer is in the affirmative, for it has become clear enough, firstly, that punishment is part and parcel of a political course of action by which a society countervails what it perceives as threats to its self-defined order; and, secondly, that law is self-imposed restraint on this policy of self-defence. So the word 'legal' is called upon to conceptually add up something to 'punishment', the latter being primarily a political notion. It is, therefore, in my view not precise enough to characterize legal punishment as 'canalized exercise

18. Cf. Vandekerckhove [1985].

of power'[19], as such a formula would neglect the demand that an order of positive law should meet to account for its own questionability or relativity. To the extent that punishing is a political instrument, criminal law is primarily principled restraint of political instrumentality. In other words, law should be enforced by legal means. Indeed, from a philosophical point of view we are heading towards a form of dualism in the relationship between law and power, which becomes manifest in legal punishment. But we also mitigate this dualism by saying that what is acknowledged in such restraint is the irreducible provisional, i.e., political character of the principles involved in such self-imposed restraint.

It is important, therefore, to acknowledge that this dualism between law and power is a philosophical insight, which cannot exhaust the whole range of the relationship. As a philosophical insight it is not directly available on either of both poles, neither on the side of positive law, nor on the side of actual politics. So, from the philosophical thesis that law should be enforced by legal means, we cannot infer the legal policy that all methods and tactics of criminal investigation are to be approved by explicit legislation. There will always be a realm of discretion by, for instance, investigating and prosecuting forces of the legal system, in which they themselves, from their political position, have to reflect on what criminal law enforcement allows and requires, without an appeal to a fashionable form of the pre-Napoléontic 'référé au législateur'. Exercising discretion is not acting arbitrarily; rather, it equals judging on the balance of (legal) reasons. That is not the prerogative of the legislator or the judge; it is not even the prerogative of officials. It is part and parcel of the definition of citizenship.

Although philosophy reveals the opposition between law and power in legal punishment, it also reveals its relativity. Neither the representatives of law, nor those involved in political action can put the opposition at work in justifying their courses of action from their respective points of view, i.e. as legal or political agents. Philosophical insight here does not warrant the conclusion that in the areas of law and politics themselves we will have to give one of the terms predominance over the other. Or, to phrase the point in the vocabulary of the discussion referred to at the be-

19. See Foqué - 't Hart [1990: 15], who use this terminology in order to indicate a position which is, in their view, on the right track, but philosophically unsatisfactory. I think that even the track is not right.

ginning of this chapter: It does not confront us with the choice between either criminal legal policy that aims at legal protection of citizens against coercion by state authority or one that wants to protect society against criminal citizens.[20] It does not create, in short, what Kelsen used to call 'the myth of Ormuzd and Ahriman in state-theoretical disguise'.

20. In Foqué and 't Hart [1989] deep and extensive arguments are produced against this alleged dilemma and the one-sided choices made. I agree largely with them. On the other hand, in my contribution to the volume of papers dealing with their book (see Van Roermund, Groenhuijsen and Witteveen [1993h]) I criticize the impression they give that each and every dual relation between law and power has to be refuted on philosophical grounds. I also mitigate the gap they construct between their position and A. Peters'.

CHAPTER 9

THE LAW OF OBLIGATIONS - AND THE FUN OF SEEING PLACES

By now it may have become clear that 'narrativity' is a category that, from a philosophical point of view, has little to do with storytelling in the ordinary sense of the word. It pertains, rather, to what constitutes the organization and boundaries of knowledge. We learned that knowledge does not consist exhaustively in reducing the singularity of things by subsumption under general terms that would represent them. Instead, we met different strategies to account for singularity as constitutive of knowledge avoiding the pitfall of quasi-criticism, that all general terms of knowledge can be reduced to singular ones. We acknowledged the importance of 'stand-points' or 'points of view' as points of departure rather than arrival. These places (in the ancient terminology 'topoi' or 'loci') do not constitute justifying reasons in themselves, but they enable us to look around for such reasons. The fact that they are 'given' does not give them any a priori justification. On the contrary, they stand in need of justification. But this can only be achieved if we manage to leave the point of view we have used, exchange it for another one that we believe to be valid, and then look around from this new one to find reasons for the old. To the extent that, then, we take a new standpoint for granted, we should acknowledge that it loses its justificatory force. The constant interpellation of dual points of view that are constitutive of one another, generating interception, suspension, proviso of definitive judgment, has been the constant theme in this book. Especially the concept of law, as it entails judgment backed up with coercion, has been its central focus. In the preceding chapters, both constitutional law and criminal law were investigated to gain a better understanding of our hypothesis.

In this final chapter, a plunge into private law will corroborate the account, allowing us at the same time to enlarge its scope. I intend to analyse a famous jurisprudential debate on the law of obligations, claiming that my hypothesis can bring some light to the perpetual circles of the turns it seems to go. All along my analysis will be dependent on the interplay of 'places' exchanging their status as 'point of departure' and 'point of arrival' in search of justification. What I want to clarify (once more) is how these characteristically 'narrative' phenomena reveal themselves in deceivingly innocent elements of legal discourse, as, for instance, prepositions.

1 Places, prompts and prepositions: an announcement

Before embarking on the law of obligations, I will show that (some) prepositions in legal rules assign places to legal actors, and that these places function as prompts of argumentation: they make you take a position from where you can say or argue (only) certain things, and from where you have to acknowledge the validity of (only) certain arguments; arguments which you could challenge, if only you were not at that particular place. Since they thus precede arguments, propositions, concepts and their ilk, prepositions will turn out to present the frame for what is considered to be a favourite image of thinking: representation. This framework allows one to note that there is also something outside: a different, but constitutive order of thinking compared to the order of propositions, and even presuppositions. Avoiding the step from acknowledging representations to saluting representationalism will remain our epistemological goal throughout. This will allow us to pay tribute to speech acts without regarding them as the final *analysans* of propositions.

I will introduce my general points by way of a rather trivial example: interpreting the symbols in a lift - which is already complicated enough. I will analyse them as icons for rules, only to support the reverse hypothesis: that rules can or should be analysed only if their iconic aspect is taken into account. Taking it into account entails understanding the rule as a mirror in which we can see (or rather, imagine) ourselves acting at different places. These places, however, are not just different; they are connected in the sense that being an actor at one place involves regarding the other place as marking the ground for justification of your actions, and vice versa. In other words: the relationship of these places is such that the source of reasonableness is at the place where you are *not*. It is never congruent with your place of acting. It is possible to take the other place to act from, but that does not change the healthy predicament. To put it in rather glamorous terms: Reasonableness is indexical; once you move from here to there, there becomes here, and vice versa. The caveat to be added is the one that constitutes the body of this book: the indices and icons are dependent on narrative elaboration to work at all. This general idea allows us to explain why a pragmatic account of rationality is not tantamount to a pragmatic account of truth or validity.

After this linguistic-epistemic part of the argument, I shall turn to the law of obligations to give the hypothesis a specific legal cut. I will try to discover the stands which some basic rules of the new Dutch Civil Code invite their readers to take. I shall elaborate on that by exploring a famous theoretical discussion on obligations by Atiyah and Fried, which focuses on the prepositional distinction of external and internal. I will distinguish three shifts in the position which Atiyah takes on the internal-external axis which he presents to frame his discussion with Fried on contractual obligations. I will highlight that, in the final analysis, the standpoint from which either of them argues has to account for a semantic ground of validity which the other defends, but which turns into a pragmatic standpoint as soon as it is appealed to.

2 Prompts: a semiosis of some domestic buttons

Most people can operate liftdoors in perfect accordance with their wishes to have them open or closed, as the case may be, by pushing either of two buttons. Not uncommonly, these buttons have the following icons: >||< and <||>. Perhaps my readers belong to the happy group of 'most people' who see immediately which button to push to have the doors open and which to have them close. I do not. Moreover, I manipulate these buttons exactly opposite to most people, feeling pretty sure that I do it right or that (this time) I will do it right. My colleagues - who are all normal - keep telling me that this is what the manufacturer had in mind:

<||>   >||<

DOORS OPEN   DOORS CLOSED

On closer examination I even have to admit that these words are clearly written underneath the buttons. But the icons suggest that I can afford to skip the reading and to go by the simple drawings. That is, after all, what icons are for. However, every time I trust the suggestion, my hand goes to the button which will make the doors move into the direction I do not want them to move into.

To strengthen my self-confidence in the face of such an abnormality I framed an explanatory hypothesis, which allows both my colleagues and me to emerge as perfectly reasonable beings. Here it is. The normals see these icons, > and <, as arrows. The power that should open or close the doors comes from the direction opposite to that in which the arrow points. For the happy majority this is the more adequate picture:

<-- ¦¦ --> and --> ¦¦ <--.

Thus, <¦¦> pushes the doors away from each other, opening the door, while >¦¦< pushes the doors towards each other, closing it. My handicap is that I have a different reading of the symbols < and >. I happen to see them not as arrows, but as angle brackets, in more or less this way:

--< ¦¦ >-- and >-- ¦¦ --<

And brackets include and exclude. They hold together and separate; at least in logic they do. And if you do not like to see logic and operating lifts conflated, there are plenty of other pictures to read in > and <. One of my other favourites is to see them as the slightly curved lines of hands *en profile*. No doubt hands hold together and separate in a rather straightforward sense. Still another possibility for me is to read > and < as a stylized comic drawing of the impact of some force: they indicate the effect rather than the cause. Whatever picture you prefer, it boils down to an image in which the power originates from the direction in which the points of < and > point. That is why I recognize <¦¦> as a 'pushing together of doors'; consequently, I operate the corresponding button in order to close the doors. With >¦¦< it is the other way round: the 'hands' separate the two half-doors, suggesting to me that they are capable of opening them.

Now, the intriguing part of this explanation is not so much the difference between my colleagues and me; it is, rather, the striking similarity in the way we all seem to relate to these symbols which is borne out only by the difference. The similarity is threefold.

(1) Both normals and I work with the same category of 'power' or 'force': the power that makes lift doors open and close. We believe that the symbols refer to such a phenomenon.

(2) We both localize the source and the orientation of this power, as coming from and going into different directions. When normals are in the lift, they locate the source of power where the asterisk is in scheme [1]:

[1] < ¦*¦ > *> ¦¦ <*

Apparently, I localize it in the opposite way [2]:

[2] *< ¦¦ >* > ¦*¦ <

(3) We imagine ourselves at the place of the asterisks in [1] and [2]: it is *our* opening and closing the doors of the lift. If power is involved in these kinds of actions, we see ourselves as the source of that power. Indeed, the icon seems to invoke our projecting ourselves on that particular spot within its own framework. The icon is a mirror, and we are prompted to step 'through the looking-glass': from a place *in front of* and *external* to the icon to a place *in the framework of* or *internal* to the icon.

This triad of reference, localization and identification is what I would like to call a prompt. It comes close to what Döpke and Schwarz (1981: 21f), in their account of linguistic prepositions, called 'localisation actantielle'.

There is still another amazing thing apart from the difference between the normals and myself: on second thought, we cannot do without one another's prompts. Depending on where we locate our respective standpoints, the other prompt gets a certain legitimacy, as it fills in what our own standpoint is not able to account for. I may be perfectly right in seeing the icons as hands that push the doors together till they close; but, as there are *two* hands in that case, this presupposes that the forces come from different directions. Reversely, the normals may be right in seeing the icons as arrows indicating the direction of the forces; but they, in turn, take for granted that these forces have to be guided or co-ordinated in order that the doors meet at a certain point. One who favours 'direction of forces' still has to account for co-ordination, and one who is impressed by 'co-ordination' still has to account for the different directions of the forces. So, we should all be happy, and acknowledge that prompts do not replace or exhaust arguments; on the contrary, they allow us to see arguments and to discover that the validity of arguments is dependent on the prompt you are invited to follow up.[1)]

Finally, I would like to draw attention to the text printed underneath the buttons, which is supposed to clarify their operative force: the phrases DOORS OPEN and DOORS CLOSED. With regard to these phrases I am normal: I have no hesitation about their meaning and I am convinced that all reasonable people I know are willing to join my interpretation. But that is quite astonishing given the fact that the phrases are very elliptic indeed. They are short for some more complicated utterance. But we are pretty certain that [3], [4], [5] and [6] below - though possible readings in other contexts - are lousy candidates for clarifying DOORS OPEN when we are standing in lifts:

[3] The doors are open.
[4] If the doors are open, then push this button.
[5] Open the doors!
[6] If the doors are closed, then push this button

Reading [3] misses the point by taking the text in the alethic mode, whereas it is deontic; [4] is an advice to the contrary of what is meant, since you are expected to push the button in question when the doors are not open; [5] is wrong in many ways, one of which is that it is categorical instead of conditional, and [6] is downright dangerous, especially when you are moving in an antique lift, which may open its doors between two floors. What we want DOORS OPEN to mean is probably something long-winded like [7]:

[7] If the doors are closed and you want them open, then push this button.

1. I would have no objection if someone were to point out to me that this is what Aristotle meant by the key term of his *Topoi*.

The complicated reading [7] seems rather adequate, although I can think of some amendments.[2] For present purposes, we may note that we have a structure of a condition which is a conjunction of a statement of fact and a wish, followed by a directive on how to act. I submit that this is a good candidate for the general structure of what we call *rules*. Now, if the meaning of the icon does not just entail, but is equivalent to this rule [7], we may safely conclude that, inversely, the rule entails the iconic meaning. To state this in a Peircean/Wittgensteinian way: Rules are iconic. To follow, indeed to interpret, a rule is not to apply a syllogism to one's intentions, but to step through the looking-glass, i.e. to project oneself as an observer in front of the rule to a form of behaviour as an actor from the perspective which the rule is prompting to. In order to 'interpret' the rule, one has to take the position which is the vanishing point of that perspective. The lines converging in that point are indicated by prepositions.

This is not to say that all (spatial) prepositions in a text contribute to that effect. What we will be looking for are conceptual structures that are eventually built along axes like 'before/after', 'up/down', 'on top of/underneath', 'inside/outside', 'from/to', etc.[3] These can hide in perfectly non-prepositional terms like 'fundamental rights' (up/down), or 'access to justice' (inside/outside).[4]

2. These would have to do with the fact that a lot of safety mechanisms are presupposed in the wiring of the buttons. These could be transformed into, or traced back to, elements of the wish to open the doors of the lift in a certain way. (You do not want the doors to open at your wish while the lift is moving?)

3. See Döpke and Schwarz [1981: 22]: '(...) les indications [qui] signalent l'endroit où se trouvent un actant ou les actants (...).' '(...) on peut, en principe, englober la localisation actantielle dans la localisation propositionelle en dérivant l'information relative à la localisation des actants de l'information que le syntagme prépositionel fournit au sujet de la localisation de l'état de choses considéré comme un tout.'

4. See also Van Roermund [1987] and chapter 3 of this book for an analysis of Locke's critique of the 'substances' by means of topological metaphors and spatial prepositions. For a most original (pragmatic) semantics of prepositions, see Vandeloise [1986].

3 Places and legal rules[5)]

Let us, however, not jump to theoretical conclusion, but patiently examine in what sense pictures, places, prepositions and prompts are involved in legal thinking. I concentrate on the law of obligations as it emerges from the first rules of the new Dutch Civil Code.[6)] The first article reads as follows[7)]:

> [6:1 BW] Obligations can only arise if this flows from statutory law.

Article 6:1 can probably be dubbed as the mother of semiotic riddles in the legal history of the Netherlands. To unravel its secrets, I will look at it as an icon on a lift button. The article has triggered a jurisprudential discussion that I would describe as one about prompts. In my reconstruction it centres around the places which the prepositional structure indicated by FROM points to, in order to render the proper prompt or 'localisation actantielle' towards the law of obligations. I want to point out that there are indeed two readings; one normal, one abnormal, if you like. Both readings will turn out to be feasible from a certain standpoint. Problems arise when they leave the other standpoint unaccounted for. By broadening the scope of the argument in the next section I will show the two standpoints condition each other.

The first article of Book 6 BW (on obligations) contains the very strong suggestion, right at the doorstep of the law of obligations, that there is an exclusive relationship between the emergence of obligations and statutory law (or as the Dutch text gives, 'de wet', i.e. the law in the sense of 'la loi', 'das Gesetz'). This relationship, whatever it may be, is expressed by the preposition FROM. In a 'normal' reading of the article,

5. This and the following section are, to a large extent, based on my inaugural address [1990a].
6. In 1991 a major part of the Dutch Civil Code law, especially the law of obligations, was officially replaced by a new Code, within the framework of the large postwar legal project in the Netherlands of the parliamentary restatement of the entire statutory civil law.
7. The translations given are unofficial ones, with little respect paid to the standards of comparative law. Note, in particular, that 'reasonableness and equity' is more or less a set formula in Dutch law and is, in the context of obligations, more or less equivalent to 'good faith' and 'duties of care'. Equity here does not refer to a supplementary institution of the law.

FROM is conceived of as indicating a relationship of validity. Indeed, at other places of this particular book of the Civil Code provisions are found to the effect that contracts, torts, etc. raise obligations. So at first sight, nothing is wrong: [6:1] is a sort of meta-provision establishing a hierarchical order: first the law declares that it is, itself, the 'source' of obligations, then it performs as it has declared by ruling when it is apt to ascribe obligations.

Let us, although for a moment, savour this peace of mind. Article 6:1 was supposed to put an end to the alleged ambiguities concealed in its predecessor, art. 1269 of the Civil Code (old). Those who are familiar with the French *Code civil* will recognise it:

> [LOB.1] Obligations arise either from contract or from the law (la loi).

Instead of the hierarchical model of object levels and meta-levels in Article 6:1 Civil Code with one token of FROM, [LOB.1] presents a juxtapositional one-step model, with two tokens of FROM. The reason for the 'correction' seems to be clear: art. 1269 was believed to be a contamination of two ideas: the old idea of Roman law, formulated by Gaius, that obligations can arise either 'contractu' or 'delictu', and the modern idea of Revolutionary law that only statutory law can be the source of legal consequences. The Civil Code retains only the latter idea; consequently, it determines that obligations are in order in the cases of (roughly) contract, tort, negotiorum gestio and non-indebted payments. Most lawyers think that this is a welcome improvement.

But not everybody was happy, as not everyone believed that art. 1269 Civil Code (old) was a vicious contamination or otherwise inadequate classification. There is, some lawyers say, a reading of the article which is faithful to tradition and is not contaminated by revolutionary ideology. They regard the distinction 'either from contract or from the law' as *rather* adequate, since it expresses that obligations may arise either from gettings-together which were intended to evoke legal consequences (contracts) or from more accidental harmful clashes of interests for which there should be remedies whether they are intended or not. They may point out, for instance, that it does make a difference whether parties have willfully decided to undertake an obligation or not, with regard, for instance, to questions of liability, the kind of evidence required, the burden of proof, etc. It is the legal relevancy of this distinction that statutory law may express, but in no way the distinction becomes legally relevant because statutory law expresses it. Still more is to be said, though. These lawyers think that this distinction is not only adequate, but also very relevant (as Gaius had already discovered) once you come to see that these goings-on are not just occasions to be subsumed under a statutory rule, but are themselves grounds or valid reasons for obligations. The rule could not have stated other (types of) occasions to attach obligations to, so the source of validity is in these types of facts rather than in the rule.

Now, the protagonists of art. 6:1 Civil Code may say that the antagonists are slightly muddleheaded in not making a clear-cut distinction between grounds, criteria or good reasons to ascribe obligations on the one hand and good occasions to do so on the other. Indeed, they are in good scholarly company. Aristotle taught us the difference between (i) the criteria for claiming some truth and (ii) the grounds on which something is true.[8)] We should distinguish between types of occasions for claiming and grounds for testing, as we do in understanding a phrase like [8]

[8] The dog howls; so my neighbour is ill.

The howling dog is, in all probability, a typical situation, a sign, which one has learned to interpret as sufficiently reliable to claim that the man next door is ill (pragmatic justification); usually, we do not mean that the dog's howling is the cause of his illness (semantic justification). Now, can we not make an analogy as to (valid) claims to obligatoriness and liability? Applied to the law of obligations, it comes down to this: contract, along with several other types of situations like unjust enrichment and tort, are mentioned in the law as giving sufficient reason to claim performance, liability, remedies and their ilk. For the protagonists, the FROM in art. 6:1 Civil Code suggests that statutory law is something quite different from (types of) facts in giving rise to obligations. It is the ground to found obligations on, not the occasion to claim them at. Facts are occasions, rules are grounds. So the former 'give rise' to obligations in a way different from that of the latter.

8. Cf. *Analytica posteriora* I, 13: '(...) for it is not because the planets do not twinkle that they are near, but because they are near that they do not twinkle.'

But that will not do for the antagonists[9] and the supporters of good old art. 1269. The deepest reason why they regret the loss of art. 1269 is not that the new law makes a distinction between grounds and occasions for obligations while the old one does not. The latter did, too, but in a much more adequate way: it acknowledged certain types of fact as both a proper occasion to claim and a ground to found obligations. The new law suggests that statutory law (being, as a system, the source of valid obligations) can enumerate the occasions for obligations, which it cannot. This is not because there are so many, or because they are unforeseeable, but because the source of the validity of obligations is not in the system of formal statutory law. The most such a formal rule of law can do is to provide legal subjects with a guideline of how to evaluate situations as to their consequences regarding legal obligations. Perhaps art. 1269 was a contamination, but at least it had the advantage of not closing what is necessarily open-ended: the set of types of situations where liability is in order. So the text is read as in [LOB.4]:

[LOB.4] Obligations arise either from situations like contracts or from whatever else the law as a whole requires us to evaluate in terms of civil liability.

In the 'normal' reading of art. 6:1 Civil Code, contract may give rise to obligations as being a type of situation which allows one to claim liability; but it is the formal rule of law which gives rise to obligations as providing a reason or a ground to which this claim is to be tested and to be held valid (or not, as the case may be). The FROM in art. 6:1 Civil Code is implicative: it transmits legal validity via semantic justification. This implicative FROM is to be distinguished from a merely consecutive FROM, which tells you in which type of occasion you may assume obligations pragmatically. In the 'abnormal' or at least old-fashioned reading it is the other way around: because obligations are founded in contracts, etc., the law cannot but state (consecutively) that this is the case. They see a different FROM in the law of obligations. Contracts or torts are not just types of obligation provoking situations. Better: if they are, it is because they are the very ground, the source, the reason of obligations. So why

9. They are in fact rather limited. A celebrated example is Schoordijk [1979]; in a different sense Van Dunné [1971] and Nieskens-Isphording [1991] are critical.

does the law claim that it is itself the source? Quite the opposite is true, and the law knows that. Yes, now we come to think of it: it is as if the Dutch Code is not quite sure whether it says something lawful. For is not it a bit odd, this two-staged hierarchical model of validity, in which the law first says and then does, where in general it is typical of the law to speak in a performative way, that is, to do what one says in saying what one does, in one fell swoop? Article 1269 acknowledged that obligations can arise FROM contracts on a par with the law, that is in the implicative sense, and not only the consecutive sense of FROM. Article 6:1 Civil Code kills legal thinking, and is therefore illegal (still it was enacted).

To reconcile these two 'rational' readings, we will have to determine the standpoints from which they are formulated. This will be done in section 4.

4 The Atiyah-Fried debate

Most students in jurisprudence are familiar with the Atiyah-Fried debate[10)] on the sources of contractual obligation, and they will probably agree that this is typically a debate in which every thesis can be infinitely reversed by the debaters, as they do not share the same paradigm of looking at the law. Both scholars are answering different, but perfectly legitimate questions from opposite standpoints. What I would like to do is to show that these standpoints are not just opposite, but also mutually necessary conditions. Thus, I hope to contribute to at least part of the solution of the riddle discussed in the previous section about what art. 6:1 Civil Code wants us to do when it declares that obligations only arise if this flows from formal statutory law. I will be very brief in sketching the explicit theses defended by Atiyah and Fried, to spend more (but not enough) space to the analysis of shifts in focus.

Atiyah advocates something close to the following

[AT] Contracts to do *x/y* are not binding on the single ground that there have been promises to do *x/y* from both sides. They are or become binding by virtue of unpaid-for benefits (that should be repaid), detrimental reliances (that

10. See Atiyah [1979a], [1981], [1986]; Fried [1981].

should be remedied), or (in rare cases) frustrated reasonable expectations (that should be fulfilled). So there is no gap between contracts on the one hand, torts etc. on the other.[11)]

In contrast and direct criticism to Atiyah, Fried has defended what looks like the following:

[FT] Contracts to do *x/y* are binding by virtue of the mutual promises to do *x/y* expressed by an appeal to a convention that is publicly acknowledged as undertaking an obligation. Whether unpaid-for benefits should be repaid, detrimental reliance should be remedied or frustrated expectation should be fulfilled, depends on whether there is this appeal or not. This is not to say that contracts are the only source of liability; there are others, such as torts etc.

Theses [AT] and [FT] are, to a large extent, the Anglo-American counterparts of the two readings of FROM given in section 3. The fact that [AT] mentions material parameters instead of statutory law may seem to be a vast difference at first, but this gradually fades away once one comes to ask what it is that the formal rules of the law of obligations try to regiment. Some Dutch legal scholars would go as far as holding that, indeed, the whole law of obligations comes down to regimenting undue enrichment in society, which is very close to Atiyah's view indeed. On the other hand, Atiyah comes close to the continental code when he explains that his parameters boil down to a basic legal rule of conferring property in property-owning society. The inverse readings of FROM in art. 6:1 Civil Code, as well as the inverse theses of [AT] and [FT], are to be seen as efforts to get hold of what is 'undue' and what is not in some general sense.

At the risk of overstating my point, I am inclined to think of [AT] and [FT] as the two inverse readings of the puzzling buttons in the lift. There seems to be a cogent logic in both readings. But we cannot affirm them both at the same time. We may try to make an synthesis out of [FT] and [AT] by the same trick as was applied in the case of art. 6:1 BW. That is,

11. 'To do *x/y*' is my idiom for what is exchanged in a contract: A is to do *x* in exchange for B's doing *y*, and vice versa.

we may want to distinguish, in an Aristotelian fashion, between the criteria for claiming liability and the grounds on which these claims are granted. At least what Atiyah says seems to boil down to the thesis that a contract, a promise or, for that matter, any other form of voluntary behaviour, can only be a criterion for claiming liability, not a ground for granting it. Grounds are benefits, reliances and (sometimes) reasonable expectations. However, this is too short a way around the problem. Apart from the fact that the distinction between criteria and grounds is not as undisputed as suggested, Fried would definitely not agree. Even if he were to accept the distinction itself, he would stress that the act of promising to undertake some obligation, is both: apart from a criterion to claim liability (appeal to a convention), it is also the very ground for being bound by the promise. We have to take the unorthodox way. At least some coherence will be restored, once we detect several places to stand in the picture drawn by [FT] and [AT].

4.1 Internal-external

Atiyah grounds his approach by making a distinction between an internal and an external perspective on contractual obligation. I want to show that the meaning of these prepositional terms shifts in the course of his argument, till it comes close to something that Fried must have had in mind. On the other hand, to lay out what Fried had in mind we will have to appeal to something very close to Atiyah's concern. Thus, I will argue, the two perspectives evoke each other without ever converging into one.

In an explicit statement Atiyah affirms that the external perspective has to do with the function which the making of a contract or, for that matter, a promise, has in society, and with the social mechanisms which guarantee that one will usually comply with it. These functions and mechanisms can be referred to as: reliability, both as a condition and as an effect of social co-operation. This social context [1981: 122ff) has to be taken into account if we want to answer the question whether a certain promise is binding or not. Atiyah thinks that it is nonsense

> '(...) to discuss the source of the (...) obligation to perform a promise without having some regard to the question *why* promises are given, and *why* they are (normally) performed' [1981: 143].

The answer to these *why's* is: Promises are usually given in order to encourage people to act in reliance on them, and they are usually performed because in the long run it is in the interest of the promisor to do so and to pose as a reliable co-person.

Atiyah distinguishes this external point of view from the internal one: the point of view of those who think that the point of moral reflection is to help people in finding a guiding principle to answer the question 'what is the right thing to do', for instance whether and when it is right to keep one's promise. The internal point of view is that of 'the moral sense of the individual', the individual who asks herself what she should do in order to act morally or legally right. Atiyah is willing to concede that there is some truth in saying that conventions are not to be regarded externally from their own perspective:

> 'They arise from the moral sense of individuals who make up society, and in that sense they can be said to have an internal element.' [1981: 124]

But this truth cannot exempt us from referring to the global purpose and practice of the convention of promising in giving an account of why and when promises or contracts are binding. In Atiyah's view, the law's perspective is primarily the external one.

What Atiyah seems to aim at in opposing internal and external points of view is the (relative) opposition between the social and the individual. That is, at least, what the quotations given above suggest. But then we should object that this opposition, even if relative, is not construed in a philosophically adequate way. It is not construed from one and the same point of view itself, nor made in one and the same respect. From the very start Atiyah conceives of the individual as practical, and of the social as theoretical: the individual person who asks herself 'what should I do?' in opposition to the functions and mechanisms that could be traced by a theory of society as a union 'with more than one person' [1981: 126] with regard to causes and effects of social co-operation. This makes the distinction inadequate. In order to construe it consistently, Atiyah would have to make a choice as to how to conceive of both the individual and the social: either as practical or as theoretical. If we presume that what he meant to analyse was the individual and the social in a practical perspective, than he should have conceived of society as a union 'with more than *the first* person'.

Is this philosophical scholasticism? It is not. What is at stake is an impossible confusion of viewpoints. One may admit that in order to judge the binding force of a promise or a contract one has to take into account the effectivity and functionality of a certain convention which is used to express and to generate reliability. But not in the relationship between promisor and promisee. A promisor cannot mortgage his promise by stipulating that he will perform by virtue of the expectation that the convention which underlies his promising will have the effect that is described to it by a theory of society: reliability in social co-operation. He who appeals to the convention of promising implies, and has (on demand) to give proof of, the presupposition that he does not do so for strategic reasons alone. By 'strategic reasons' I mean: reasons which acknowledge the convention precisely *in as far as* the rationale of the convention is or will be in force. This is to say in the case of promising: in as far as it is true that social co-operation will be furthered by the appeal to the convention. In the very case that a person would make it clear (in advance) that the performance of his promise will be dependent on what the world (the promise convention included) will look like at the time of the expected execution, she would disqualify herself as one who can be relied upon in social co-operation. Thus, the promisor cannot practically use in his promising what he himself theoretically knows about promising (although he can use it, for instance, in the choice to make a particular promise or not, or not to make any promise ever at all. For conventions and institutions there is a general rule that says: they are only useful if we do not ask about their use at the very moment we appeal to them. That is why there are conflicting points of view built into Atiyah's primary opposition between the internal and the external perspective. And that, by the way, is what Fried has emphasised in a different context when he said:

> 'In general we can get the social, collective benefits of trust only if we are faithful for the sake of trust itself, not just for the sake of the resulting benefits.' [1981: 83]

It is not surprising, then, that we observe Atiyah gliding into a different idiom regarding the internal-external distinction. Indeed, his own distinction seems to 'prompt' him to adopt a different standpoint, and he gradually assumes the practical approach for both terms: the individual and the social. At the outset, as we have seen, the external perspective regarded the preservation OF society as the effect of certain mechanisms such as contract and promise. But not long after that announcement the meaning of the preposition 'of' is changed from an objective to a subjective genitive, bringing the practical point of view into the open. Society is not only what is in fact preserved, it is also what does the preserving, perceiving *self*-preservation as *the right thing to do*. But that, remember, was the internal point of view! In spite of his belief that law takes the external standpoint, Atiyah is prompted to take the internal one in giving an account of society as an *instance* that is permitted to set the rules which it deems appropriate to its preservation. It is up to society (or the law in general) to set the conditions of behaviour that will generate obligations.

> 'Obligations within the social group *can* just be created because the social group is in charge of the rules of the group, and does just create the rules. Since the rules are designed for regulating the relations between members of the group, it is natural for the group to create the rules. The position of the individual thus differs from that of the group. He cannot just create moral rules and moral obligations by what he does, because he is not in charge of relations between himself and other members of the group.' [1981: 129]

Atiyah leaves the shift of the theoretical to the practical viewpoint implicit until chapter 7 of his [1981]. Or so it seems. There he introduces the internal-external distinction once more, this time - as he himself points out - to take the internal point of view in Hart's sense. Hart [1961: 86ff] used the term 'internal' to indicate the practical perspective of those who participate in creating, obeying and applying the law, and who have to ask themselves constantly what would be (legally) the right thing to do? But once we are under the strong impression that Atiyah has restored the coherence of his argument, the argument lapses into yet another distinction underneath 'internal' and 'external': this time he aims at the difference between an objective, i.e. valid, versus a subjective claim to being bound.

> 'From this, internal viewpoint, we can see that the promise is not the *reason* for the obligation, any more than the judge's decision is *to him* a reason for the law which he declares. The oddity is that the promisor is himself the judge, but he also retains his character as a promisor. Thus, having in his capacity as judge conclusively determined what is beneficial, and how much it is worth, etc., he thereafter becomes bound, in his capacity as promisor, by his own decision as judge. Hence, the external viewpoint may become appropriate even for the promisor himself, once he has made a promise.' [1981: 201]

This last point, the objectifiability of intentions, may well be the point which it is all about.

4.2 Perspectivism

Globally, an intention is the first-person perspective of practical thinking, i.e. the perspective of some person asking herself: What am I to do? If one promises to do x, one does not only form and utter an intention to do x, one also claims the objectifiability of what one is to do. By objectifiability I mean to baptise a set of perhaps very different predicates such as 'realisability', 'desirability', 'permissibility', 'predictability', 'reliability', etc. These are - at least in different cases - all aspects of what amounts to the promised acting being right, apt, valid or justified.[12)] Now it is self-contradictory to make a claim to objectifiability and to intend, at the same time so to speak, to establish the standards that will be used in deciding whether the claim should be granted or not. Testing one's own preferences against one's own preferred standards is no testing at all. One who claims objectifiability for his intention has to acknowledge a certain authority from the point of view of a 'third person' to decide on the validity of his intention. By 'third person' I mean the perspective that a first person as an actor has to acknowledge if and when he makes a claim regarding the validity of his intention towards some other person, i.e. a second person. As soon as he makes that claim he acknowledges (i) that he himself does not determine the testing conditions and (ii) that these testing conditions are not even determined by a deal between him and a second person (as in the case of consensus). For the first person, this counterperspective has the form of an instance of judging. The third-person instance is recognized by the first person as one that holds the standards for what counts as an adequate practical interpretation, i.e., an adequate compliance with the promise.[13)] From the first-person perspec-

12. That I use the word 'objectifiability' instead of justifiability finds no reason in this chapter, but in a more embracing context where I relate alethic and deontic objectifiability to each other. See Van Roermund [1990d, ch.4].

13. That is why the analysis of a promise as an intention to do something plus the intention not to change that first intention, makes no sense: there is no third-person perspective recognized.

tive, the promise is the source for claiming validity, the third-person standards, however, are the source for testing and deciding on the claim, and recognising or ascribing validity of what was promised - to return to our main line of argument.

So far Atiyah seems to be right as far as his primary thesis AT is concerned. But chances reverse quickly when we discover that the one who has to decide from the third-person perspective, is - from his own perspective - a first person, too; that is, one who - by deciding on the claim - makes a claim himself, which, by necessity, has to be found valid by reference to standards he did not set himself. Indeed, 'Society is in charge of the rules of society' - as Atiyah would like to have it - only up to a certain point. At least two problems emerge with this formula. Firstly, there will only be rules of society if society takes on the form of a law-enacting body that can be 'in charge'. This requires a theory of authorization and representation, which we will neglect at this point. Secondly, and more importantly in this context, for this law-enacting body the question to answer in deciding on the claims before it is exactly the same question as that which Atiyah dubbed the internal-individual question: What is the right thing to do in a certain situation? The perspective of that question is surely internal, but by no means individual. That is to say, it is again - but this time for the instance that gives a ruling - the viewpoint of the first person, more particularly the first person-in-action, who asks herself what she is to do and has to find her way blindfoldedly, without a guarantee in advance.[14)] From the practical perspective of the legislator or the judge, the obligation that follows from certain types of facts is a normative ascription that cannot be justified merely from the point of view of the legislator or the judge. Even if society can be conceived of as a body that is 'in charge', it cannot be conceived of as a body that can attach obligations to facts *arbitrarily*. This, I submit, is the reason that explains both why Fried's thesis [FT] has a plausibility which seems equal to that of [AT] and why Atiyah constantly shifts the ground of the argument in defending [AT].

14. Cf. Wittgenstein, *Philos. Invest.*, par. 219: 'I obey the rule blindly.' What he meant - or said, if you want to argue for a wrong translation here - was rather: blindfoldedly. Then his statement comes in line with what is said in the famous conversation between Lyotard and Thébaut, *Au juste*, p. 30: 'On juge sans critère. On est dans la position du prudent aristotélicien qui juge du juste et de l'injuste sans critère.'

Of course Atiyah could try to fight perspectivism by saying: 'Right. To avoid arbitrariness in attaching obligations to certain types of fact, the criteria of unpaid-for benefit and detrimental reliance come into play in the first place.' But that seems a little too short as a defence. *Why* do benefit and reliance come into play as non-arbitrary criteria for being bound? We may answer like Atiyah would do: because there is a general rule of law in 'property-owning society', which says that a duty of care is in place where one actor has made, or tends to make, another actor dependent on him as far as the latter's property is concerned. Sometimes (not always) one is held liable, for instance when one has enriched oneself at the expense of another or has done harm to another; also when one has performed in exchange for the other to perform and the performance of the latter is still executory, or when one has relied in good faith on the promise of another that he would perform his part of the deal. But this is not enough. Unpaid-for benefits and detrimental reliance are not always sufficient grounds to make someone liable, unless he is a party to a contract. To judge whether liability is in order, the law looks at these situations from specific points of view, especially what parties wanted, what they already performed in exchange, but sometimes also what they can take. It monitors indications to the effect that parties have made it clear more or less explicitly that in property they *wanted* to be dependent on each other. The mere fact that parties wanted to be dependent on each other in this particular respect is for the law-enacting or law-applying authorities one of the very good reasons to say that a claim to obligation is really valid. From the perspective of the legal authority the dependence wanted is a sufficient ground for obligation and, indeed, a ground for ascribing validity, not just a criterion for claiming validity. Like Barnett [1986] and Atiyah I would think that this wanting phenomenologically amounts to different forms of assent and consent.

Now Fried may interrupt to cash his cheque and say: 'Right. The promise and the consent of parties, the one towards the other, the meeting of wills, the consent to the offer, this is all not only a reason to claim obligation, but a ground for acknowledging the justifiability of the obligation in a contract, apart from unjust enrichments and torts.' But that alleged victory is also a short one. I did not say that the will of the parties can create obligations from its own perspective as the will of the parties. It can only claim the validity of such an obligation, anticipating - to the best of its knowledge - the grounds of validity regarding (freely accepted) dependence of properties, which it, by necesssity, is not to determine itself.

This is not to say that the obligations of the parties cannot be cancelled as long as the contract is wholly executory (like Fried and Atiyah both acknowledge). This is obvious, since in these cases *sometimes* dependence of property will not be strong yet. It is, on the other hand, also not to say that where the agreement of wills ends, the contract also has to end, and principles of tort and unjust enrichment have to come in to regiment legal consequences (as Fried believes) because there is no contract any more. That would amount to saying that the law of contract by definition has to do with contracts that are valid without any problem. To repeat: Making a contract is, from the perspective of the parties, to claim a specific, legal relationship, anticipating grounds of validity that, in the final analysis, one has not to determine as parties. When that relationship shipwrecks on certain grounds of validity that turn out not to be fulfilled (e.g., in the case of error or *imprévision*), this does not mean that the relationship was not claimed and that it is not still the primary perspective from where to look for a solution. That is precisely what the judge does.

4.3 Prompting

Now the ground is prepared to look at the law of obligations as an icon. It invites us to answer to a prompt where we have to locate ourselves with regard to obligations. Either we are one of the parties that wants to undertake an obligation; and then we start by appealing to the convention of promising or some equivalent form of social behaviour and anticipate society's standards for the adequacy of our mutual performances. Or we are in the position of the judge; then we start with the rationale of the convention and anticipate the good reasons parties may have had to be mutually dependent in matters of property. Whatever position we take, the position we do not take is the one that is to be responded to. It is like the indexical references of here and there: as soon as our position changes form here to there, there becomes here. And note that there is no middle ground between here and there! As a party to a contract we primarily have to act in response to the question of what a judge would say who is in charge of upholding the societal standards of undue enrichment; as a judge of the contract we primarily have to decide in response to the question what the parties involved consented to. I add 'primarily', because it is clear that this perspectivism entails an infinite reflection of mirror images of hypotheses. To decide in response to what the parties involved consented to is to decide in response to what these parties consented to in an alleged effort to act in response to what a judge would say ..., etc. This, I think, is fine: it grounds the view that, in the final analysis, law is a matter of a special sort of politics: one that is open to acknowledging in advance the standpoint of the other as counting against one.

The consequences of this view are perhaps rather shocking. Let me just mention two of them, neither of which will be argued for in detail. The first is that, since making claims is a matter of discourse and speech acts, and justifying claims is a matter of practical thinking, the level of speech acts and the level of practical thinking become intertwined without either one losing its distinctive character. There is no once-and-for-all distinction between what counts as criteria for making the claim and what counts as grounds to grant the claim: these two change places when we change places. The second consequence is that it becomes pointless to look for a conceptual 'synthesis' between theses like [AT] and [FT]. There isn't any. Their opposition is not of a propositional, but of a prepositional kind: it is a difference of places which is already decided on before any propositions are put forward. These places determine what references we can make, which references we can intercept and which of our references are intercepted.

EPILOGUE

The title of this book is purposively ambiguous. It can be read as either a classical summation of topics for discussion, or as a thumbnail sketch of the main issue of the book: law as both narrative and reality. Let me confess that, for a change, the second reading would be better than the first one. Indeed, with kind regards to Heidegger, the emphasis was not so much on either law, or narrative, or reality, as it was on the word 'and'. How can law be conceived of as both narrative and reality, without there being a synthesis to warrant the mediation between the two poles?

It is sometimes objected that, without such a theoretical warrant, mediation would come down to sheer decisionism. Decisionism would be the view that conflicts in society can and should only end by whatever decision those in power take, which would, allegedly, imply arbitrariness and tyranny. Now quite apart from the question whether the use of power is compatible with arbitrariness and tyranny if only for a short period of time, my hypothesis heads towards a different notion of decision. I agree that conflicts in society cannot always be solved by agreement and that they have to be ended by authoritative decision. But I have tried to show that such decisions, which the representatives of the law are called upon to take, are stretched between the poles of narrative and reality, and that this is how they mediate between them. There is, I have showed, mediation without a warranting synthesis, by virtue of political decisions that give an account of a society's identity in terms that convey self-imposed self-restraint rather than making this identity the only thing that counts. These forms of self-restraint, and nothing more pretentious, are what I mean by the law.

BIBLIOGRAPHY

Aarnio, A.: 1979a
Denkweisen der Rechtswissenschaft. Einführung in die Theorie der rechtswissenschaftlichen Forschung (Forschungen aus Staat und Recht, 48), Wien-New York, Springer.

Aarnio, A.: 1979b
Linguistic Philosophy and Legal Theory. Some Problems of Legal Argumentation. In: W.J. Krawietz et al. (eds.), *Argumentation und Hermeneutik in der Jurisprudenz*, Berlin, Duncker und Humblot, pp. 17-42.

Aarnio, A.: 1981
On Truth and the Acceptability of Interpretative Propositions in Legal Dogmatics. In: A. Aarnio et al. (eds.), *Methodologie und Erkenntnistheorie der juristischen Argumentation*, Berlin, Duncker und Humblot, pp. 33-52.

Aarnio, A.: 1987
The Rational as Reasonable. A Treatise on Legal Justification. Dordrecht, Reidel.

Aristoteles: 1975
The Metaphysics (The Loeb Classical Library). Cambridge (Mass.), Harvard University Press - London, Heineman.

Adorno, Th.W.: 1966
Negative Dialektik. Frankfurt a.M., Suhrkamp.

Atiyah, P.: 1979a
The Rise and Fall of Freedom of Contract. Oxford, Clarendon Press.

Atiyah, P.S.: 1979b
Promises and the Law of Contract. In: *Mind*, 88, pp. 410-418.

Atiyah, P.: 1981
Promises, Morals and Law. London, Oxford University Press.

Atiyah, P.: 1986
Essays on Contract. Oxford, Oxford University Press.

Austin, J.L.: 1962
How to do things with words (The William James Lectures delivered at Harvard University in 1955). Ed. by J.O. Urmson. Oxford, Clarendon Press.

Baker, G.P. and P.M.S. Hacker: 1984
Critical Study: On Misunderstanding Wittgenstein: Kripke's Private Language Argument. In: *Synthese*, 58, pp. 407-450.

Bal, M.: 1980
Narratologie. De theorie van vertellen en verhalen. Muiderberg, Coutinho.

Barnett, R. E.: 1986
A Consent Theory of Contract. In: *Columbia Law Rev.*, 86, pp. 269-321.

Baudrillard, J.: 1977
Oublier Foucault. Paris, Galilée.

Bellingen, J. van: 1985
Diskriminierung und Gleichheit als rechtsphilosophisches Problem bei Carl Schmitt. In: F. de Pauw and M. Weyembergh (eds.), *Gelijkheid en conservatisme/Gleichheit und Konservatismus* (Serie Rechtsfilosofie en rechtstheorie, 4), Zwolle, Tjeenk Willink, pp. 163-192.

Benda, E.: 1983
Die Menschenwürde. In: E. Benda, W. Maihofer and H.J. Vogel (eds.), *Handbuch des Verfassungsrechts der Bundesrepublik Deutschland*, Berlin-New York, De Gruyter, pp. 107-128.

Bergh, G.C.J.J. van den, and J.M. Broekman: 1979
Recht en taal. Deventer, Kluwer.

Black, J.M.: 1980
Lebensform and Sprachspiel in Wittgenstein's Later Work. In E. Leinfellner e.a. (eds.), *Wittgenstein and His Impact on Contemporary Thought.* Wien, Schriftenreihe der Wittgenstein-Gesellschaft, pp. 325-331.

Blanpain, R.: 1977
De Belgische arbeidsverhoudingen: een momentopname van 'tripartisme' in perspectief. In: *Dertig jaar Belgische arbeidsverhoudingen*, Deventer, Kluwer, pp. 69-86.

Bourdieu, P.: 1982
Ce que parler veut dire, l'économie des échanges linguistiques. Paris, Fayard.

Bratman, M.: 1983
Castaneda's theory of thought and action. In: J. Tomberlin (ed.), *Agent, Language and the Structure of the World. Essays presented to H.-N. Castaneda, with his replies.* Indianapolis, Hackett Publishing Company, pp. 149-169.

Brint, M., and W. Weaver (eds.): 1991
Pragmatism in Law and Society. Boulder, Westview Press.

Broekman, J.M.: 1971
Strukturalismus. Moskau--Prag--Paris. München, Karl Alber.

Broekman, J.M.: 1973
Recht en structuralisme. In: *Rechtsfilosofie en Rechtstheorie*, 2, pp. 1-46.

Broekman, J.M.: 1978
Sprechakt und Intersubjektivität. In: B. Waldenfels et al. (eds.), *Phänomenologie und Marxismus*, Frankfurt, Suhrkamp, Vol. 3, pp. 66-114.

Broekman, J.M.: 1980
Juristischer Diskurs und Rechtstheorie. In: *Rechtstheorie*, 11, pp. 17-46.

Broekman, J.M.: 1982a [1979]
Recht en antropologie. Antwerpen, Standaard Wetenschappelijke Uitgeverij.

Broekman, J.M.: 1982b
Der juristischer Diskurs. In: *ARSP*, Suppl. Vol. 1,2, pp. 123-127.
Broekman, J.M.: 1993
Recht, rechtsfilosofie en rechtstheorie. Antwerpen, Kluwer.
Broekman, J.M., and A.C. 't Hart: 1980
Normverleggend gedrag en justitieel beleid. Leuven, Acco - Zwolle, Tjeenk Willink.
Cappelletti, M.: 1982
Accès à la justice: comme programme de réforme et comme méthode de pensée. In: *Windsor Yearbook of Access to Justice*, 2, pp. 193-208.
Cappelletti, M. and Garth, B.: 1970
Access to Justice: The World-Wide Movement to Make Rights Effective; A General Report. In: M. Cappelletti and Br. Garth (eds.), *Access to Justice*, vol. I, *A world survey*, Book I, Alphen a/d Rijn-Milan, pp. 1-124.
Carrole, L.: 1865 [1954]
Alice in Wonderland & Through the Looking-Glass and Other Writings. London, Collins.
Castañeda, H.-N.: 1974
Thinking and the Structure of the World. Discours d'ontologie. In: *Philosophia*, 4, pp. 3-40.
Castañeda, H.-N.: 1975
Thinking and Doing: The Philosophical Foundations of Institutions. Dordrecht-Boston, Reidel.
Castañeda, H.-N.: 1979
Fiction and Reality: Their Fundamental Connections. An Essay on the Ontology of Total Experience. In: *Poetics*, 8, pp. 31-62 (renewed version in Castañeda (1989)).
Castañeda, H.-N.: 1980
On Philosophical Method. s.l., Indiana University Publications.
Castañeda, H.-N.: 1982a
Sprache und Erfahrung. Texte zu einer neuen Ontologie. Eingeleitet und übers. v. H. Pape, Frankfurt a.M., Suhrkamp.
Castañeda, H.-N.: 1982b
Deontic Logic as a Tool for the Analysis of Institutions. In: *Epistemologia*, 5, pp. 27-56.
Castañeda, H.-N.: 1984
Ought, Reasons, Motivations, and the Unity of the Social Sciences: The Metatheory of the Ought-Is Problem. In: A. Peczenik - L. Lindahl - B. van Roermund (eds.), *Theory of Legal Science*. Dordrecht - Boston - Lancaster, Reidel, pp. 71-96.

Castañeda, H.-N.: 1988
The Semantics of Thinking, Dia-Philosophical Pluralism, and Guise Theory. In: *Metaphilosophy*, 19, pp. 79-104.

Castañeda, H.-N.: 1989
Thinking, Language and Experience. Minneapolis, University of Minnesota Press.

Chamberlain, D.F.: 1990
Narrative in Fiction. A Phenomenological Mediation of Reader, Text and World. Toronto, University of Toronto Press.

Cohen, M. (ed.): 1984
Ronald Dworkin and Contemporary Jurisprudence. London, Duckworth.

Compagnon, A.: 1979
La seconde main, ou la travail de citation, Paris, Seuil.

Cover, R.: 1983 [1992]
Nomos and Narrative. In: M. Minow et al. (eds.), *Narrative, Violence, and the Law*, Ann Arbor, University of Michigan Press (original in *Harvard Law Review*).

Crombag, H.F.M., P.J. van Koppen, and W.A. Wagenaar: 1992
Dubieuze zaken: de psychologie van strafrechtelijk bewijs. Amsterdam, Contact.

Culler, J.: 1981
The Pursuit of Signs: Semiotics, Literature, Deconstruction. Ithaca (NY), Cornell University Press.

Culler, J.: 1983
On Deconstruction. Theory and Criticism after Structuralism. London, Henley.

Debray, R.: 1981
Critique de la raison politique. Paris, Gallimard.

De Man, P.: 1979a
The Epistemology of Metaphor. In: Sh. Sacks (ed.), *On Metaphor*, London, University of Chicago Press, pp. 11-28.

De Man, P.: 1979b
Allegories of Reading. Figural Language in Rousseau, Nietzsche, Rilke and Proust. New Haven-London, Yale University Press.

Derrida, J., 1972
Marges de la philosophie (Coll. 'Critique'), Paris, Minuit.

Derrida, J. et. al.: 1985
Préjugés. Devant la loi. In: J. Derrida et al. *La Faculté de juger,* Paris, Minuit, pp. 87-139.

Diederiks, H.A., and H.W. Roodenburg (eds.): 1991
Misdaad, zoen en straf: aspekten van de middeleeuwse strafrechtsgeschiedenis in de Nederlanden. Hilversum, Verloren.

Donner, A.M.: 1986
Over representatie. In: *Tussen het echte en het gemaakte.* Zwolle, Tjeenk Willink, pp. 107-116.
Döpke, W., and Schwarze, Chr.: 1981
Le role des prépositions locales dans la constitution sémantique de la phrase. In: Chr. Schwarze (ed.), *Analyse des prépositions*, Tübingen, Niemeyer Verlag, pp. 19-28.
Dunné, J. van: 1971
Normatieve uitleg van rechtshandelingen, een onderzoek naar de grondslagen van het geldende verbintenissenrecht. Deventer, Kluwer.
Dworkin, R.M.: 1977a
Taking Rights Seriously. London, Duckworth.
Dworkin, R.: 1977b
No Right Answer? In: P.M.S. Hacker and J. Raz (eds.), *Law, Morality and Society, Essays in Honour of H.L.A. Hart.* Oxford, Oxford University Press, pp. 58-84.
Dworkin, R.: 1983a
Law as Interpretation. In: W.J.T. Mitchell (ed.), *The Politics of Interpretation,* Chicago, The University of Chicago Press, pp. 287-314.
Dworkin, R.: 1983b
My Reply to Stanley Fish (and Walter Benn Michaels): Please Don't Talk about Objectivity Any More. In: W.J.T. Mitchell (ed.), *The Politics of Interpretation.* Chicago - London, University of Chicago Press, pp. 287-314.
Dworkin, R.: 1985
A Matter of Principle. Cambridge (Mass.), Harvard University Press.
Dworkin, R.: 1986
Law's Empire. London, Fontana.
Eggens, J.: 1950 [1959]
De bronnen van verbintenis. In: *Verzamelde privaatrechtelijke opstellen*, Alphen a.d. Rijn, Samsom, pp. 236-256.
Engisch, K.: 1957
Einführung in das juristische Denken. Stuttgart, Kohlhammer.
Erp, J.H.M.: 1990
Contract als rechtsbetrekking. Een rechtsvergelijkende studie. Zwolle, Tjeenk Willink.
Esser, J.: 1970
Vorverständnis und Methodenwahl in der Rechtsfindung. Rationalitätsgarantien der richterlichen Entscheidungspraxis. Frankfurt a.M., Athenäum Verlag.
Esser, J.: 1972
Möglichkeiten und Grenzen des dogmatischen Denkens im modernen Zivilrecht. In: *Archiv für civilistische Praxis*, 172, pp. 97-130.

Esser, J.: 1974
Dogmatik zwischen Theorie und Praxis. In: Fr. Baus et al. (eds.), *Funktionswandel der Privatrechtsinstitutionen* (Festschrift L. Raiser), Tübingen, Mohr, pp. 517-539.

Esser, J.: 1979
Juristisches Argumentieren im Wandel des Rechtsfindungskonzepts unseres Jahrhunderts. Sitzungsbericht der Heidelberger Akademie der Wissenschaften, Philosophisch-historische Klasse, 1979, 1. Heidelberg.

Ewald, Fr.: 1986a
L'État providence. Paris, Grasset.

Ewald, Fr.: 1986b
A Concept of Social Law. In: G. Teubner (eds.), *Dilemmas of Law in the Welfare State*, Berlin, De Gruyter, pp. 40-75.

Fish, S.: 1983
Working on the Chain Gang: Interpretation in the Law and in Literary Criticism. In: W.J.T. Mitchell (ed.), *The Politics of Interpretation.* Chicago - London, University of Chicago Press, pp. 271-286.

Fish, S.: 1989
Doing What Comes Naturally. Oxford, University Press.

Foqué, R.: 1987
Het belang van het recht. In: *Recht en legitimiteit* (Serie Rechtstheorie 5), Zwolle, Tjeenk Willink.

Foqué, R., and J. van Bellingen: 1985
Juridisch conservatisme en concreet en ordeningsdenken. In: F. de Pauw and M. Weyembergh (eds.), *Gelijkheid en Conservatisme/Gleichheit und Konservatismus*, (Serie Rechtsfilosofie en Rechtstheorie, 4), Zwolle, pp. 1983-210.

Foqué, R., and G. van der Wal: 1988
La situation exceptionelle en procès. In: *Rev. interdisc. d'études juridiques*, Numéro spécial anniversaire 1978-1988, pp. 63-84.

Foqué, R., and A.C. Hart: 1990
Instrumentaliteit en rechtsbescherming. Grondslagen van een strafrechtelijke waardendiscussie. Arnhem, Gouda Quint - Antwerpen, Kluwer Rechtswetenschappen.

Forster, E.M.: 1927 [1974]
Aspects of the Novel and Related Writings. London, E. Arnold.

Foucault, M.: 1975
Surveiller et punir, naissance de la prison. Paris, Gallimard, Bibliotheque des histoires.

Foucault, M.: 1976
La Volonté de savoir. Histoire de la sexualité I. Paris, Gallimard.

Fried, Ch.: 1981
Contract as Promise. A Theory of Contractual Obligation. Cambridge (Mass.)-London, Harvard University Press.

Freud, S.: 1913 [1944]
Totem und Tabu, IV: Die infantile Widerkehr des Totemismus. In: *Gesammelte Werke*, Bd IX. Frankfurt a.M., Fischer, pp. 122-194.

Freud, S.: 1918 [1969]
Aus der Geschichte einer infantilen Neurose [Der Wolfsmann] (1918 [1914]). In: *Studienausgabe*, hrsg. v. A. Mitscherlich u.a., Vol. VIII, Frankfurt, Fischer.

Frommel, M.: 1981
Die Rezeption der Hermeneutik bei Karl Larenz und Josef Esser (Münchener Universitätsschriften, Jur. Fak. Abhandlungen zur rechtsw. Grundlagenforschung, Vol. 47), Ebelsbach, Gremer.

Gadamer, H.G.: 1975
Wahrheit und Methode. Grundzüge einer philosophischen Hermeneutik. 3. erw. Aufl., Tübingen, Mohr/Siebeck.

Galston, M.: 1994
Taking Aristotle Seriously: Republican-Oriented Legal Theory and Moral Foundation of Deliberative Democracy. In: *California Law Review*, 82, pp. 329-399.

Gerhardt, V.: 1983
Das 'Prinzip des Gleichgewichts', zum Verhältnis von Recht und Macht bei Nietzsche. In: *Nietzsche Studien*, 12, pp. 111-133.

Giese, B.: 1975
Das Würde-Konzept. Eine normfunktionale Explikation des Begriffes 'Würde' in Art. 1 Abs. 1 Gg (Schriften zur Rechtstheorie, 45), Berlin, Duncker und Humblot

Habermas, J., 1992
Faktizität und Geltung. Beiträge zur Diskurstheorie des Rechts und des demokratischen Rechtsstaats. 2. Aufl., Frankfurt a. M., Suhrkamp.

Hart, A.C. 't: 1979
Recht en staat in het denken van Giambattista Vico. Alphen a.d. Rijn, H.D. Tjeenk Willink, diss. Leuven 1978.

Hart, A.C. 't: 1983
Strafrecht en beleid. Essays. Leuven, Acco - Zwolle,Tjeenk Willink.

Hart, A.C. 't: 1991
Recht als schild van Perseus. Voordrachten over strafrechtstheorie. Arnhem, Gouda Quint - Antwerpen, Kluwer Rechtswetenschappen.

Hart, H.L.A.: 1961
The Concept of Law. Oxford, Oxford University Press.

Haverkate, G.: 1977
Gewissheitsverluste im juristischen Denken, zur politischen Funktion der juristischen Methode (Schriften zur Rechtstheorie, 73), Berlin, Duncker und Humblot.

Hegel, G.W.F.: 1827 [1989]
Enzyklopädie der philosophischen Wissenschaften im Grundrisse. Hamburg, Meiner.

Hegel, G.W.F.: 1821 [1955]
Grundlinien der Philosophie des Rechts. In: J. Hoffmeister (eds.), *Gesammelte Werke,* 4, Hamburg, Meiner.

Heijden, E.J.J. van der: 1928
De toerekenbare schijn en de bronnen der verbintenis. Haarlem, Erven F. Bohn.

Herberger, M.: 1981
Dogmatik, Zur Geschichte von Begriff und Methode in Medizin und Jurisprudenz. Frankfurt, Ius Commune, 12, Klostermann.

Hobbes, Th.: 1973
Leviathan (Everyman's Library). Introd. by K.R. Minogue, London-New York.

Hubmann, H.: 1967
Das Persönlichkeitsrecht. Köln-Graz, Böhlau.

Jackson, B.S.: 1985
Semiotics and Legal Theory. London, Routledge and Kegan Paul.

Jackson, B.S.: 1988
Law, Fact and Narrative Coherence (Legal Semiotics Monographs, 1), Roby, Deborah Charles Publications.

Jhering, R. von: 1924 [1980]
Scherz und Ernst in der Jurisprudenz. Darmstadt, WBG.

Kalmthout, A.M. van, and P.J.P. Tak: 1988-1992
Sanctions-systems in the Member-States of the Council of Europe. Deprivation of Liberty, Community Service and Other Substitutes (2 vols.). Deventer - Boston, Kluwer Law and Taxation Publishers.

Kalmthout, A. M. van: 1996
Death on Request: The Dutch Approach. In: *Revue internationale de droit pénale/International Review of Penal Law,* 67: (forthcoming).

Kant, I.: 1797/1798 [1975]
Die Metaphysik der Sitten. In: *Werke,* Vol. 7, Darmstadt, WBG.

Kaufmann, M.: 1988
Recht ohne Regel? Philosophische Prinzipien in Carl Schmitts Staats- und Rechtslehre. Freiburg, Alber.

Kelsen, H.: 1926
Zur Soziologie der Demokratie. In: *WRS,* pp. 1729-1741.

Kelsen, H.: 1927
Demokratie. In: *WRS*, pp. 1743-1776.
Kelsen, H.: 1929
Wesen und Entwicklung der Staatsgerichtsbarkeit. In: *WRS*, pp. 1813-1871.
Kelsen, H.: 1931
Wer soll der Hüter der Verfassung sein? In: *WRS*, pp. 1873-1922.
Kelsen, H.: 1933
Staatsform und Weltanschauung. In: *WRS*, pp. 1923-1942.
Kelsen, H.: 1932 [1967]
Verteidigung der Demokratie. In: N. Leser (ed.), *Demokratie und Sozialismus. Ausgewählte Aufsätze*, Wien, Verlag der Wiener Volksbuchhandlung, pp. 60-68.
Kelsen, H.: 1960 [1976]
Reine Rechtslehre. Mit einem Anhang: Das Problem der Gerechtigkeit. Wien, Deuticke.
Kelsen, H.: 1979
Algemeine Theorie der Normen. K. Ringhofer and R. Walter (eds.), Wien, Manz.
Kelsen, H., Merkl, A., and A. Verdross: 1968
Die Wiener Rechtstheoretische Schule (WRS). Wien, 2, Europa Verlag.
Kriele, M.: 1983
Freiheit und Gleichheit. In: E. Benda et al. (eds.), *Handbuch der Verfassungsrechts der Bundesrepublik Deutschland*, Berlin, De Gruyter, pp. 129-167.
Köndgen, J.: 1981
Selbstbindung ohne Vertrag. Zur Haftung aus geschäftsbezogenem Handeln. Tübingen, Mohr.
Krawietz, W.: 1984
Recht als Regelsystem. Darmstadt, Wissenschaftliche Buchgesellschaft.
Kripke, S.: 1982
Wittgenstein on Rules and Private Language. An Elementary Exposition. Oxford, Blackwell.
Kruithof, R.: 1986
Leven en dood van het contract. In: *Rechtskundig Weekblad*, pp. 2731-2768.
Ladeur, K.-H.: 1990
From the Deductive to the Argumentative Rationality of Law. In: P. Nerhot (ed.), *Law, Interpretation and Reality. Essays in Epistemology, Hermeneutics and Jurisprudence*, Dordrecht, Kluwer, Academic Publishers, pp. 169-192.
Landowski, E.: 1988
Toward a Semiotic and Narrative Approach to Law. In: *International Journal for the Semiotics of Law*, 1, pp. 79-106.

Langemeijer, G.E.: 1973
Inleiding tot de studie van de wijsbegeerte des rechts. Zwolle, Tjeenk Willink.

Larenz, K.: 1979
Methodenlehre der Rechtswissenschaft. 4, Aufl., Berlin, Springer.

LaTorre, M.: 1990
Degenerated Law. Jurists and Nazism. In: *Ratio Juris*, 3, pp. 95-99.

Lefort, Cl.: 1981
L'Invention democratique. Les limites de la domination totalitaire. Paris, Fayard.

Lefort, Cl.: 1986
Essais sur le politique (XIXe-XXe siècles). Paris, Seuil.

Lefort, Cl.: 1992
Écrire. A l'épreuve du politique, Paris, Calmann-Lévy.

Lewis, D.: 1975
Adverbs of Quantification. In: E. Keenan (ed.), *Formal Semantics of Natural Language*, Cambridge, Cambridge University Press, pp. 3-15.

Lindahl, H.: 1995
Welfare and Enlightenment. An Enquiry into the Rational Foundations of the Welfare State. Leuven, Leuven University Press.

Locke, J.: 1690 [1979]
An Essay Concerning Human Understanding. Oxford, Clarendon Press.

Locke, J.: 1690 [1990]
Two Treatises of Government. Cambridge, Cambridge University Press.

Loose, D.: 1989
Claude Lefort: een politieke filosofie van de mensenrechten. In: *Rechtsfilosofie en rechtstheorie*, 18, pp. 130-157.

Luhmann, N.: 1986
The Self-reproduction of Law and its Limits. In: G. Teubner (ed.): *Dilemmas of Law in the Welfare State* (European University Institute, Series A 3), Berlin-New York, De Gruyter, pp. 111-127.

Luijpen, W.: 1982
Rechtvaardigheid. Zwolle, Tjeenk Willink.

Lyotard, J.-Fr. and Thebaud, J.L.: 1979
Au juste. Paris, Bourgois.

Lyotard, J.-Fr.: 1981
Discussions, ou: phraser 'après Auschwitz'. In: Ph. Lacoue-Labarthe and J.L. Nancy (eds.), *Les Fins de l'homme* (à partir du travail de J. Derrida), Paris, pp. 283-316.

MacCormick, D.N.: 1984
Coherence in Legal Justification. In: A. Peczenik, L. Lindahl and B. van Roermund (eds.), *Theory of Legal Science*, Dordrecht, Reidel.

MacCormick, D.N., and O. Weinberger: 1986
An Institutional Theory of Law. New Approaches to Legal Positivism. Dordrecht, Reidel.
MacCormick, D.N.: 1992
Further Thoughts on Institutional Facts. In: *International Journal for the Semiotics of Law*, 5, pp. 3-15.
Maihofer, W. (ed.): 1962
Naturrecht oder Rechtspositivismus. Darmstadt, WBG.
Maihofer, W.: 1968
Rechtsstaat und menschliche Würde. Frankfurt a.M., Suhrkamp.
Maihofer, W. (ed.): 1973
Begriff und Wesen des Rechts. Darmstadt, WBG.
Maus, I.: 1976
Bürgerliche Rechtstheorie und Faschismus. Zur sozialen Funktion und aktuellen Wirkung der Theorie Carl Schmitts. München, Fink.
Maus, I.: 1986
Rechtstheorie und politische Theorie im Industriekapitalismus. München, Fink.
Mertens, T.J.M.: 1990
Kritische filosofie en politiek: Immanuel Kant over oorlog en vrede. Nijmegen, Gerard Noodt Instituut.
Mertens, T.J.M.: 1991
Categorische beginselen van het strafrecht. In: *Rechtsfilosofie en rechtstheorie*, 20, pp. 31-49.
Métall, R.A.: 1969
Hans Kelsen. Leben und Werk. Wien, Manz.
Mitchell, W.J.T. (ed.): 1980-1981
On Narrative. Chicago, Chicago University Press.
Mols, G.P.M.F., and Th. A. de Roos: 1992,
Naar een algemene strafbaarheid van de voorbereidingshandeling. In: *Nederlands Juristenblad*, 67, pp. 221-225.
Münch, I. von: 1985
Grundgesetzkommentar. München, Beck, Vol. 1.
Nerhot, P. (ed.): 1990
Law, Interpretation and Reality. Essays in Epistemology, Hermeneutics and Jurisprudence. Dordrecht-Boston, Kluwer Academic Publishers.
Nieskens-Isphording, B.W.M.: 1991
Het fait accompli in het vermogensrecht. Deventer, Kluwer.
Nussbaum, M.: 1994
Scepticism about practical reason in literature and law. In: *Harvard Law Review*, 107: 714-744.

Nussbaum, M.: 1995
Poetic Justice. The Literary Imagination and Public Life. Boston, Beacon Press.
NN.:1985:
Rapport van de Staatscommissie Euthanasie. dl. 1, 's-Gravenhage.
Parret, H.: 1983
Wittgenstein II bis. In: *Tijdschrift voor Filosofie*, Leuven, 45, pp. 261-290.
Pater, W.A. de: 1965
Les Topiques d'Aristote et la dialectique platonicienne, méthodologie de la définition. (Études Thomistes, X), Fribourg, St. Paul.
Peczenik, A., L. Lindahl, and B. van Roermund (eds.): 1984
Theory of Legal Science. Proceedings of the Conference on Legal Theory and Philosophy of Science, Lund, 1983, Dordrecht, Reidel.
Perelman, Ch.: 1976
Logique juridique, nouvelle rhétorique. Paris, Dalloz.
Plantinga, A.: 1983
Guise Theory. In: J. Tomberlin (ed.), *Agent, Language and the Structure of the World. Essays presented to H.-N. Castaneda, with his replies.* Indianapolis, Hackett Publishing Company, pp. 43-78.
Posner, R.A.: 1988
Law and Literature: A Misunderstood Relation. Cambridge (Mass.), Harvard University Press.
Preuss, U.K.: 1986
The Concept of Rights and the Welfare State. In: G. Teubner (ed.), *Dilemmas of Law in the Welfare State*, Berlin-New York, De Gruyter, pp. 151-172.
Prisching, M.: 1988
Hans Kelsen und Carl Schmitt. Zur Konfrontation zweier staatstheoretischer Modelle. In: W. Krawietz and O. Weinberger (eds.), *Reine Rechtslehre im Spiegel ihrer Fortsetzer und Kritiker*, Berlin, Duncker und Humblot.
Putnam, H.: 1979
Meaning and the Moral Sciences. Boston, Routledge and Kegan Paul.
Readings, B.: 1991
Introducing Lyotard. Art and Politics. London, Routledge and Kegan Paul.
Richir, M., 1991
Du sublime en politique. Paris, Payot.
Ricoeur, P.: 1977
Ideologie und Ideologiekritik. In: B. Waldenfels - J. Broekman, A. Pazanin, *Phänomenologie und Marxismus*, Bd. 1, Frankfurt a.M., Suhrkamp, pp. 197-233.

Ricoeur, P.: 1979
The Metaphorical Process as Cognition, Imagination and Feeling. In: S. Sacks (ed.), *On Metaphor*, London, University of Chicago Press, pp. 141-157.

Ricoeur, P.: 1983a
Die Metapher und das Hauptproblem der Hermeneutik. In: A. Haverkamp (ed.) *Theorie der Metapher*, Darmstadt, WBG.

Ricoeur, P.: 1983-1985
Temps et récit. Paris, Seuil, 3 vols.

Roermund, B. van: 1983
Wetten en weten. "Theorie van het recht": een wijsgerige kritiek. Leuven, Acco - Zwolle, Tjeenk Willink.

Roermund, B. van: 1984
Regel en waarheid - wijsgerige aantekeningen omtrent rechtsdogmatiek. In: *Rechtsfilosofie en Rechtstheorie*, 13, pp. 205-228.

Roermund, B. van: 1987
Justice, Rights and Human Dignity. Some Aspects of Coherence in the Legal Concept of a Person. In: *The Windsor Yearbook of Access to Justice*, 7, pp. 46-65.

Roermund, B. van: 1988a
On 'Narrative Coherence' in Legal Contexts. In: C. Faralli and E. Pattaro (eds.), *Reason in Law*, Milan, Giuffré, Vol. III, pp. 159-170.

Roermund, B. van: 1988b
De rechtsfilosofische sporen van het structuralisme. In: O. Kamstra et al., *Nederlandse rechtswetenschap*, Zwolle, Tjeenk Willink, pp. 263-281.

Roermund, B. van: 1988c
Jean-Jacques Rousseau en zijn politieke filosofie. In: S. van den Braak and B. van Roermund (translat.), *J.-J. Rousseau, Het maatschappelijk verdrag; of, Beginselen van staatsinrichting*, Tilburg, Tilburg University Press, pp. 145-166.

Roermund, B. van: 1989
De algemeenheid van de wet en de singulariteit van het individu bij Rousseau. In: *Rechtsfilosofie en rechtstheorie*, 18, pp. 19-34.

Roermund, B. van: 1990a
Wet en belofte. Overdenkingen omtrent gebondenheid uit overeenkomst. Nijmegen, Ars Aequi Libri.

Roermund, B. van: 1990b
Narrative Coherence and the Guises of Legalism. In: P. Nerhot (ed.), *Law, Interpretation and Reality. Essays in Epistemology, Hermeneutics and Jurisprudence*, Dordrecht-Boston, Kluwer Academic Publishers.

Roermund, B. van: 1990c
Parlementarisme en politiek, Kelsen over vertegenwoordiging. In: L. Heyde et al., *Filosofie en democratie*, Tilburg, Tilburg University Press, pp. 41-69.
Roermund, B. van: 1990d
Themis' terzijde. Omtrekken van rechtsfilosofie. Nijmegen, Ars Aequi Libri.
Roermund, B. van: 1991a
Nóg een categorisch beginsel van strafrecht? In: *Rechtsfilosofie en rechtstheorie*, 20, pp. 128-136.
Roermund, B. van: 1991b
The Instituting of Brute Facts. In: *International Journal for the Semiotics of Law*, 4, pp. 279-308.
Roermund, B. van: 1993a
Recht, verhaal en werkelijkheid. Bussum, Coutinho.
Roermund, B. van: 1993b
Seeing Places: On Prepositions in Law. In: *The International Journal for the Semiotics of Law / Revue internationale de sémiotique juridique*, 6, 1993, pp. 249-270.
Roermund, B. van: 1993c
Dualisme en dualisme is twee. In: G.C.G.J. van Roermund et al. (eds.), *Symposium strafrecht, vervolg van een grondslagendebat*, Arnhem, Gouda Quint, pp. 265-289.
Roermund, B. van: 1994
'Law is Narrative, Not Literature'. In: W.J. Witteveen (ed.), *Law, Rhetoric and Literature* (Special Dutch Journal for Legal Philosophy and Legal Theory), 23, 3, 1994), Zwolle, Tjeenk Willink, pp. 221-227.
Rousseau, J.-J.: 1791 [1865-1870]
Essai sur l'origine des langues. In: *Oeuvres complètes*, Paris, I. Hachette, pp. 370-408.
Rousseau, J.-J.: 1755 [1964a]
Discours sur l'origine et les fondements de l'inégalité parmi les hommes. In: *Oeuvres complètes*, t.III (Pléiade), Paris, Gallimard.
Rousseau, J.-J.: 1762 [1964b]
Du contrat social. t.III (Pléiade), Paris, Gallimard.
Sartre, J.P.: 1939
L'enfance d'un chef, In: *Le Mur*, Paris.
Scheler, M.: 1916 [1966]
Der Formalismus in der Ethik und die materiale Wertethik. Neue Versuch der Grundlegung eines ethischen Personalismus. (5. Aufl.), Bern-München, Francke Verlag.

Schmitt, C.: 1922 [1934]
Politische Theologie. Vier Kapitel zur Lehre von der Souveränität. Leipzig, Duncker und Humblot.

Schmitt, C.: 1923/1926 [1985]
Die geistesgeschichtliche Lage des heutigen Parlamentarismus. Berlin, Duncker und Humblot.

Schmitt, C.: 1927 [1963]
Der Begriff des Politischen. Berlin, Duncker und Humblot.

Schmitt, C.: 1928 [1970]
Verfassungslehre. (5. Aufl.), Berlin, Duncker und Humblot.

Schmitt, C.: 1931 [1969]
Der Hüter der Verfassung. Berlin, Duncker und Humblot.

Schmitt, C., 1932 [1979] (orig. 1927)
Der Begriff des Politischen. Text von 1932 mit einem Vorwort und drei Corollarien, Nachdr. d. Aufl. von 1963, Berlin, Duncker und Humblot,

Schmitt, C.: 1965
Verfassungslehre. Berlin, Duncker und Humblot.

Schmitt, C., 1970 [1984]
Politische Theologie II. Die Legende der Eledigung jeder politischer Theologie. (2. Aufl.), Berlin, Duncker und Humblot.

Scholten, P.: 1931
Algemeen deel. Zwolle, Tjeenk Willink.

Schoordijk, H.C.F.: 1979
Algemeen gedeelte verbintenissenrecht volgens het NBW. Deventer, Kluwer.

Schreckenberger, W.: 1978
Rhetorische Semiotik, Analyse von Texten des Grundgesetzes und von rhetorischen Grundstrukturen der Argumentation des Bundesverfassungsgerichts. Freiburg-München, Alber.

Seuren, P.A.M.: 1975
Tussen taal en denken, een bijdrage tot de empirische funderingen van de semantiek. Utrecht, Scheltema en Holkema.

Sloterdijk, P.: 1983
Kritik der zynischen Vernunft. Frankfurt, Suhrkamp.

Smith, A.: 1978
Lectures on Jurisprudence. Ed. by R.K. Meek, D.D. Raphael and P.G. Stein (eds.), Oxford, Clarendon Press.

Sutorius, E.Ph.R.: 1984
Vrijwillige euthanasie of de gewetensfunctie van een rechtspolitiek conflict. In: *Nederlands Juristenblad*, 59, pp. 50-57.

Steiner, G.: 1975
After Babel. London, Oxford University Press.

Strauss, L.: 1953
Natural Right and History. Chicago, University of Chicago Press.

Strawson, P.F.: 1959
Individuals. An Essay in Descriptive Metaphysics. London, Methuen.

Tindemans, K.: 1996
Recht en tragedie. De scène van de wet in de antieke polis. Leuven (diss.).

Tomberlin, J.E. (ed.): 1983
Agent, Language and the Structure of the World: Essays in Honor of H. Castañeda, with his Replies. Indianapolis, Hackett.

Ullmer-Ehrich, V.: 1981
L'usage des prépositions indexicales dans un discours descriptif - la perspective deictique et la perspective inhérente. In: Chr. Schwarze (ed.), *Analyse des prépositions.* Tübingen, Niemeyer Verlag, pp. 224-250.

Vandekerckhove, L.: 1985
Van straffen gesproken. De bestraffing van zelfdoding in het oude Europa. Tielt-Weesp, Lannoo.

Vandeloise, Cl.: 1986
L'espace en français. Sémantique des prépositions spatiales. Paris, Du Seuil.

Verhoeven, C.: 1966
Het grote gebeuren. Utrecht, Ambo.

Viehweg, Th.: 1953
Topik und Jurisprudenz. Ein Beitrag zur rechtswissenschaftlichen Grundlagenforschung. München, Beck Verlag.

Vranken, J.B.M.: 1989
Mededelings-, informatie- en onderzoeksplichten in het verbintenissenrecht. Zwolle, Tjeenk Willink.

Waard, R. de: 1992
Strafbaarstelling van voorbereidingshandelingen. In: *Nederlands Juristenblad,* 67, pp. 213-220.

Weisberg, R.: 1992
Poethics, and Other Strategies of Law and Literature. New York, Columbia University Press.

Weissenborn, J.: 1981
L'acquisition des prépositions spatiales: problèmes cognitifs et linguistiques. In: Chr. Schwarze (ed.), *Analyse des prépositions,* Tübingen, Niemeyer Verlag, pp. 251-285.

Weyembergh, M.: 1988
La fin du politique et la problématique de l'exclusion. In: M. Weyembergh and J.M. Piret (eds.), *La fin du politique - Das Ende des Politischen*, Brussel, Vrije Universiteit Brussel.

White, H.: 1981
The Value of Narrativity in the Representation of Reality. In: W.J.T. Mitchell (ed.), *On Narrative,* Chicago-London, University of Chicago Press, pp. 1-23.

White, H.: 1987
The Content of the Form. Narrative Discourse and Historical Representation. Baltimore, Johns Hopkins University Press.

White, J.B.: 1973
The Legal Imagination. Studies in the Nature of Legal Thought and Expression. Boston - Toronto, Little, Brown and Company.

White, J.B.: 1985
Heracles' Bow. Essays on the Rhetoric and Poetics of the Law. Madison, University of Wisconsin Press

White, J.B.: 1990
Justice as translation. An Essay in Cultural and Legal Criticism. Chicago, University of Chicago Press, 1990.

Wieacker, Fr.: 1952
Privatrechtsgeschichte der Neuzeit. Göttingen, Vandenhoeck und Ruprecht.

Wieacker, J.: 1970
Zur praktischen Leistung der Rechtsdogmatik. In: R. Bubner (ed.), *Hermeneutik und Dialektik* (Festschrift H.G. Gadamer), Tübingen, Mohr. pp. 311-336.

Witteveen, W.J.: 1988
De retoriek in het recht. Zwolle, Tjeenk Willink.

Witteveen, W.J.: 1990
Het verhaal in het recht. In: F. Ankersmit et al., *Op verhaal komen. Over narrativiteit in de mens- en cultuurwetenschappen*, Kampen, Kok Agora, pp. 179-203.

Witteveen, W.J.: 1991
Evenwicht van machten. Zwolle, Tjeenk Willink.

Wittgenstein, L.: 1933-1935 [1969]
The Blue and Brown Books. Oxford, Blackwell.

Wittgenstein, L. 1930 [1970c]
Philosophische Bemerkungen. In: *Schriften*, Frankfurt, Suhrkamp, Vol. 2.

Wittgenstein, L.: 1932-1934 [1970b]
Philosophische Grammatik. In: *Schriften*, Frankfurt, Suhrkamp, Vol. 4.

Wittgenstein, L.: 1953 [1970a]
Philosophische Unterschungen/Philosophical Investigations. In: *Schriften*, Frankfurt, Suhrkamp, Vol. 1.

Wittgenstein, L.: 1969 [1984]
Über Gewißheit. In: *Schriften*, Frankfurt, Suhrkamp, Vol. 8.
Wright, G.H. von: 1982
Wittgenstein on Certainty. In: G.H. von Wright (ed.), *Wittgenstein*, Oxford, Blackwell.

Law and Philosophy Library

1. E. Bulygin, J.-L. Gardies and I. Niiniluoto (eds.): *Man, Law and Modern Forms of Life*. With an Introduction by M.D. Bayles. 1985 ISBN 90-277-1869-5
2. W. Sadurski: *Giving Desert Its Due*. Social Justice and Legal Theory. 1985 ISBN 90-277-1941-1
3. N. MacCormick and O. Weinberger: *An Institutional Theory of Law*. New Approaches to Legal Positivism. 1986 ISBN 90-277-2079-7
4. A. Aarnio: *The Rational as Reasonable*. A Treatise on Legal Justification. 1987 ISBN 90-277-2276-5
5. M.D. Bayles: *Principles of Law*. A Normative Analysis. 1987 ISBN 90-277-2412-1; Pb: 90-277-2413-X
6. A. Soeteman: *Logic in Law*. Remarks on Logic and Rationality in Normative Reasoning, Especially in Law. 1989 ISBN 0-7923-0042-4
7. C.T. Sistare: *Responsibility and Criminal Liability*. 1989 ISBN 0-7923-0396-2
8. A. Peczenik: *On Law and Reason*. 1989 ISBN 0-7923-0444-6
9. W. Sadurski: *Moral Pluralism and Legal Neutrality*. 1990 ISBN 0-7923-0565-5
10. M.D. Bayles: *Procedural Justice*. Allocating to Individuals. 1990 ISBN 0-7923-0567-1
11. P. Nerhot (ed.): *Law, Interpretation and Reality*. Essays in Epistemology, Hermeneutics and Jurisprudence. 1990 ISBN 0-7923-0593-0
12. A.W. Norrie: *Law, Ideology and Punishment*. Retrieval and Critique of the Liberal Ideal of Criminal Justice. 1991 ISBN 0-7923-1013-6
13. P. Nerhot (ed.): *Legal Knowledge and Analogy*. Fragments of Legal Epistemology, Hermeneutics and Linguistics. 1991 ISBN 0-7923-1065-9
14. O. Weinberger: *Law, Institution and Legal Politics*. Fundamental Problems of Legal Theory and Social Philosophy. 1991 ISBN 0-7923-1143-4
15. J. Wróblewski: *The Judicial Application of Law*. Edited by Z. Bańkowski and N. MacCormick. 1992 ISBN 0-7923-1569-3
16. T. Wilhelmsson: *Critical Studies in Private Law*. A Treatise on Need-Rational Principles in Modern Law. 1992 ISBN 0-7923-1659-2
17. M.D. Bayles: *Hart's Legal Philosophy*. An Examination. 1992 ISBN 0-7923-1981-8
18. D.W.P. Ruiter: *Institutional Legal Facts*. Legal Powers and their Effects. 1993 ISBN 0-7923-2441-2
19. J. Schonsheck: *On Criminalization*. An Essay in the Philosophy of the Criminal Law. 1994 ISBN 0-7923-2663-6
20. R.P. Malloy and J. Evensky (eds.): *Adam Smith and the Philosophy of Law and Economics*. 1994 ISBN 0-7923-2796-9
21. Z. Bankowski, I. White and U. Hahn (eds.): *Informatics and the Foundations of Legal Reasoning*. 1995 ISBN 0-7923-3455-8
22. E. Lagerspetz: *The Opposite Mirrors*. An Essay on the Conventionalist Theory of Institutions. 1995 ISBN 0-7923-3325-X
23. M. van Hees: *Rights and Decisions*. Formal Models of Law and Liberalism. 1995 ISBN 0-7923-3754-9
24. B. Anderson: *"Discovery" in Legal Decision-Making*. 1996 ISBN 0-7923-3981-9

Law and Philosophy Library

25. S. Urbina: *Reason, Democracy, Society.* A Study on the Basis of Legal Thinking. 1996
ISBN 0-7923-4262-3
26. E. Attwooll: *The Tapestry of the Law.* Scotland, Legal Culture and Legal Theory. 1997
ISBN 0-7923-4310-7
27. J.C. Hage: *Reasoning with Rules.* An Essay on Legal Reasoning and Its Underlying Logic. 1997
ISBN 0-7923-4325-5
28. R.A. Hillman: *The Richness of Contract Law.* An Analysis and Critique of Contemporary Theories of Contract Law. 1997
ISBN 0-7923-4336-0
29. C. Wellman: *An Approach to Rights.* Studies in the Philosophy of Law and Morals. 1997
ISBN 0-7923-4467-7
30. B. van Roermund: *Law, Narrative and Reality.* An Essay in Intercepting Politics. 1997
ISBN 0-7923-4621-1

KLUWER ACADEMIC PUBLISHERS – DORDRECHT / BOSTON / LONDON